LOVING
WHAT IS

LOVING
WHAT IS

*Four Questions That
Can Change Your Life*

BYRON KATIE

Written with Stephen Mitchell

HARMONY BOOKS
New York

Published by Harmony Books, New York, New York.
Member of the Crown Publishing Group,
a division of Random House, Inc.
www.randomhouse.com

HARMONY BOOKS is a registered trademark and the
Harmony Books colophon is a trademark of Random House, Inc.

Printed in the United States of America

Design by David Bullen

Library of Congress Cataloging-in-Publication Data
is available on request.

ISBN 0-609-60874-6

10 9 8 7 6 5 4 3 2 1

FIRST EDITION

To Adam Joseph Lewis

and to Michael

Contents

Introduction

The more clearly you understand yourself and your emotions,
the more you become a lover of what is.
Baruch Spinoza

The first time I watched The Work, I realized that I was witnessing something truly remarkable. What I saw was a succession of people, young and old, educated and uneducated, who were learning to question their own thoughts, the thoughts that were most painful to them. With the lovingly incisive help of Byron Katie (everyone calls her Katie), these people were finding their way not only toward the resolution of their immediate problems, but also toward a state of mind in which the deepest questions are resolved. I have spent a good part of my life studying and translating the classic texts of the great spiritual traditions, and I recognized something very similar in process here. At the core of these traditions—in works such as the Book of Job, the Tao Te Ching, and the Bhagavad Gita —there is an intense questioning about life and death, and a profound, joyful wisdom that emerges as an answer. That wisdom, it seemed to me, was the place Katie was standing in, and the direction where these people were headed.

As I watched from my seat in a crowded community center, five men and women, one after another, were learning freedom through the very thoughts that had caused their suffering, thoughts such as "My husband betrayed me" or "My mother doesn't love me enough." Simply by asking four questions and listening to the answers they found inside themselves, these people were opening their minds to profound, spacious, and life-transforming insights. I saw a man who had been suffering for decades from anger and resentment toward his alcoholic father light up before my eyes within forty-five minutes. I saw a woman who had been almost too frightened to speak, because she had just found out that her cancer was spreading, end the session in a glow of understanding and acceptance. Three out of the five people had never done The Work before, yet the process didn't seem to be more difficult for them than it was for the other two, nor were their realizations any less profound. They all began by realizing a truth so basic that it is usually invisible: the fact that (in the words of the Greek philosopher Epictetus) "we are disturbed not by what happens to us, but by our thoughts about what happens." As soon as they grasped that truth, their whole understanding changed.

Before people have experienced The Work of Byron Katie for themselves, they often think that it is too simple to be effective. But its simplicity is precisely what makes it so effective. Over the past two years, since first encountering it and meeting Katie, I have done The Work many times, on thoughts I hadn't even been aware of. And I've watched more than a thousand people do it in public events across the United States and Europe, on the whole gamut of human problems: from major illnesses, the deaths of parents and children, sexual and psychological abuse, addictions, financial insecurity, professional problems, and social issues to the usual frustrations of daily life. (Having a reserved seat at all Katie's events is one of the privileges of being married to her.) Again and again, I have seen The Work quickly and radically transform the way people think about their problems. And as the thinking changes, the problems disappear.

"Suffering is optional," Katie says. Whenever we experience a stressful feeling—anything from mild discomfort to intense sorrow, rage, or despair—we can be certain that there is a specific thought causing our reaction, whether or not we are conscious of it. The way to end our stress is to investigate the thinking that lies behind it, and anyone can do this by himself with a piece of paper and a pen. The Work's four questions, which you will see in context later in this introduction, reveal where our thinking isn't true for us. Through this process—Katie also calls it "inquiry"—we discover that all the concepts and judgments that we believe or take for granted are distortions of things as they really are. When we believe our thoughts instead of what is really true for us, we experience the kinds of emotional distress that we call suffering. Suffering is a natural alarm, warning us that we're attaching to a thought; when we don't listen, we come to accept this suffering as an inevitable part of life. It's not.

The Work has striking similarities with the Zen koan and the Socratic dialogue. But it doesn't stem from any tradition, Eastern or Western. It is American, homegrown, and mainstream, having originated in the mind of an ordinary woman who had no intention of originating anything.

To realize your true nature, you must wait for the right
moment and the right conditions. When the time comes, you are
awakened as if from a dream. You understand that what you
have found is your own and doesn't come from anywhere outside.
Buddhist Sutra

The Work was born on a February morning in 1986 when Byron Kathleen Reid, a forty-three-year-old woman from a small town in the high desert of southern California, woke up on the floor of a halfway house.

In the midst of an ordinary life—two marriages, three children, a successful career—Katie had entered a ten-year-long downward spiral into rage, paranoia, and despair. For two years she was so depressed that she could seldom manage to leave her house; she stayed in bed for weeks at a time, doing business by telephone from her bedroom, unable even to bathe or brush her teeth. Her children would tiptoe past her door to avoid her outbursts of rage. Finally, she checked in to a halfway house for women with eating disorders, the only facility that her insurance company would pay for. The other residents were so frightened of her that she was placed alone in an attic room.

One morning, a week or so later, as she lay on the floor (she had been feeling too unworthy to sleep in a bed), Katie woke up without any concepts of who or what she was. "There was no me," she says.

All my rage, all the thoughts that had been troubling me, my whole world, *the* whole world, was gone. At the same time, laughter welled up from the depths and just poured out. Everything was unrecognizable. It was as if something else had woken up. *It* opened its eyes. *It* was looking through Katie's eyes. And it was so delighted! It was intoxicated with joy. There was nothing separate, nothing unacceptable to it; everything was its very own self.

When Katie returned home, her family and friends felt that she was a different person. Her daughter, Roxann, who was sixteen at the time, says,

We knew that the constant storm was over. She had always yelled at me and my brothers and criticized us; I used to be scared to be in the same room with her. Now she seemed completely peaceful. She would sit still for hours on the window seat or out in the desert. She was joyful and innocent, like a child, and she seemed to be filled with love. People in trouble started knocking on our door, asking her for help. She'd sit with them and ask them questions—mainly, "Is that true?" When I'd come home miserable, with a problem like "My boyfriend doesn't love me anymore," Mom would look at me as if she knew that wasn't possible, and she'd ask me, "Honey, how could that be true?" as if I had just told her that we were living in China.

Once people understood that the old Katie wasn't coming back, they began to speculate about what had happened to her. Had some miracle occurred? She wasn't much help to them: It was a long time before she could describe her experience intelligibly. She would talk about a freedom that had woken up inside her. She also said that, through an inner questioning, she had realized that all her old thoughts were untrue.

Shortly after Katie got back from the halfway house, her home began to fill with people who had heard about her and had come to learn. She was able to communicate her inner inquiry in the form of specific questions that anyone who wanted freedom could apply on his own, without her. Soon she began to be invited to meet with small gatherings in people's living rooms. Her hosts often asked her if she was "enlightened." She would answer, "I'm just someone who knows the difference between what hurts and what doesn't."

In 1992 she was invited to northern California, and The Work spread very fast from there. Katie accepted every invitation. She has been on the road almost constantly since 1993, demonstrating The Work in church basements, community centers, and hotel meeting rooms, in front of small and large audiences (admission is always free). And The Work has found its way into all kinds of organizations, from corporations, law firms, and therapists' offices to hospitals, prisons, churches, and schools. It is now popular in other parts of the world where Katie has traveled. All across America and Europe, there are groups of people who meet regularly to do The Work.

Katie often says that the only way to understand The Work is to experience it. But it's worth noting that inquiry fits precisely with current research into the biology of mind. Contemporary neuroscience identifies a particular part of the brain, sometimes called "the interpreter," as the source of the familiar internal narrative that gives us our sense of self. Two prominent neuroscientists have recently characterized the quirky, undependable quality of the tale told by the interpreter. Antonio Damasio describes it this way: "Perhaps the most important revelation is precisely this: that the left cerebral hemisphere of humans is prone to fabricating verbal narratives that do not necessarily accord with the truth." And Michael Gazzaniga writes: "The left brain weaves its story in order to convince itself and you that it is in full control. . . . What is so adaptive about having what amounts to a spin doctor in the left brain? The interpreter is really trying to keep our personal story together. To do that, we have to learn to lie to ourselves." These insights, based on solid experimental work, show that we tend to believe our own press releases. Often when we think we're being rational, we're being spun by our own thinking. That trait explains how we get ourselves into the painful positions that Katie recognized in her own suffering. The self-questioning she discovered uses a different, less-known capacity of the mind to find a way out of its self-made trap.

After doing The Work, many people report an immediate sense of release and freedom from thoughts that were making them miserable. But if The Work depended on a momentary experience, it would be far less useful than it is. The Work is an ongoing and deepening process of self-realization, not a quick fix. "It's more than a technique," Katie says. "It brings to life, from deep within us, an innate aspect of our being."

The deeper you go into The Work, the more powerful you realize it is.

People who have been practicing inquiry for a while often say, "The Work is no longer something I do. *It* is doing *me.*" They describe how, without any conscious intention, the mind notices each stressful thought and undoes it before it can cause any suffering. Their internal argument with reality has disappeared, and they find that what remains is love—love for themselves, for other people, and for whatever life brings. The title of this book describes their experience: Loving what is becomes as easy and natural as breathing.

Considering that, all hatred driven hence,
The [mind] recovers radical innocence
And learns at last that it is self-delighting,
Self-appeasing, self-affrighting,
And that its own sweet will is Heaven's will.
William Butler Yeats

I have waited until now to introduce the four questions to you, because they don't make much sense out of context. The best way to meet them is to see how they function in an actual example of The Work. You'll also meet what Katie calls the "turnaround," which is a way of looking at reversed versions of a statement that you believe.

The following dialogue with Katie took place before an audience of about two hundred people. Mary, the woman who is sitting opposite Katie on the stage, has filled out a one-page Worksheet that asked her to write down her thoughts about someone who upsets her. The instructions are: "Allow yourself to be as judgmental and petty as you really feel. Don't try to be 'spiritual' or kind." The pettier we can be when writing, the more likely it is that we'll benefit from The Work. You'll see that Mary hasn't held back at all. She is a forceful woman, perhaps forty years old, slim, attractive, and dressed in expensive-looking exercise clothes. At the beginning of the dialogue, her anger and impatience are palpable.

A first experience of The Work, as a reader or onlooker, can be uncomfortable. It helps to remember that all the participants—Mary, Katie, and the audience—are on the same side here; all of them are looking for the truth. If Katie ever seems to be mocking or derisive, you'll notice that she's making fun of the thought that is causing Mary's suffering, never of Mary herself.

Toward the middle of the dialogue, when Katie asks, "Do you really want to know the truth?" she doesn't mean her truth, or any abstract, predetermined truth, but Mary's truth, the truth that is hidden behind her troubling thoughts. Mary has entered the dialogue in the first place because she trusts that Katie can help her discover where she is lying to herself. She welcomes Katie's persistence.

You'll also notice right away that Katie is very free in her use of terms of endearment. One CEO, before a workshop that Katie gave to his top executives, felt that he had to issue a warning: "If she holds your hand and calls you 'sweetheart' or 'honey,' please don't get excited. She does this with everyone."

Mary [reading the statements from her Worksheet]: I hate my husband because he drives me crazy—everything about him, including the way he breathes. What disappoints me is that I don't love him anymore, and our relationship is a charade. I want him to be more successful, to not want to have sex with me, to get in shape, to get a life outside of me and the children, to not touch me anymore, and to be powerful. My husband shouldn't fool himself that he's good at our business. He should create more success. My husband is a wimp. He's needy and lazy. He's fooling himself. I refuse to keep living a lie. I refuse to keep living my relationship as an imposter.

Katie: Does that pretty well sum it up? [The audience bursts into laughter, and Mary laughs along with them.] By the sound of the laughter, it seems as though you speak for a lot of people in this room. So, let's start at the top and see if we can begin to understand what's going on.

Mary: I hate my husband because he drives me crazy—everything about him, including the way he breathes.

Katie: "Your husband drives you crazy"—is it true? [This is the first of the four questions: **Is it true?**]

Mary: Yes.

Katie: Okay. What's an example of that, sweetheart? He breathes?

Mary: He breathes. When we're doing conference calls for our business, I can hear his breath on the other end of the telephone, and I want to scream.

Katie: So, "His breath drives you crazy" — is that true?

Mary: Yes.

Katie: Can you absolutely know that that's true? [The second question: **Can you absolutely know that it's true?**]

Mary: Yes!

Katie: We can all relate to that. I hear that it really is true for you. In my experience, it can't be your husband's breath that's driving you crazy; it has to be your *thoughts* about his breath that are driving you crazy. So let's take a closer look and see if that's true. What are your thoughts about his breath on the phone?

Mary: That he should be more aware that he's breathing loudly during a conference call.

Katie: How do you react when you think that thought? [The third question: **How do you react when you think that thought?**]

Mary: I feel like I want to kill him.

Katie: So what's more painful—the thought you attach to about his breathing or his breathing?

Mary: The breathing is more painful. I'm comfortable with the thought that I want to kill him. [Mary laughs, and so does the audience.]

Katie: You can keep that thought. That's the beautiful thing about The Work. You can keep all your thoughts.

Mary: I've never done The Work before, so I don't know any of the "right" answers.

Katie: Your answers are perfect, sweetheart. Don't rehearse. So he's breathing on the phone and you have the thought that he should be more aware, and he's not. What's the next thought?

Mary: It brings up every terrible thought I have about him.

Katie: Okay, and he's still breathing. "He should stop breathing into the phone on the conference call"—what's the reality of it? Does he?

Mary: No. I've told him to stop.

Katie: And he still does it. That's reality. What's true is always what's happening, not the story about what *should* be happening. "He should stop breathing on the phone"—is it true?

Mary [after a pause]: No. It's not true. He's doing it. That's what's true. That's reality.

Katie: So how do you react when you think the thought that he should stop breathing on the phone, and he doesn't?

Mary: How do I react? I want out. It feels uncomfortable because I know I want out and I know I'm not going anywhere.

Katie: Let's move back to inquiry, honey, rather than moving further into your story, your interpretation of what's happening. Do you really want to know the truth?

Mary: Yes.

Katie: Okay. It helps if we stick to one written statement at a time. Can you see a reason to drop the thought that he should stop breathing on the phone? [This is an additional question that Katie sometimes asks.] For those of you new to The Work, if you hear that I'm asking Mary to drop her story, let me make it very clear: I'm not. This is not about getting rid of thoughts or about overcoming, improving, or surrendering them. None of that. This is about realizing for yourself internal cause and effect. The question is simply "Can you *see a reason* to drop this thought?"

Mary: Yes, I can. It would be a lot more enjoyable to do conference calls without this thought.

Katie: That's a good reason. Can you find a stress-free reason to keep this thought, this lie, that he should stop breathing on the phone? [A second additional question]

Mary: No.

Katie: Who would you be without that thought? [The fourth question:

Who would you be without the thought?] Who would you be, while you're on a conference call with your husband, if you didn't have the ability to think that thought?

Mary: I'd be much happier. I'd be more powerful. I wouldn't be distracted.

Katie: Yes, sweetheart. That's it. It's not his breathing that is causing your problem. It's your *thoughts* about his breathing, because you haven't investigated them to see that they oppose reality in the moment. Let's look at your next statement.

Mary: I don't love him anymore.

Katie: Is that true?

Mary: Yes.

Katie: Okay. Good. I hear that, and do you really want to know the truth?

Mary: Yes.

Katie: Okay. Be still. There's no right or wrong answer. "You don't love him"—is that true? [Mary is silent.] If you had to answer honestly either yes or no, right now, and you had to live forever with your answer—your truth or your lie—what would your answer be? "You don't love him"—is that true? [There is a long pause. Then Mary begins to cry.]

Mary: No. It's not true.

Katie: That's a very courageous answer. If we answer it that way, with what's really true for ourselves, we think that there may be no way out. "Is it true?" is just a question! We're terrified to answer the simplest question honestly, because we project what that may mean in the imagined future. We think we have to do something about it. How do you react when you believe the thought that you don't love him?

Mary: It makes my whole life a stupid charade.

Katie: Can you see a reason to drop this thought that you don't love him? And I'm not asking you to drop the thought.

Mary: Yes, I can see a reason to drop it.

Katie: Can you think of one stress-free reason to keep the thought?

Mary [after a long pause]: I think if I keep my story, then I can keep him from wanting to have sex all the time.

Katie: Is that a stress-free reason? It seems stressful to me.

Mary: I guess it is.

Katie: Can you find one stress-free reason to keep that thought?

Mary: Oh, I see. No. There aren't any stress-free reasons to keep the story.

Katie: Fascinating. Who would you be, standing with your husband, without the thought that you don't love him?

Mary: It would be great. It would be fabulous. That's what I want.

Katie: I'm hearing that *with* the thought, it's stressful. And *without* the thought, it's fabulous. So what does your husband have to do with your unhappiness? We're just noticing here. So, "I don't love my husband"—turn it around. [After the four questions comes the **turnaround**.]

Mary: I do love my husband.

Katie: Feel it. It has nothing to do with him, does it?

Mary: No. It really doesn't. I do love my husband, and you're right, it doesn't have anything to do with him.

Katie: And sometimes you think you hate him, and *that* doesn't have any-thing to do with him, either. The man's just breathing. You tell the story that you love him, or you tell the story that you hate him. It doesn't take two people to have a happy marriage. It only takes one: you! There's another turnaround.

Mary: I don't love myself. I can relate to that one.

Katie: And you may think that if you divorce him, then you'll feel good. But if you haven't investigated your thinking, you'll attach these same con-cepts onto whoever comes into your life next. We don't attach to people or to things; we attach to uninvestigated concepts that we believe to be true in the moment. Let's look at the next statement on your Worksheet.

Mary: I want my husband not to be needy, not to be dependent on me, to be more successful, to not want to have sex with me, to get in shape, to get a life outside of me and the children, and to be more powerful. Those are just a few.

Katie: Let's turn that whole statement around.

Mary: I want me not to be needy. I want me not to be dependent on him. I want me to be more successful. I want me to want to have sex with him.

I want me to get in shape. I want me to get a life outside of him and the children. I want me to be more powerful.

Katie: So, "He shouldn't be needy"—is it true? What's the reality of it? Is he?

Mary: He's needy.

Katie: "He shouldn't be needy" is a lie, because the guy is needy, according to you. So, how do you react when you think the thought "He shouldn't be needy," and in your reality he is needy?

Mary: I just want to run away all the time.

Katie: Who would you be in his presence without the thought "He shouldn't be needy"?

Mary: What I just understood is that I could be with him in a space of love, instead of just having my defenses up. It's like if I notice any bit of neediness, I'm out of there. I've got to run. That's what I do with my life.

Katie: When he's acting needy, in your opinion, you don't say no honestly. You run away or want to run away instead of being honest with yourself and him.

Mary: That's true.

Katie: Well, it would have to be. You have to call him needy until you can get some clarity and honest communication going with yourself. So let's be clear. You be him and be very needy. I'll take the role of clarity.

Mary: Mr. Needy comes in and says, "I just had the best phone call. You've got to hear about it. It was this guy, and he's going to be fabulous in the business. And I had another call. . . ." You know, he just goes on and on. Meanwhile, I'm busy. I've got a deadline.

Katie: "Sweetheart, I hear that you had a wonderful phone call. I love that, and I would also like you to leave the room now. I have a deadline to meet."

Mary: "We have to talk about our plans. When are we going to Hawaii? We have to figure out what airlines . . ."

Katie: "I hear that you want to talk about our plans for Hawaii, so let's discuss this at dinner tonight. I really want you to leave the room now. I have a deadline to meet."

Mary: "If one of your girlfriends called, you would talk to her for an hour. Now you can't listen to me for two minutes?"

Katie: "You could be right, and I want you to leave the room now. It may sound cold, but it's not. I just have a deadline to meet."

Mary: I don't do it like that. Usually I'm mean to him. I just seethe.

Katie: You *have* to be mean, because you're afraid to tell the truth and say no. You don't say, "Sweetheart, I would like you to leave. I have a deadline," because you want something from him. What scam are you running on yourself and on him? What do you want from him?

Mary: I am never straightforward with anybody.

Katie: Because you want something from us. What is it?

Mary: I can't stand when somebody doesn't like me. I don't want disharmony.

Katie: So you want our approval.

Mary: Yes, and I want to maintain harmony.

Katie: Sweetheart, "If your husband approves of what you say and what you do, then there is harmony in your home"—is that true? Does it work? Is there harmony in your home?

Mary: No.

Katie: You trade your integrity for harmony in the home. It doesn't work. Spare yourself from seeking love, approval, or appreciation—from anyone. And watch what happens in reality, just for fun. Read your statement again.

Mary: I want my husband not to be needy.

Katie: All right. Turn it around.

Mary: I want me not to be needy.

Katie: Yes, you need all this harmony. You need his approval. You need his breathing to change. You need his sexuality to change for you. Who's the needy one? Who is dependent on whom? So let's turn the whole list around.

Mary: I want myself not to be needy, not to be dependent . . .

Katie: On your husband, perhaps?

Mary: I want myself to be more successful. I want myself to not want to have sex with me.

Katie: That one could be really legitimate if you sit with it. How many times do you tell the story of how he has sex with you and you hate it?

Mary: Constantly.

Katie: Yes. You're having sex with him in your mind and thinking how terrible that is. You tell the story, over and over, of what it's like having sex with your husband. That story is what's repelling you, not your husband. Sex without a story has never repelled anyone. It just is what it is. You're having sex or you're not. It's our thoughts about sex that repel us. Write that one out too, honey. You could write a whole Worksheet on your husband and sexuality.

Mary: I get it.

Katie: Okay, turn the next statement around.

Mary: I want me to get in shape. But I *am* in shape.

Katie: Oh, really? How about mentally?

Mary: Oh. I could work on that.

Katie: Are you doing the best you can?

Mary: Yes.

Katie: Well, maybe he is, too. "He's supposed to be in shape"—is that true?

Mary: No. He's not in shape.

Katie: How do you react when you believe the thought that he should be in shape, and he's not? How do you treat him? What do you say? What do you do?

Mary: Everything is subtle. I show him my muscles. I don't ever look at him with approval. I don't ever admire him. I don't ever do anything kind in that direction.

Katie: Okay, close your eyes. Look at yourself looking at him that way. Now look at his face. [There is a pause. Mary sighs.] Keep your eyes closed. Look at him again. Who would you be, standing there with him, without the thought that he should be in shape?

Mary: I would look at him and see how handsome he is.

Katie: Yes, angel. And you'd see how much you love him. Isn't that fascinating? This is very exciting. So let's just be there a moment. Look at how you treat him, and he still wants to go to Hawaii with you. That's amazing!

Mary: What's amazing about this guy is that I am so horrible and mean, and he loves me without conditions. It drives me nuts.

Katie: "He drives you nuts"—is that true?

Mary: No. So far, it's been my thinking that drives me nuts.

Katie: So let's go back. "He should get in shape"—turn it around.

Mary: I should get in shape. I should get my thinking in shape.

Katie: Yes. Every time you look at him and are repulsed, get your thinking in shape. Judge your husband, write it down, ask four questions, and turn it around. But only if you are tired of the pain. Okay, honey, I think you've got it. Just continue through the rest of the statements on your Worksheet in the same manner. I love sitting with you. And welcome to inquiry. Welcome to The Work.

Step aside from all thinking,
and there is nowhere you can't go.
Seng-ts'an (the Third Founding Teacher of Zen)

In *Loving What Is,* Katie has given you everything you need in order to do The Work by yourself or with others. The book will guide you, step by step, through the whole process, and along the way it will show you many people doing The Work directly with Katie. These one-on-one dialogues, in which Katie brings her clarity to the most complicated human problems, are examples—dramatic examples, some of them—of how ordinary people can find their own freedom through inquiry.

Stephen Mitchell

The Work is merely four questions; it's not

even a thing. It has no motive, no strings.

It's nothing without your answers.

These four questions will join any program

you've got and enhance it. Any religion you

have — they'll enhance it. If you have no

religion, they will bring you joy. And they'll

burn up anything that isn't true for you.

They'll burn through to the reality

that has always been waiting.

How to Read This Book

The purpose of this book is your happiness. The Work has worked for thousands of people, and *Loving What Is* will show you exactly how to use it in your own life.

You begin with the problems that irritate or depress you. The book will show you how to write them down in a form that is easy to investigate. Then it will introduce the four questions and show you how to apply them to your problems. At this point, you'll be able to see how The Work can reveal solutions that are simple, radical, and life-changing.

There are exercises that will teach you how to use The Work with increasing depth and precision and show you how it can function in every situation. After doing The Work on the people in your life, you'll learn how to do it on the issues that cause you the most pain—money, for example, illness, injustice, self-hatred, or the fear of death. You'll also learn how to recognize the underlying beliefs that hide reality from your eyes and how to work with the self-judgments that upset you.

Throughout the book, there will be many examples of people just like you doing The Work—people who believe that their problems are unsolvable, who are sure that they have to suffer for the rest of their lives because a beloved child died or because they live with someone they no longer love. You will meet a mother distraught over a crying baby, a woman living in fear about the stock market, people terrorized by their thoughts about childhood trauma or just trying to get along with a difficult co-worker. You'll see how they came to find a way out of their suffering; and perhaps through them and the practical insights on the pages ahead, you'll find a way out of your own.

Everyone learns The Work in their own way. Some learn the process primarily by watching how the dialogues unfold. (I encourage you to read them actively—looking inside yourself for your own answers as you read.) Others learn The Work strictly by doing it: inquiring into whatever is troubling them at the time, pen and paper in hand. I suggest that you read chapter 2, and possibly chapter 5 as well, in order to absorb the basic instructions. You might then read each dialogue in sequence—but only if this feels helpful. If you feel like skipping around and going to the dialogues whose topics particularly interest you, that's fine. Or you might prefer to follow the thread of instructions as they continue throughout the book and dip into a dialogue only now and then. I trust that you'll do whatever works best for you.

We are entering the dimension

where we have control—

the inside.

1.

A Few Basic
Principles

What I love about The Work is that it allows you to go inside and find your own happiness, to experience what already exists within you, unchanging, immovable, ever-present, ever-waiting. No teacher is necessary. You are the teacher you've been waiting for. You are the one who can end your own suffering.

I often say, "Don't believe anything I say." I want you to discover what's true for you, not for me. Still, many people have found the following principles to be helpful for getting started in The Work.

Noticing When Your Thoughts
Argue with Reality

The only time we suffer is when we believe a thought that argues with what is. When the mind is perfectly clear, what is is what we want.

If you want reality to be different than it is, you might as well try to teach a cat to bark. You can try and try, and in the end the cat will look up at you and say, "Meow." Wanting reality to be different than it is is hopeless. You can spend the rest of your life trying to teach a cat to bark.

And yet, if you pay attention, you'll notice that you think thoughts like this dozens of times a day. "People should be kinder." "Children should be well-behaved." "My neighbors should take better care of their lawn." "The line at the grocery store should move faster." "My husband (or wife) should agree with me." "I should be thinner (or prettier or more success- ful)." These thoughts are ways of wanting reality to be different than it is. If you think that this sounds depressing, you're right. All the stress that we feel is caused by arguing with what is.

After I woke up to reality in 1986, people often referred to me as the woman who made friends with the wind. Barstow is a desert town where the wind blows a lot of the time, and everyone hated it; people even moved from there because they couldn't stand the wind. The reason I made friends with the wind—with reality—is that I discovered I didn't have a choice. I realized that it's quite insane to oppose it. When I argue with reality, I lose—but only 100 percent of the time. How do I know that the wind should blow? It's blowing!

People new to The Work often say to me, "But it would be disempow- ering to stop my argument with reality. If I simply accept reality, I'll become passive. I may even lose the desire to act." I answer them with a question: "Can you really know that that's true?" Which is more empow- ering?—"I wish I hadn't lost my job" or "I lost my job; what can I do now?"

The Work reveals that what you think shouldn't have happened *should* have happened. It should have happened because it did, and no thinking in the world can change it. This doesn't mean that you condone it or approve of it. It just means that you can see things without resistance and without the confusion of your inner struggle. No one wants their children to get sick, no one wants to be in a car accident; but when these things happen, how can it be helpful to mentally argue with them? We know better than to do that, yet we do it, because we don't know how to stop.

I am a lover of what is, not because I'm a spiritual person, but because it hurts when I argue with reality. We can know that reality is good just as it is, because when we argue with it, we experience tension and frustra- tion. We don't feel natural or balanced. When we stop opposing reality, action becomes simple, fluid, kind, and fearless.

Staying in Your Own Business

I can find only three kinds of business in the universe: mine, yours, and God's. (For me, the word *God* means "reality." Reality is God, because it rules. Anything that's out of my control, your control, and everyone else's control—I call that God's business.)

Much of our stress comes from mentally living out of our own business. When I think, "You need to get a job, I want you to be happy, you should be on time, you need to take better care of yourself," I am in your business. When I'm worried about earthquakes, floods, war, or when I will die, I am in God's business. If I am mentally in your business or in God's business, the effect is separation. I noticed this early in 1986. When I mentally went into my mother's business, for example, with a thought like "My mother should understand me," I immediately experienced a feeling of loneliness. And I realized that every time in my life that I had felt hurt or lonely, I had been in someone else's business.

If you are living your life and I am mentally living your life, who is here living mine? We're both over there. Being mentally in your business keeps me from being present in my own. I am separate from myself, wondering why my life doesn't work.

To think that I know what's best for anyone else is to be out of my business. Even in the name of love, it is pure arrogance, and the result is tension, anxiety, and fear. Do I know what's right for myself? That is my only business. Let me work with that before I try to solve your problems for you.

If you understand the three kinds of business enough to stay in your own business, it could free your life in a way that you can't even imagine. The next time you're feeling stress or discomfort, ask yourself whose business you're in mentally, and you may burst out laughing! That question can bring you back to yourself. And you may come to see that you've never really been present, that you've been mentally living in other people's business all your life. Just to notice that you're in someone else's business can bring you back to your own wonderful self.

And if you practice it for a while, you may come to see that you don't have any business either and that your life runs perfectly well on its own.

Meeting Your Thoughts
with Understanding

A thought is harmless unless we believe it. It is not our thoughts, but the *attachment* to our thoughts, that causes suffering. Attaching to a thought means believing that it's true, without inquiring. A belief is a thought that we've been attaching to, often for years.

Most people think that they *are* what their thoughts tell them they are. One day I noticed that I wasn't breathing—I was being breathed. Then I also noticed, to my amazement, that I wasn't thinking—that I was actually being thought and that thinking isn't personal. Do you wake up in the morning and say to yourself, "I think I won't think today"? It's too late: You're already thinking! Thoughts just appear. They come out of nothing and go back to nothing, like clouds moving across the empty sky. They come to pass, not to stay. There is no harm in them until we attach to them as if they were true.

No one has ever been able to control his thinking, although people may tell the story of how they have. I don't let go of my thoughts—I meet them with understanding. Then *they* let go of *me*.

Thoughts are like the breeze or the leaves on the trees or the raindrops falling. They appear like that, and through inquiry we can make friends with them. Would you argue with a raindrop? Raindrops aren't personal, and neither are thoughts. Once a painful concept is met with understanding, the next time it appears you may find it interesting. What used to be the nightmare is now just interesting. The next time it appears, you may find it funny. The next time, you may not even notice it. This is the power of loving what is.

Becoming Aware of Your Stories

I often use the word *story* to talk about thoughts, or sequences of thoughts, that we convince ourselves are real. A story may be about the past, the present, or the future; it may be about what things should be, what they could be, or why they are. Stories appear in our minds hundreds of times a day—when someone gets up without a word and walks out of the room, when someone doesn't smile or doesn't return a phone call, or when a stranger *does* smile; before you open an important letter, or after you feel an unfamiliar sensation in your chest; when your boss invites you to come to his office, or when your partner talks to you in a certain tone of voice. Stories are the untested, uninvestigated theories that tell us what all these things mean. We don't even realize that they're just theories.

Once, as I walked into the ladies' room at a restaurant near my home, a woman came out of the single stall. We smiled at each other, and, as I closed the door, she began to sing and wash her hands. "What a lovely voice!" I thought. Then, as I heard her leave, I noticed that the toilet seat was dripping wet. "How could anyone be so rude?" I thought. "And how did she manage to pee all over the seat? Was she standing on it?" Then it came to me that she was a man—a transvestite, singing falsetto in the women's restroom. It crossed my mind to go after her (him) and let him know what a mess he'd made. As I cleaned the toilet seat, I thought about everything I'd say to him. Then I flushed the toilet. The water shot up out of the bowl and flooded the seat. And I just stood there laughing.

In this case, the natural course of events was kind enough to expose my story before it went any further. Usually it doesn't; before I found inquiry, I had no way to stop this kind of thinking. Small stories bred bigger ones; bigger stories bred major theories about life, how terrible it was, and how the world was a dangerous place. I ended up feeling too frightened and depressed to leave my bedroom.

When you're operating on uninvestigated theories of what's going on and you aren't even aware of it, you're in what I call "the dream." Often the dream becomes troubling; sometimes it even turns into a nightmare. At times like these, you may want to test the truth of your theories by doing The Work on them. The Work always leaves you with less of your uncomfortable story. Who would you be without it? How much of your world is made up of unexamined stories? You never know until you inquire.

Looking for the Thought
Behind the Suffering

I have never experienced a stressful feeling that wasn't caused by attaching to an untrue thought. Behind every uncomfortable feeling, there's a thought that isn't true for us. "The wind shouldn't be blowing." "My husband should agree with me." We think the thought that argues with reality, then we have a stressful feeling, and then we act on that feeling, creating more stress for ourselves. Rather than understand the original cause—a thought—we try to change our stressful feelings by looking outside ourselves. We try to change someone else, or we reach for sex, food, alcohol, drugs, or money in order to find temporary comfort and the illusion of control.

It is easy to be swept away by some overwhelming feeling, so it's helpful to remember that any stressful feeling is like a compassionate alarm clock that says, "You're caught in the dream." Depression, pain, and fear are gifts that say, "Sweetheart, take a look at your thinking right now. You're living in a story that isn't true for you." Living an untruth is always stressful. But if we don't honor the alarm clock, we try to alter and manipulate the feeling by reaching outside ourselves. We're usually aware of the feeling before the thought. That's why I say it's an alarm clock that lets you know you're in a thought that you may want to investigate. And investigating an untrue thought through The Work always leads you back to who you really are. It hurts to believe you're other than who you are, to live any story other than happiness.

If you put your hand into a fire, does anyone have to tell you to move it? Do you have to decide? No: When your hand starts to burn, it moves. You don't have to direct it; the hand moves itself. In the same way, once you understand, through inquiry, that an untrue thought causes suffering, you move away from it. Before the thought, you weren't suffering; with the thought, you're suffering; when you recognize that the thought isn't true, again there is no suffering. That is how The Work functions. "How do I react when I think that thought?" Hand in the fire. "Who would I be without it?" Out of the flames. We look at the thought, we feel our hand in the fire, and we naturally move back to the original position; we don't have to be told. And the next time the thought arises, the mind automatically moves from the fire. The Work invites us into the awareness of internal cause and effect. When we recognize this, all our suffering begins to unravel on its own.

Inquiry

I use the word *inquiry* as synonymous with The Work. To *inquire* or to *investigate* is to put a thought or a story up against the four questions and turnaround (explained in the next chapter). Inquiry is a way to end confusion and to experience internal peace, even in a world of apparent chaos. Above all else, inquiry is about realizing that all the answers we ever need are always available inside us.

Inquiry is more than a technique: It brings to life, from deep within us, an innate aspect of our being. When practiced for a while, inquiry takes on its own life within you. It appears whenever thoughts appear, as their balance and mate. This internal partnership leaves you clear and free to live as a kind, fluid, fearless, amused listener, a student of yourself, and a friend who can be trusted not to resent, criticize, or hold a grudge. Eventually, realization is experienced automatically, as a way of life. Peace and joy naturally, inevitably, and irreversibly make their way into every corner of your mind, into every relationship and experience. The process is so subtle that you may not even have any conscious awareness of it. You may only know that you used to hurt and now you don't.

You're either attaching

to your thoughts

or inquiring.

There's no other choice.

2.

The Great Undoing

The one criticism of The Work I consistently hear is that it's just too simple. People say, "Freedom can't be this simple!" I answer, "Can you really know that that's true?"

Judge your neighbor, write it down, ask four questions, turn it around. Who would imagine that freedom could be so simple?

Putting the Mind on Paper

The first step in The Work is to write down your judgments about any stressful situation in your life, past, present, or future—about a person you dislike or worry about, a situation with someone who angers or frightens or saddens you, or someone you're ambivalent or confused about. Write your judgments down, just the way you think them. (Use a blank sheet of paper; or, if you have access to the Internet, you can go to http://www.thework.org, to the section called "Do The Work," where you'll find a Judge-Your-Neighbor Worksheet to download and print.)

Don't be surprised if you find this difficult. For thousands of years, we have been taught not to judge—but let's face it, we still do it all the time. The truth is that we all have judgments running in our heads. Through The Work we finally have permission to let those judgments speak out, or even scream out, on paper. We find that even the most vile thoughts can be met with unconditional love.

I encourage you to write about someone—parent, lover, enemy—

whom you haven't yet totally forgiven. This is the most powerful place to begin. Even if you've forgiven that person 99 percent, you aren't free until your forgiveness is complete. The 1 percent you haven't forgiven them is the very place where you're stuck in all your other relationships (including the relationship with yourself).

I strongly suggest that if you are new to inquiry, you not write about yourself at first. If you start by judging yourself, your answers come with a motive and with solutions that haven't worked. Judging someone else, then inquiring and turning it around, is the direct path to understanding. You can judge yourself later, when you have been doing inquiry long enough to trust the power of truth.

If you begin by pointing the finger of blame outward, then the focus isn't on you. You can just let loose and be uncensored. We're often quite sure about what other people need to do, how they should live, whom they should be with. We have 20/20 vision about other people, but not about ourselves.

When you do The Work, you see who you are by seeing who you think other people are. Eventually you come to see that everything outside you is a reflection of your own thinking. You are the storyteller, the projector of all stories, and the world is the projected image of your thoughts.

Since the beginning of time, people have been trying to change the world so that they can be happy. This hasn't ever worked, because it approaches the problem backward. What The Work gives us is a way to change the projector—mind—rather than the projected. It's like having a piece of lint on a projector's lens. We think there's a flaw on the screen, and we try to change this person and that person, whomever the flaw appears to be on next. But it's futile to try to change the projected images. Once we realize where the lint is, we can clear the lens itself. This is the end of suffering, and the beginning of a little joy in paradise.

People often say to me, "Why should I judge my neighbor? I already know that it's all about me." I say, "I understand. And please trust the process. Judge your neighbor, and follow the simple directions." Here are some examples of people you may want to write about: mother, father, wife, husband, children, siblings, partner, neighbor, friend, enemy, roommate, boss, teacher, employee, co-worker, teammate, salesmen, customers, men, women, authorities, God. Often, the more personal your choice is, the more potent The Work can be.

Later, as you become skilled in The Work, you may want to investigate your judgments about issues such as death, money, health, your body, your addictions, and even your own self-criticisms. (See chapter 6, "Doing The Work on Work and Money"; chapter 7, "Doing The Work on Self-Judgments"; and chapter 11, "Doing The Work on the Body and Addictions.") In fact, once you are ready, you can write about and inquire into any uncomfortable thought that appears in your mind. When you realize that every stressful moment you experience is a gift that points you to your own freedom, life becomes very kind and abundant beyond all limits.

Why and How to Write on the Worksheet

Please avoid the temptation to continue without writing down your judgments. If you try to do The Work in your head, without putting your thoughts on paper, the mind will outsmart you. Before you're even aware of it, it will be off and running into another story to corroborate your first statement. But though the mind can justify itself faster than the speed of light, it can be stopped through the act of writing. Once the mind is stopped on paper, thoughts remain stable, and inquiry can easily be applied.

Write down your thoughts without trying to censor them. Sit with your pen and paper and just wait. The words will come. The story will come. And if you really want to know the truth, if you're not afraid to see your story on paper, the ego will write like a maniac. It doesn't care; it's totally uninhibited. This is the day the ego has been waiting for. Give it its life on paper. It has been waiting for you to stop, just once, and really listen to it. It will tell you everything, like a child. Then, when the mind is expressed on paper, you can inquire.

I invite you to be judgmental, harsh, childish, and petty. Write with the spontaneity of a child who is sad, angry, confused, or frightened. Don't try to be wise, spiritual, or kind. This is the time to be totally honest and uncensored about how you feel. Allow your feelings to express themselves, without any fear of consequences or any threat of punishment.

People who have been in The Work for a while get pettier and pettier on their Worksheets, as they try to find the sticking-points that are left. Beliefs just get more subtle, more invisible, as problems dissolve. They're just the last little children calling out, "Yoo-hoo! Here I am! Come and find me!" The more you do The Work, the more uncensored you become and the pettier you like to get, because it becomes hard to find something that will upset you. Eventually, you can't find a problem. That's an experience I hear from thousands of people.

Write down the thoughts and stories that are running through you, the ones that really cause you pain—the anger, the resentment, the sadness. Point the finger of blame first at people who have hurt you, the ones who have been closest to you, people you're jealous of, people you can't stand, people who have disappointed you. "My husband left me." "My partner infected me with AIDS." "My mother didn't love me." "My children don't respect me." "My friend betrayed me." "I hate my boss." "I hate my neighbors; they're ruining my life." Write about what you read this morning in the newspaper, about people being murdered or losing their homes through famine or war. Write about the checker at the grocery store who was too slow or about the driver who cut you off on the freeway. Every story is a variation on a single theme: *This shouldn't be happening. I shouldn't have to experience this. God is unjust. Life isn't fair.*

People new to The Work sometimes think, "I don't know what to write. Why should I do The Work anyway? I'm not angry at anyone. Nothing's really bothering me." If you don't know what to write about, wait. Life will give you a topic. Maybe a friend didn't call you back when she said she would, and you're disappointed. Maybe when you were five years old, your mother punished you for something you didn't do. Maybe you're upset or frightened when you read the newspaper or think about the suffering in the world.

Put on paper the part of the mind that is saying these things. You can't stop the story inside your head, however long you try. It's not possible. But when you put the story on paper and write it just the way the mind is telling it, with all your suffering and frustration and rage and sadness, then you can take a look at what is swirling around inside you. You can see it brought into the material world, in physical form. And finally, through The Work, you can begin to understand it.

When a child gets lost, he may feel sheer terror. It can be just as frightening when you're lost inside the mind's chaos. But when you enter The Work, it is possible to find order and to learn the way back home. It doesn't matter what street you walk down, there's something familiar; you know where you are. You could be kidnapped and someone hides you away for a month and then throws you blindfolded out of a car, but when you take off the blindfold and look at the buildings and streets, you begin to recognize a phone booth or a grocery store, and everything becomes familiar. You know what to do to find your way home. That is how The Work functions. Once the mind is met with understanding, it can always find its way back home. There is no place where you can remain lost or confused.

The Judge-Your-Neighbor Worksheet

After my life changed in 1986, I spent a lot of time in the desert near my home, just listening to myself. Stories arose inside me that had been troubling mankind forever. Sooner or later, I witnessed every concept, it seemed, and I discovered that even though I was alone in the desert, the whole world was with me. And it sounded like this: "I want," "I need," "they should," "they shouldn't," "I'm angry because," "I'm sad," "I'll never," "I don't want to." These phrases, which repeated themselves over and over in my mind, became the basis for the six sets of queries on the Judge-Your-Neighbor Worksheet. The purpose of the Worksheet is to help you put your painful stories and judgments into writing; it's designed to draw out judgments that otherwise might be difficult to uncover.

The judgments you write on the Worksheet will become the material that you'll use to do The Work. You'll put each written statement — one by one — up against the four questions and let each of them lead you to the truth.

On the next page, you'll find an example of a completed Judge-Your-

Neighbor Worksheet. I have written about my second husband, Paul, in this example (included here with his permission); these are the kinds of thoughts that I used to have about him before my life changed. As you read, you're invited to replace Paul's name with the appropriate name in your life.

1. **Who angers or saddens or disappoints you? What is it about them that you didn't or still don't like?**
   I don't like (I am angry at, or saddened, frightened, confused, etc., by) (name) *Paul* because *he doesn't listen to me. I'm angry at Paul because he doesn't appreciate me. I'm angry at Paul because he wakes me at midnight and doesn't care about my health. I don't like Paul because he argues with everything I say. I'm saddened by Paul because he is so angry.*

2. **How do you want them to change? What do you want them to do?**
   I want (name) *Paul to give me his full attention. I want Paul to love me completely. I want Paul to be considerate of my needs. I want Paul to agree with me. I want Paul to get more exercise.*

3. **What is it that they should or shouldn't do, be, think, or feel?**
   (Name) *Paul shouldn't watch so much television. Paul should stop smoking. Paul should tell me that he loves me. He shouldn't ignore me. He shouldn't criticize me in front of our children and friends.*

4. **Do you need anything from them? What do they need to give you or do in order for you to be happy?**
   I need (name) *Paul to listen to me. I need Paul to stop lying to me. I need Paul to share his feelings and be emotionally available. I need Paul to be gentle and kind and patient.*

5. **What do you think of them? Make a list.**
   (Name) *Paul is dishonest. Paul is reckless. Paul is childish. He thinks he doesn't have to follow the rules. Paul is uncaring and unavailable. Paul is irresponsible.*

6. **What is it that you don't ever want to experience with that person, thing, or situation again?**
I don't ever want or I refuse to *live with Paul if he doesn't change. I refuse to watch Paul ruin his health. I don't ever want to argue with Paul again. I don't ever want to be lied to by Paul again.*

Inquiry:
The Four Questions and Turnaround

1. Is it true?
2. Can you absolutely know that it's true?
3. How do you react when you think that thought?
4. Who would you be without the thought?
   and
   Turn it around.

Now, using the four questions, let's investigate the first statement from number 1 on the example: *I don't like Paul because he doesn't listen to me.* As you read along, think of someone you haven't totally forgiven yet.

1. Is it true? Ask yourself, "Is it true that Paul doesn't listen to me?" Be still. If you really want to know the truth, the answer will rise to meet the question. Let the mind ask the question, and wait for the answer that surfaces.

2. Can you absolutely know that it's true? Consider these questions: "Can I really know that it's true that Paul doesn't listen to me? Can I ever really know when someone is listening or not? Am I sometimes not listening even when I appear to be?"

3. How do you react when you think that thought? At this point, examine how you react and how you treat Paul when you think the thought "Paul doesn't listen to me." Make a list. For example: "I give him 'the look.' I interrupt him. I punish him by not paying attention to him. I start talking faster and louder and try to force him to listen and understand." Continue making your list as you go inside, and see how you treat yourself in that situation and how that feels. "I shut down. I isolate myself. I eat and sleep a lot, and I watch television for days. I feel depressed and lonely." Be still and realize how you react when you believe the thought "Paul doesn't listen to me."

4. Who would you be without the thought? Now consider who you would be if you couldn't think the thought "Paul doesn't listen to me." Close your eyes and imagine Paul not listening to you. Imagine you don't have the thought that Paul doesn't listen (or that he even should listen). Take your time. Notice what is revealed to you. What do you see? How does that feel?

Turn it around. The original statement "I don't like Paul because he doesn't listen to me," when reversed, could become "I don't like myself because I don't listen to Paul." Is that as true or truer for you? Are you listening to Paul when you're thinking about him not listening to you? Continue to find other examples of how you don't listen (to someone you work with or care about, for example).

Another turnaround that could be as true or truer is "I don't like myself because I don't listen to myself." When you're mentally out of your business and thinking about what Paul should be doing, are you listening to yourself? Do you put your own life on hold when you believe that he should listen? Can you hear how you talk to Paul when you believe that he should listen?

After sitting with the turnarounds, you would continue a typical inquiry with the next statement written in number 1 on the Worksheet— *I'm angry at Paul because he doesn't appreciate me*—and then with every other statement on the Worksheet.

The turnarounds are *your* prescription for health, peace, and happiness. Can you give yourself the medicine that you have been prescribing for others?

Your Turn: The Worksheet

Now you know enough to try out The Work. First you'll put your thoughts on paper. It's not time to inquire with the four questions yet; we'll do that later. Simply pick a person or situation and write, using short, simple sentences. Remember to *point the finger of blame or judgment outward*. You may write from your present position or from your point of view as a five-year-old or twenty-five-year-old. Please do *not* write about yourself yet.

1. **Who angers or saddens or disappoints you? What is it about them that you didn't or still don't like?** (Remember: Be harsh, childish, and petty.) I don't like (I am angry at, or saddened, frightened, confused, etc., by) (name) because _____.

2. **How do you want them to change? What do you want them to do?** I want (name) to _____.

3. **What is it that they should or shouldn't do, be, think, or feel?** (Name) should (shouldn't) _____.

4. **Do you need anything from them? What do they need to give you or do in order for you to be happy?** (Pretend it's your birthday and you can have anything you want. Go for it!) I need (name) to _____.

5. **What do you think of them? Make a list.** (Don't be rational or kind.) (Name) is _____.

6. **What is it that you don't ever want to experience with that person, thing, or situation again?** I don't ever want or I refuse to _____.

[Note: Sometimes you may find yourself upset without knowing why. There is always an internal story, but occasionally it can be hard to find. If you feel blocked with the Judge-Your-Neighbor Worksheet, see "When the Story Is Hard to Find," pages 163–165.]

Your Turn: The Inquiry

One by one, put each statement on the Judge-Your-Neighbor Worksheet up against the four questions, and then turn around the statement you're working on. (If you need help, refer back to the example on pages 14–15.) Throughout this process, practice being open to possibilities beyond what you think you know. There's nothing more exciting than discovering the don't-know mind.

It's like diving. Keep asking the question and wait. Let the answer find you. I call it the heart meeting the mind: the gentler polarity of mind (which I call the heart) meeting the polarity that is confused because it hasn't been investigated. When the mind asks sincerely, the heart will respond. Many of you will begin to experience revelations about yourself and your world, revelations that can transform your whole life, forever.

Take the time now to give yourself a taste of The Work. Look at the first statement that you have written on number 1 of your Worksheet. Now ask yourself the following questions:

1. Is it true?

Take your time. The Work is about discovering what is true from the deepest part of yourself. It may not coincide with anything you've ever considered before. But when you experience your own answer, you'll know it. Just be gentle, sit with it, and let it take you deeper in.

There are no right or wrong answers to these questions. You are listening for *your* answers now, not other people's, and not anything you have been taught. This can be very unsettling, because you're entering the unknown. As you continue to dive deeper, allow the truth within you to rise and meet the question. Be gentle as you give yourself to inquiry. Let this experience have you completely.

2. Can you absolutely know that it's true?

This is an opportunity to go deeper into the unknown, to find the answers that live beneath what we think we know. All I can tell you about this realm is that what lives beneath the nightmare is a good thing. Do you really want to know the truth?

If your answer to question 2 is yes, you can simply move on to the next question. But you may find it useful to pause and rewrite your statement in order to uncover your interpretation of it. Often it is the interpretation, which may be hidden from you, that causes you pain. For a detailed explanation of rewriting, see pages 69–72.

3. How do you react when you think that thought?

Make a list. How do you treat yourself, how do you treat the person you've written about, when you think that thought? What do you do? Be specific. Make a list of your actions. What do you say to that person when you think that thought? List the things you say. How do you live when you believe that thought? List how each reaction feels physically inside you. Where do you feel it? How does it feel (tingling, hot, etc.)? What is the self-talk that goes on in your head when you think that thought?

4. Who would you be without the thought?

Close your eyes and wait. Imagine yourself just for a moment without the thought. Imagine that you didn't have the ability to think the thought as you stand in the presence of that person (or in that situation). What do you see? How does it feel? How is the situation different? List the possibilities for living your life without this concept. For example, how would you treat that person differently in the same situation without the thought? Does this feel kinder inside you?

Turn it around.

To do the turnaround, rewrite your statement. This time, write it as if it were written about you. Where you have written someone's name, put yourself. Instead of "he" or "she," put "I." For example, "Paul should be kind to me" turns around to "I should be kind to myself" and "I should be kind to Paul." Another type is a 180-degree turnaround to the extreme opposite: "Paul shouldn't be kind to me." He shouldn't be kind, because he isn't (in my opinion). This isn't an issue of morality but of what's actually true.

You may come to see that there are three or four or more turnarounds in one sentence. Or there may be just one or two that feel true for you. (The turnaround for statement number 6 on the Worksheet is different from the usual turnaround. We take the statement and replace "I don't ever want to …" with "I am willing to …" and then "I look forward to. …") See pages 76–83 for help with turnarounds.

Consider whether or not the turned-around statement is as true as or truer than your original statement. For example, the turnaround "I should be kind to myself" does seem as true as or truer than the original statement, because when I think that Paul should be kind to me, I get angry and resentful, and I cause myself a lot of stress. This is not a kind thing to do. If I were kind to myself, I wouldn't have to wait for kindness from others. "I should be kind to Paul"—that too is at least as true as the original statement. When I think that Paul should be kind to me and I get angry and resentful, I treat Paul very unkindly, especially in my mind. Let me begin with myself and act as I'd like Paul to act. As for "Paul shouldn't be kind to me," that is certainly truer than its opposite. He shouldn't be kind, because he isn't. That's the reality of it.

The Inquiry Continued

Now it's time for you to continue applying the four questions and the turnaround to your own judgments, one at a time. Read all the sentences you have written on your Judge-Your-Neighbor Worksheet. Then, one by one, investigate each statement by asking yourself:

1. Is it true?
2. Can I absolutely know that it's true?
3. How do I react when I think that thought?
4. Who would I be without the thought?
   and then
   Turn it around.

If you try The Work now and it doesn't seem to work for you, that's fine. Just move on to the next chapter, or do The Work on a different person and come back to this one later. Don't stop to worry about whether The Work is working or not. You're just beginning to learn how to do it.

It's like riding a bike. All you need to do is keep wobbling on. As you read the dialogues, you'll get a better feel for it. And you won't necessarily be the first to notice that it's working. You may find, as many people have, that it doesn't seem to have any effect now, but you have already shifted in ways you can't feel yet. The Work can be very subtle and profound.

Everyone is a mirror image

of yourself—

your own thinking

coming back at you.

3.

Entering the Dialogues

In reading the dialogues in this book, it is important to understand that there is no essential difference between what the facilitator does (in these examples, it happens to be me) and what a person doing The Work alone does. You are the teacher and healer you've been waiting for. This book is designed to help you do The Work by yourself. It's not necessary to work with a facilitator, though that can be very powerful. It can also be useful to watch someone else do The Work with a facilitator and, as you watch, to look inside for your own answers. Participating in this way helps you learn how to question yourself.

Many of the following chapters contain dialogues with men and women doing The Work. These are edited transcripts of conversations taped during workshops that I have given over the past year or two. At a typical workshop, several participants volunteer to sit with me, one by one, in front of the audience and read what they have written on their Judge-Your-Neighbor Worksheet. Then they are guided into the power of the four questions and the turnaround, and thus into their own self-induced realizations.

I have discovered that in every language and every country I have visited, there are no new thoughts. They're all recycled. The same thoughts arise in each mind one way or another, sooner or later. That's why anyone's Work can be your Work also. Read these dialogues as if they were written by you. Don't just read the workshop participants' answers. Go inside and discover your own. Get as emotionally involved and as close to them as you can. Discover where and when you have experienced what you're reading about.

You'll notice that I don't always ask the four questions in the order you've learned. I sometimes vary the usual order, I leave out questions, zeroing in on just one or two, and sometimes I skip the questions entirely and go directly to the turnaround. Even though the usual order of the questions works well, after a while it may not be necessary to ask them in order. You don't have to begin with "Is it true?" You can start with any question; "Who would you be without that thought?" might be the first one, if that feels right. Just one of these questions can set you free if you inquire deeply from within. And the questions become internalized as inquiry lives its life in you. But until this happens, the deepest shifts happen when you ask all four questions and the turnaround in the suggested order. That's why I strongly recommend that those new to The Work stay with this form.

Notice that I sometimes ask two subsidiary questions: "Can you see a reason to drop that thought?" and "Can you find one stress-free reason to keep the thought?" These are follow-ups to the third question, "How do you react when you think that thought?" They can be very useful.

Notice also that when I feel it is appropriate, I will help someone find the story that is the real cause of their suffering and that may be hidden from their awareness. This may involve looking more deeply at the original statement to find the statement behind it. Or it may involve shifting the inquiry from the written statements to a painful statement that they've just spontaneously made. (When you do The Work on your own, and a new painful thought or deeper story appears, you may want to write it down to include in your inquiry.)

Please understand that The Work does not condone any harmful action. To hear it as justifying anything that is less than kind is to misinterpret it. If you find something in the following pages that sounds cold, uncaring, unloving, or unkind, I invite you to be gentle with it. Breathe through it. Feel and experience what arises in *you*. Go inside yourself and answer the four questions. Experience inquiry for yourself.

If you can't relate to one of the following examples as closely as you would like to, try substituting someone who is significant in your life for what's written. For example, if the participant's issue is with a friend, and you substitute the word *husband, wife, lover, mother, father,* or *boss,* you may find that his Work turned out to be your Work. We think we are doing The Work on people, but actually we're working on our *thoughts* about people. (You can write an entire Worksheet on your mother, for example, and later find that your relationship with your daughter has dramatically improved, because you were attached to the very same thoughts about her, though you weren't aware of it.)

The Work allows you to go inside and experience the peace that already exists within you. That peace is unchanging, immovable, and ever-present. The Work takes you there. It is a true homecoming.

[Note: To help you follow the process of inquiry, the four questions are printed in boldface in chapter 4.]

If I had a prayer, it would be this:

"God, spare me from the desire

for love, approval, or appreciation.

Amen."

4.

Doing The Work on Couples and Family Life

My experience is that the teachers we need most are the people we're living with now. Our spouses, parents, and children are the clearest masters we could hope for. Again and again, they will show us the truth we don't want to see, until we see it.

After I returned home from the halfway house in 1986 with a radically different understanding of the world and of myself, I found that nothing my husband or my children did could upset me. Inquiry was alive inside me, and every thought I had was met by a wordless questioning. When Paul did something that would have angered me before, and the thought "He should" appeared in my mind, all I felt was gratitude and laughter. The man might have been walking on the carpets with mud all over his shoes, or dropping his clothes everywhere, or shouting at me, waving his arms, his face red, and if "He should" appeared in my mind, I just laughed at myself, because I knew what it led to; I knew it led to "I should." "He should stop screaming"? *I* should stop screaming, mentally, about him, before I remind him to take off his muddy shoes.

I remember sitting on the living room couch with my eyes closed, and Paul came into the room and saw me, and he stormed up to me, shouting, "Jesus Christ, Kate, what the hell is the matter with you?" It was a simple question. So I went inside and asked myself, "What the hell *is* the matter with you, Katie?" It wasn't personal. Could I just find an answer to that question? Well, there had been one instant when I'd had the thought that Paul shouldn't have been shouting, though the reality was that he *was* shouting. Ah. *That's* what was the matter with me. So I said, "Sweetheart, the matter with me is that I had the thought that you shouldn't be shouting, and it didn't feel right. Thank you for asking. Now it feels right again."

During those first few months, my children would seek me out and tell me what they really thought of the woman they'd known as their mother—things they would have been punished for saying before. For example, Bobby, my older son, trusted me enough to say, "You always favored Ross over me. You always loved him the most." (Ross is my younger son.) And I was finally the mother who could listen. I went inside with it and got still. "Could this be true? Could he be right?" And since I had invited my children to speak honestly, because I really wanted to know the truth, I found it. So I said, "Honey, I see it. You're right. I was very confused." I felt such love for him as my teacher who had lived through all that pain, and such love for the woman who thought she preferred one child over another.

People often ask me if I had a religion before 1986, and I say yes—it was "My children should pick up their socks." This was my religion, and I was totally devoted to it, even though it never worked. Then one day, after The Work was alive in me, I realized that it simply wasn't true. The reality was that day after day, they left their socks on the floor, after all my years of preaching and nagging and punishing them. I saw that *I* was the one who should pick up the socks if I wanted them picked up. My children were perfectly happy with their socks on the floor. Who had the problem? It was me. It was my thoughts about the socks on the floor that had made my life difficult, not the socks themselves. And who had the solution? Again, me. I realized that I could be right, or I could be free. It took just a few moments for me to pick up the socks, without any thought of my children. And an amazing thing began to happen. I realized that I loved picking up their socks. It was for me, not for them. It stopped being a chore in that moment, and it became a pleasure to pick them up and see the uncluttered floor. Eventually, they noticed my pleasure and began to pick up their socks on their own, without my having to suggest it.

Our parents, our children, our spouses, and our friends will press every button we have, again and again, until we realize what it is that we don't want to know about ourselves, yet. They will point us to our freedom every time.

I Want My Son to Talk to Me

In this dialogue, a mother comes to understand her son's apparent neglect. When she realizes that her sadness, resentment, and guilt have nothing to do with him and have everything to do with her own thinking, she opens the possibility of change, for herself and also for her son. We don't have to wait for our children to change before we can be happy. We may even come to discover that the very situation we dislike is what we've been looking for—the entrance into ourselves.

———————

Elisabeth [reading from her Worksheet]: *I am angry at Christopher because he stopped contacting me and doesn't invite me to meet his family. I'm saddened because he doesn't talk to me.*

Katie: Good. Continue.

Elisabeth: I want Christopher to talk to me from time to time, to invite me to meet him, his wife, and his kids. He should stand up to his wife and tell her that he doesn't want to exclude his mother. And he should stop blaming me. I need Christopher to accept me, to accept my way of life. And I need him to understand that I did my best. Christopher is a coward, resentful, arrogant, and rigid. I don't ever want to feel him rejecting me, or not contacting me anymore.

Katie: Okay. So we'll take some of these thoughts to inquiry now. At this point, we're going to look at our thinking, ask four questions, and turn it around. And see if we can find some understanding. So let's begin. Read the first statement again.

Elisabeth: I'm angry at Christopher because he stopped contacting me and doesn't invite me to meet his family.

Katie: Is that true? Is that really true? [There is a long pause.] Just answer yes or no, sweetheart. There's no trickery in these questions. It's not better if you answer one way or another. This is simply to go inside for yourself and see what's really true. And maybe to go inside again under that. And under that. "He doesn't contact you or invite you to meet his family"—is **that true?**

Elisabeth: Well, sometimes.

Katie: Good. "Sometimes" is more honest, because you've just revealed that he does invite you. "He doesn't invite you to meet his family"—is **that true?** The answer simply is no.

Elisabeth: I see that.

Katie: And **how do you react when you think the thought?**

Elisabeth: It makes me totally tense. My mind is agitated every time the phone rings.

Katie: Can you see a reason to drop the thought "He doesn't invite me to meet his family"? And I'm not asking you to drop it. Just simply, can you see a reason to drop this lie that argues with reality?

Elisabeth: Yes.

Katie: Give me a peaceful reason to keep this story, a reason that doesn't cause you stress.

Elisabeth [after a long pause]: I can't find one.

Katie: Let's work with the thought "I want my son to call me." I can tell you my experience—that I don't ever want my sons to call me. I want them to live the way they want to live. I want them to call whoever they want to call, and I love that it's often me. It wasn't always that way. **Who would you be without the thought** "I want my son to call me. I want him to invite me into his family whether he wants to or not"?

Elisabeth: I would be a person who could breathe and enjoy life.

Katie: And you'd be intimate with him, with no separation, whether he visits you or not. Intimate with him in here, in the heart. Let's **turn this** first statement **around.**

Elisabeth: I'm angry and saddened at me because I stopped contacting me.

Katie: Yes. You've been mentally living in your son's business. So you've traded yourself for the dream of how your son should live. I love my sons, and I'm sure they can run their lives *at least* as well as I could run their lives. They need to see me? I trust that they're the best judges of that. If I want to see them, I let them know, and they say yes or no honestly. That's it. If they say yes, I love it. If they say no, I love it. There's nothing I can lose. That's not possible. Can you find another turnaround?

Elisabeth: I'm saddened because I don't talk to me.

Katie: You don't talk to you. You're mentally over there running his business. And then you're *feeling* all the loneliness of that. The loneliness of not being here for yourself. Okay, now read your next statement.

Elisabeth: I want Christopher to talk to me from time to time, to invite me to meet him, his wife, and his kids.

Katie: "You want him to invite you to meet his wife and children"—is **that really true?** Why do you want to be with them? What do you want them to do or say?

Elisabeth: What I actually want is for them to accept me.

Katie: **Turn it around.**

Elisabeth: What I actually want is for me to accept myself.

Katie: Why burden them with something you can give to yourself?

Elisabeth: And what I actually want is for me to accept them, the way they live.

Katie: Yes. With or without you. [Elisabeth laughs.] And I know you can do it because you thought they could do it so easily. This tells me you know the way. "If they invite you, they will accept you"—**can you absolutely know that that's true?**

Elisabeth: No.

Katie: So **how do you react when you believe the thought?**

Elisabeth: It's horrible. It gives me a headache and tension in the shoulders.

Katie: So, you want them to invite you and accept you, and then you'll have . . . what?

Elisabeth: For a few minutes, I guess I'll have something. Then when I leave, it's the same story.

Katie: You go there, and what do you get?

Elisabeth: A kind of satisfaction.

Katie: Yes. You tell the story of how they invited you, and this story makes you happy. Or you tell the story of how they don't invite you, and the story makes you sad. Nothing is happening but your story. And yet you believe that it's their action or nonaction that causes your emotions. You're deluding yourself with your own uninvestigated thoughts, in their name, bouncing off walls—happy, sad, happy, sad. "It's their fault I'm happy, it's their fault I'm sad." This is confusion. Let's look at the next one.

Elisabeth: He should stand up to his wife . . .

Katie: Is that true? Does he?

Elisabeth: No.

Katie: How do you react when you think that thought?

Elisabeth: It's horrible. It makes me suffer.

Katie: Yes, because it's not true for you. "Christopher, make war in your home, and win, so that I can come in." That's not what we want from our children. And then it moves into "He's a coward." We haven't stopped to investigate. Maybe what you perceive as his not standing up to his wife is really courage. Maybe it's love. Can you see a reason to drop the thought "He should stand up to his wife"?

Elisabeth: Yes.

Katie: Yes. Internal war is a reason. Internal war makes external war. Who would you be without this thought?

Elisabeth: Less angry.

Katie: Yes. You might even see that you have a courageous, loving son, who does what he knows to do, with a peaceful family, even though he has a mother who thinks he should stand up to his wife. How do you treat him when you think that thought? Do you give him "the look"? Just to let him know that you think he's a coward, or doing it wrong? Let's look at the next one.

Elisabeth [laughing]: Am I going to survive this up here?

Katie [laughing]: Well, hopefully not. [Loud laughter from the audience]

Elisabeth: Hopefully not.

Katie: This Work is the end of the world as we understand it to be, sweetheart. And it's the opening to reality, as it really is, in all its beauty. What is already true is much better without any plan of mine. I'm so glad of that. My life is so simple, now that I no longer rule the world in my mind. And my children and friends are very grateful. Let's look at the next statement.

Elisabeth: He should stop blaming me.

Katie: "He should stop blaming you"—is that true? Now you want to control his thinking—even who he should blame.

Elisabeth [laughing]: Oh, God!

Katie: You want to take over your son's whole mind. You know what's best for him. You even know what he should be thinking. "Excuse me, Christopher. Don't think unless I've told you what to think; don't think until I want you to." [Laughter] "And then let's work on your wife. And by the way, I love you." [More laughter]

Elisabeth: Ooooh. I knew it!

Katie: So, read it again.

Elisabeth: He should stop blaming me.

Katie: "He blames you"—is that really true?

Elisabeth: No.

Katie: How do you react when you believe that thought?

Elisabeth: Ooof. It kills me.

Katie: And what's the worst thing he could say to blame you? [To audience] What could your children say about you that you don't want to hear?

Elisabeth: "You weren't a good mother. You aren't a good mother."

Katie: Can you find it? Can you find a place where you feel you didn't do what a good mother should do?

Elisabeth: Yes.

Katie: If one of my sons said to me, "You're not a good mother," I could honestly say, "You know, sweetheart, I can find that. I travel all over the world, I'm hardly ever physically there for you and my grandchildren. Thank you for bringing that to my attention. What do you suggest?" My sons and I have everything in common. They tell me what I may not have realized for myself. I look inside myself to see if they're right, and so far they always have been. It's simply a matter of my going deep enough into the truth to find it. I can go outside and attack them and their ideas about me in the attempt to change their minds and keep my lack of awareness, or I can go inside and search for a new truth that will set me free. This is why I say that all war belongs on paper. Inquiry takes me to the answers inside. And when my children tell me, "You're a wonderful mother," I can go in and find that, too. I don't have to go out to them and say, "Oh, thank you, thank you, thank you" and live my life proving it. I can just go in and find "I'm a wonderful mother." And then I don't have to diffuse it by doing all that thank-you stuff. I can sit with both my sons, wordlessly, with tears of joy just streaming down our cheeks. Love is so big that you can die in it —die of self and be fully consumed in it. It's what you are, and it will have all of you back to itself again. So simple. My sons are always right. My daughter is always right. My friends are always right. And I get to realize it or suffer. All of it. I am everything they say I am. And anything I feel I need to defend keeps me from full realization. So, sweetheart, let's **turn that around.**

Elisabeth: I should stop blaming him.

Katie: Yes. Work on that. It's not his job to work on it. He's providing for his family. This "stop blaming" thing is your philosophy; it's for *you* to live. This will keep you very busy, and out of his business. And that's where life begins. It begins from where you are now, not from where he is. Let's look at the next statement.

Elisabeth: I need Christopher to accept me, to accept my way of life.

Katie: "Stop your life, Christopher, and accept *my* way of life." Is this what you really need? **Is this true?**

Elisabeth: No. It really isn't true.

Katie: **Turn it around. "I need me . . ."**

Elisabeth: I need me to accept him and his way of life. That feels much better.

Katie: Yes. His way of life. He has a wonderful family, he doesn't invite you with all your concepts into his life to make war with his wife, to have to appreciate you and . . .

Elisabeth: Oooh . . . Oooh.

Katie: He sounds like a very wise man.

Elisabeth: He is.

Katie: You might call and thank him. "Thank you for not inviting me. I haven't been someone you would really want to have around. And I understand now."

Elisabeth [laughing]: Yes, I can see that.

Katie: And you might also let him know that you love him and that you're working on unconditional love. So, sweetheart, there's another turn-around.

Elisabeth: I need to accept myself, and I need to accept my way of life.

Katie: Yes. Give him a break and know that it's for you to accept your way of life. I know it's a very simple matter for you to accept it, because you expected him to do it just like that! [Snaps her fingers] Let's look at the next one.

Elisabeth: I need him to understand that I did my best.

Katie: **Is that true?**

Elisabeth: No.

Katie: **How do you react when you believe this fairy tale?**

Elisabeth: I'm hurt and angry. I feel like I'm in hell.

Katie: **Who would you be without this story** of victimhood? It's the story of a dictator not having her own way. Here's the dictator: "You should tell me that I did the best that I could do." It's crazy. What would you be without this sad, sad story?

Elisabeth: I would be a free, joyful being.

Katie: Now that's very exciting. You would already be what you wanted him to see you as: a mother who did her best at the time and is loving her son now. He could never know who you really are anyway; it's not possible. I say, skip the middleman, and be happy and free from where you are right now. Once we start doing that, we become so lovable that our children are attracted to us. They have to be. The storyteller's mind, the projector of the story, has changed, so what you project as a world has to change. When I am clear, my children have to love me; they have no choice. Love is all that I'm able to project or see. The whole world is simply *my* story, projected back to me on the screen of my own perception. All of it. Let's look at the next one, sweetheart.

Elisabeth: Christopher is a coward.

Katie: **Is that true?** My goodness, look who he's been up against. A tiger. A mother tigress. [Elisabeth bursts out laughing.]

Elisabeth: Oh, a tigress, ooh. Yes, that's true. Well, he did a good job. From the very beginning.

Katie: You may want to share that with him. "He's a coward"—**turn it around.**

Elisabeth: I am a coward.

Katie: Yes. You use him for your happiness. But he's not going for it. He's a brilliant teacher. We all live with the perfect teacher. No mistake. Let's look at the next ones and **turn them around.**

Elisabeth: He's resentful. I am resentful. *He's arrogant.* I am arrogant. *He's rigid.* I am rigid.

Katie: Yes. We've been confused for a while, that's all. Just a little confusion here and there, nothing serious.

Elisabeth [crying]: I've been wanting this for so long, to stop the confusion.

Katie: I know, angel. We have all wanted this for so long. It's time now. Let's move to your last statement.

Elisabeth: I don't ever want to feel him rejecting me.

Katie: **Turn it around.** "I'm willing to feel . . ."

Elisabeth: I'm willing to feel him rejecting me.

Katie: Each time he rejects you, if you still feel pain, you can realize that your Work's not done. And he is the master. He will continue to reject you until you understand. You are responsible for not rejecting him or yourself. Take it to inquiry and give yourself your freedom. "I look forward to . . ."

Elisabeth: I look forward to feeling him reject me.

Katie: It's good that it hurts. Pain is the signal that you're confused, that you're in a lie. Judge your son, write it down, ask four questions, turn it around, and realize whatever pain is left.

Elisabeth: Okay.

Katie: You are the solution to your problem—your apparent problem. No mother or son has ever done harm. We're dealing with confusion here, that's all. Through this Work we come to realize that.

My Husband's Affair

Marisa was obviously upset when she came up on stage to sit with me; her lips were quivering, and she looked as if she was on the brink of tears. Watch how powerful inquiry can be if someone sincerely wants to know the truth, even though she is in great pain and thinks she has been terribly wronged.

———

Marisa [reading from her Worksheet]: *I'm angry at David*—that's my husband—*because he keeps saying he needs time to sort things out. I want David to express what he is feeling when he's feeling it, because I'm tired of asking. And I'm too impatient to wait.*

Katie: So, "Husbands should express what they're feeling"—**is that true?**

Marisa: Yes.

Katie: And what's the reality on this planet?

Marisa: Well, basically they don't.

Katie: So how do I know that husbands *shouldn't* express their feelings? They don't. [The audience and Marisa laugh.] Sometimes. That's reality. "Husbands should express their feelings" is just a thought that we believe without a single piece of evidence. **How do you react when you believe this lie?** Can you hear where I'm coming from when I call it a lie? It's not true that he should express his feelings, because the truth is that he doesn't, in your experience. This doesn't mean that he's not going to fully express his feelings in ten minutes or in ten days. But the reality is that right now, it's not true. So **how do you react when you think this thought?**

Marisa: I'm angry and hurt.

Katie: Yes. And how do you treat him when you believe the thought that he should express his feelings, and he doesn't?

Marisa: I feel like I'm prying, I'm demanding something.

Katie: I would drop the "I feel like." You pry and demand.

Marisa: But I . . . Oh! . . . Yes. That's exactly what I do.

Katie: And how does it feel when you pry and demand?

Marisa: It doesn't feel good at all.

Katie: Can you see a reason to drop the thought? And please don't try to drop it. My experience is that you *can't* drop a thought, because you didn't make it in the first place. So the question is simply "Can you *see a reason* to drop the thought?" Often, very good reasons can be found in your answer to question 3, "How do you react when you think that thought?" Each stressful reaction—anger, for example, or sadness, or distancing—is a good reason to drop the thought.

Marisa: Yes, I can see a reason.

Katie: Give me a stress-free reason to believe the thought that husbands should express their feelings.

Marisa: A stress-free reason?

Katie: Give me a stress-free reason to believe this.

Marisa: I really don't know how to . . .

Katie: Give me a reason that doesn't cause you pain or stress to believe the thought "My husband should express his feelings to me." How many years have you been married?

Marisa: Seventeen.

Katie: And for seventeen years, according to you, he hasn't expressed his feelings. Give me a stress-free reason to believe the thought. [There is a long pause.] It could take you a while to find one.

Marisa: Yes. I can't find a stress-free reason.

Katie: And **who would you be,** living with this man, **if you didn't believe this lie?**

Marisa: I would be a happier person.

Katie: Yes. So what I'm hearing is that your husband is not the problem.

Marisa: Yes. Because I'm the one who pries and demands.

Katie: You're the one who believes this lie that hurts so much. I hear from you that if you didn't believe it, you'd be happy. And when you do believe it, you pry and demand. So how can your husband be the problem? You're trying to alter reality. This is confusion. I'm a lover of reality. I can always count on it. And I love that it can change, too. But I'm a lover of reality just the way it is now. So read that statement again, about what you want him to do.

Marisa: I want David to express what he is feeling when he's feeling it.

Katie: **Turn it around.** "I want me . . ."

Marisa: I want me to express my feelings. But that's what I do all the time!

Katie: Yes, exactly. That's for you to live. It's your way, not his.

Marisa: Ah. I see.

Katie: You're the one who should express her feelings, because you do. He shouldn't express his, because he doesn't. You go through the house prying and demanding, fooling yourself with this lie that your way is better. How does it feel to pry?

Marisa: It doesn't feel good at all.

Katie: And you're feeling bad in his name. You're blaming it on him.

Marisa: Exactly. I see what you're saying.

Katie: You feel bad and believe that he's doing it. And all the time, it's your own misunderstanding. All right, let's look at the next statement.

Marisa: I'm tired of asking. And I'm too impatient to wait.

Katie: "You're too impatient to wait"—is that true?

Marisa: Yes.

Katie: And *are* you waiting?

Marisa: I guess I am.

Katie: I would drop the "I guess."

Marisa: I *am* waiting. Yes.

Katie: "You're too impatient to wait"—is that true?

Marisa: Yes.

Katie: And *are* you waiting?

Marisa: Yes. And I don't know how to stop it.

Katie: So, "You're too impatient to wait"—is that true? [There is a very long pause.] You *are* waiting! You're *waiting!* I heard it from your own lips!

Marisa: Oh! I see! . . . Yeah.

Katie: Got it?

Marisa: Yes.

Katie: Yes. You're *not* too impatient to wait. You're hanging in there. Seventeen years, eighteen years . . .

Marisa: Yes.

Katie: So **how do you react when you think the thought** that you're too impatient to wait? How do you treat *him* when you believe that lie?

Marisa: I don't treat him well. I close off to him. I scream at him sometimes, or cry and threaten to leave him. I say some pretty nasty things.

Katie: So give me a stress-free reason to believe this lie.

Marisa: There isn't any.

Katie: **Who would you be in your home if you didn't believe this lie?**

Marisa: I guess I would enjoy the fact that I do love him and not get caught up in the rest of it.

Katie: Yes. And the next time you speak to him, you may want to say, "You know, sweetheart, I must love you a lot, because I *am* patient. I've been fooling myself. I've been telling you I'm too impatient to wait, and it's not true."

Marisa: Yes.

Katie: That's what I love about integrity. Each time we go inside, that's where it is. It's a sweet place to live in. So let's **turn it around.** "I'm too impatient to wait"—what is the extreme opposite of that, the 180-degree turnaround?

Marisa: I'm *not* too impatient to wait.

Katie: Yes. Isn't that as true or truer?

Marisa: It's truer. Definitely truer.

Katie: Let's look at your next statement.

Marisa: I'm going to read it, because I wrote it. *David shouldn't think that I'll wait forever.* . . . [Laughing] Which I *have* been doing, of course.

Katie: So, "He shouldn't think that"—**is it true?**

Marisa: Of course not.

Katie: No. He has all the proof that you *will* wait.

Marisa [smiling and nodding her head]: Yes.

Katie: So . . . **how do you react when you think this?** You know what I love, sweetheart? The thoughts that used to send us into deep depression—these same thoughts, once understood, send us into laughter. This is the power of inquiry.

Marisa: It's amazing!

Katie: And it just leaves us with "You know, honey, I love you." Unconditional love.

Marisa: Yeah.

Katie: And it's nothing more than clarity. So **how do you react when you believe the thought** that he shouldn't think you'll wait forever?

Marisa: I'm fooling myself if I believe what I wrote.

Katie: Yes. And it's very painful to live a lie. We're like children. We're so innocent. The whole world would tell you that you're right to be impatient.

Marisa: I certainly believed it up until today.

Katie: But when you go inside, you can see what's really true. It makes sense that no one else can cause you pain. That's *your* job.

Marisa: Yes, it's a lot easier to blame it on the other person.

Katie: Well, but is that true? Maybe it's easier *not* to. And it's the truth that sets us free. I came to see that there was nothing to forgive, that *I* was the one who caused my own problems. I found just what you're finding. Let's look at your fourth statement.

Marisa: I need David to stop saying that he doesn't want to hurt me, when he keeps doing things that hurt me.

Katie: "He wants to hurt you"—**can you really know that that's true?**

Marisa: No. I can't really know that.

Katie: "He wants to hurt you"—go inside and see if it's true.

Marisa: I don't know how to answer this. He *says* he doesn't.

Katie: I would believe him. What other information do you have?

Marisa: His actions.

Katie: "He wants to hurt you"—**can you absolutely know that that's true?**

Marisa: No.

Katie: And **how do you react when you believe this?** How do you treat him?

Marisa: I don't treat him well. I basically lay on the guilt.

Katie: Basically, you act as if you want to hurt him.

Marisa: Oh! I see . . . I see.

Katie: So of course you would project that he wants to hurt you. The truth is that *you* want to hurt *him.* You're the projector of it all, the storyteller of it all.

Marisa: Is it that easy, really?

Katie: Yes, it is.

Marisa: Wow!

Katie: If I think that someone else is causing my problem, I'm insane.

Marisa: I see. So . . . we cause our own problems?

Katie: Yes, but only all of them. It's just been a misunderstanding. Your misunderstanding. Not theirs. Not ever, not even a little. Your happiness is your responsibility. This is very good news. How does it feel when you live with a man and believe that he wants to hurt you?

Marisa: It feels terrible.

Katie: So give me a stress-free reason to believe the thought that your husband wants to hurt you.

Marisa: I can't think of one.

Katie: **Who would you be,** living with your husband, **if you didn't believe this thought?**

Marisa: I'd be a very happy person. I can see that so clearly now.

Katie: "He wants to hurt me"—**turn it around.**

Marisa: I want to hurt myself. Yes. I understand that.

Katie: Is that as true or truer?

Marisa: Truer, I think.

Katie: That's how we are. We don't know another way, until we do. That's what we're here for this evening: We sit together, and we find another way. There's another turnaround. "He wants to hurt me . . ."

Marisa: I want to hurt him. Yes. That's truer, too.

Katie: And there's still another turnaround. "He wants to hurt me"— what's the 180-degree turnaround?

Marisa: He *doesn't* want to hurt me.

Katie: He could be telling you the truth. That's just as possible. Okay, I'd like to go back. "You want to hurt your husband"—is that really true?

Marisa: No. No, I don't.

Katie: No, sweetheart. None of us would ever hurt another human being if we weren't confused. That's my experience. Confusion is the only suffering on this planet. How does it feel when you hurt him?

Marisa: It doesn't feel good at all.

Katie: Yes. And that feeling is a gift. It lets you know that you've moved from your integrity. Our thoughts say, "Oh, I shouldn't hurt him." But we don't know how to stop. Have you noticed?

Marisa: Yes.

Katie: It just goes on and on. So through self-realization—the way we're experiencing it here—through these realizations, the doing changes. I was the same as you. I couldn't change. I couldn't stop hurting my children and myself. But as I realized what was true for me, with the questions alive inside me, the doing changed. The problems stopped. I didn't stop them; they stopped. It's just that simple. Now, what has he done? You said that his actions prove that he wants to hurt you. What's an example of that? Where's your proof?

Marisa: To put it simply, he had an affair, and he told me about it five months ago. The feelings they had for each other are still very much there, and they still talk and see each other. Those are the actions.

Katie: Okay. Now watch the two of them in your mind. Can you see them?

Marisa: I've seen them many times.

Katie: Now look at your husband's face. Look at him looking at her. Now look at him for just a moment without your story. Look at his eyes, look at his face. What do you see?

Marisa: Love for her. And happiness. But also hurt, because they're not together. He wants to be with her . . .

Katie: Is that true? Can you absolutely know that it's true?

Marisa: Not absolutely. No, I can't.

Katie: Who's he with?

Marisa: Oh! He's with me.

Katie: "He wants to be with her"—**is that true?**

Marisa: Umm . . . he . . .

Katie: Who's he with?

Marisa: Okay. Yes. I see what you're saying.

Katie: "He wants to be with her"—**is that true?** Who's stopping him? He's free.

Marisa: And I have made that clear, too.

Katie: So **how do you react when you think the thought** that he wants to be with her . . .

Marisa: Oh, I hurt.

Katie: . . . and he's living with you?

Marisa: I guess I'm not fully in the present. I'm not *living* the fact that he loves me and he's with me.

Katie: He's living with you, and in your mind you have him living with her. So *no one's* living with the guy! [Marisa and the audience laugh.] Here's this beautiful man, and no one's living with him! [Marisa laughs even harder.] "I want him to live with me, I want him to live with me!" Well, when are you going to begin? How do you treat him when you believe that he wants to be with her and the truth is that he's living with you?

Marisa: I don't treat him well. I push him away.

Katie: And then you wonder why he likes to sit with her.

Marisa: Yes. Yes.

Katie: Give me a stress-free reason to believe the thought that he wants to be with her when the fact is that he's with you.

Marisa: A stress-free reason?

Katie: You can't *make* him come home. He comes home because he wants to. **Who would you be if you didn't believe this thought?**

Marisa: Oh! . . . [With a big smile] I would have no problem.

Katie: "He wants to be with her"—**turn it around.**

Marisa: He wants to be with me.

Katie: Yes. That could be as true or truer.

Marisa: Yes. Yes.

Katie: I heard you say he looked happy.

Marisa: Yes.

Katie: Isn't that what you want?

Marisa: Oh, I definitely want his happiness. I've told him so. At whatever price.

Katie: "I want his happiness"—**turn it around.**

Marisa: I want my happiness.

Katie: Yes.

Marisa: Very badly.

Katie: Isn't that the truth?

Marisa: Yeah.

Katie: You want him to be happy because that makes you happy. I say, skip the middleman and be happy now. He'll follow. He has to, because he's your projection.

Marisa [laughing]: Yes.

Katie: His happiness is his responsibility.

Marisa: Definitely.

Katie: And yours is your responsibility.

Marisa: Yes. I understand.

Katie: No one can make you happy but you.

Marisa: I don't know why that is so difficult.

Katie: Maybe because you think it's *his* job to love you and make you happy when you don't know how to yourself. "I can't do it—you do it."

Marisa: It's easier to give it to somebody else.

Katie: Is that true? How could he prove that he loves you? What could he do?

Marisa: I have no idea.

Katie: Isn't that interesting! Maybe he doesn't either. [Marisa and the audience laugh.] Except maybe he can just come home and be your husband.

Marisa: Yesterday I would have told you, "He can prove it by not seeing her again." That would have made me happy. Now I can't say that.

Katie: You're seeing reality a bit more clearly. Let's look at the next statement.

Marisa: "What do I think of him?" I don't know what to say. I love him.

Katie: Turn it around.

Marisa: I love myself. That has taken me a while.

Katie: Don't you just love yourself when you love him?

Marisa: I never saw it like that. Yeah.

Katie: Let's look at the next one, angel.

Marisa: I don't ever want to feel that my happiness depends on somebody loving me.

Katie: "I am willing . . ." and read it again.

Marisa: I am willing to feel that my happiness depends on somebody loving me.

Katie: Yes, because it's going to hurt to believe that thought. And then judge him again, or whoever it is, ask four questions, turn it around, and bring yourself back to sanity, back to peace. The pain shows you what's left to investigate. It shows you what's blocking you from the awareness of love. That's what pain is for. "I look forward to . . ."

Marisa: I look forward to feeling that my happiness depends on somebody loving me?

Katie: Yes. Some of us are returning to sanity, because we're tired of the pain. We're in a hurry. No time to mess around. It's good that you think, "Oh, I'd be happier if he were different." Write it down. Put it up against inquiry.

The Baby Shouldn't Scream

If you are a caregiver—if you have children or are feeling painfully responsible for anyone—you may find this dialogue particularly useful. Sally's statements "I am responsible for my children's choices" and "I have to take care of my children" are underlying beliefs for many people (see chapter 9), and it's wonderful to watch her find some clarity about these concepts as she enters inquiry.

Sally: I'm looking for a way to work through my depression.

Katie: Okay, let's see what cause we're dealing with—what confused thoughts you're believing that aren't true for you and therefore leave you depressed.

Sally [reading from her Worksheet]: *My son irritates me when he's not responsible. He doesn't do his homework. He doesn't do his chores like I've told him to every day for the last eight years.* I mean, it's like it's new every day.

Katie: Yes, I hear you clearly. Do you hear yourself? You are such an influence on his life. For eight years, you've been giving him guidance. For eight years, it hasn't worked.

Sally: I get it, but it goes against my grain not to say anything. I can't just let him do whatever he wants. As a parent, I am responsible for my children's choices and their consequences and for the people they become.

Katie: Inquiry is for people who really want to know the truth. Do you really want to know the truth?

Sally: Yes.

Katie: The beautiful thing about this Work is that it's *your* truth as a parent, not the world's, that we're about to deal with. "You're responsible for your children's choices"—**is that true?**

Sally [after a pause]: Well, no. The truth is I haven't been able to control what he does. I don't have any control over it. But I feel like I'm supposed to.

Katie: You said, "I don't have any control over it." That's what goes against your grain. Even though you don't have control over *anything,* you think you should. The effect of this thought is anxiety, frustration, and depression.

Sally: Isn't it depressing to think that I have no control over anything? I mean, why should I even try? I get so frustrated that I don't even want to be there taking care of him. Sometimes I just don't even want to be a mom.

Katie: Is it true that you have to care for your son? Who makes you do it?

Sally: Well, no one really. I do. Hmmm. No, it's probably not true that I have to take care of him.

Katie: I would drop the "probably."

Sally: It's truer that I do *want* to take care of him—even when I don't like what he's doing.

Katie: You've just found a wonderful truth within you. This truth brings great freedom. You don't ever *have* to take care of your son again. You never had to in the first place. That means that he doesn't owe you a thing. You're not doing it for him. Now you understand that you're doing it for yourself. With this awareness, you serve your children, knowing that you're there because you want to be there, serving them and teaching them by the way you live. You do it simply because you love them, and because you like yourself when you do that. It's not about them. This is unconditional love, even though it's a totally selfish act. It's truth owning itself. Once this is experienced, self-love becomes so greedy that there's no limit to the people it can serve. That's why to love one person unconditionally is to love all people. All right, let's travel inside to the answers that you may not be aware of yet. "Your son should do his homework"—is it true?

Sally: Yes.

Katie: Can you absolutely know that it's true that he should do his homework?

Sally: I pay for him to go to a private school. I know it's true.

Katie: Yes, and can you absolutely know that it's true that he should do his homework? Does he do his homework?

Sally: Eighty percent of the time.

Katie: So, "He's supposed to do his homework 100 percent of the time" — **is that true?** What's the reality of what he has done for eight years?

Sally: What has he been doing for eight years? He only does it about 80 percent. And I'm supposed to be happy with that? To just accept it?

Katie: It doesn't matter whether you accept it or not. The reality is that he does about 80 percent. I'm not saying that he won't do 100 percent tomorrow, but for now, that's reality. Are you supposed to just accept it? Let's see . . . For eight years . . . [The audience laughs.] you've been arguing with reality, and you've always lost. The effect of that has been stress, frustration, and depression. Let's **turn this** whole thing **around.**

Sally: I irritate me when I don't do my homework and my chores. Yes, that's true. I do that. And I get really upset with myself then. Okay. I see that I'm expecting him to do more than what I'm actually doing.

Katie: When you have the thought that he should do his homework and chores, then notice the turnaround. Do *your* homework and chores — 100 percent. Could it have been your example that taught him to do 80 percent? Or maybe you do 50 percent and he does 80 percent. He could be your teacher.

Sally: That's really good. I get it. I haven't modeled 100 percent. I also got really depressed about my baby last year. He wasn't the baby I wanted him to be. He was sick all the time, and he didn't sleep much. He wasn't happy. He's still not a friendly child. He screams when he sees people. I got so depressed.

Katie: "He's not a friendly child" — **is that true? Can you absolutely know that it's true** that he's not a friendly child on the inside?

Sally: No.

Katie: **How do you react when you think that thought** about your child?

Sally: I become fearful about how people will treat him in his life. I imagine that his life will be hard, because it will be hard for people to love him, and no one will ever want to have a family with him because he's so unfriendly, and before long there is no hope for him in my mind. "He'll never have friends" is what I feel. That's why I get depressed when he sees people and begins to cry.

Katie: Who would you be without that thought?

Sally: I would be peaceful. I would just love him exactly the way that he is.

Katie: With the thought, you're depressed. Without the thought, you're not depressed. So, sweetheart, can you see that it's your uninvestigated thinking, not your child's behavior, that is depressing you? Can you see that he has nothing to do with it? "He's not supposed to scream when he sees people"—is that true?

Sally: No.

Katie: What's the reality?

Sally: He does.

Katie: How do you react when you believe the thought that he's not supposed to scream when he sees people, and he does scream?

Sally: I get depressed. I feel sad and embarrassed. My mother says that I'm spoiling him. People say he's weird. Then I think, "Oh no! He's weird! What's wrong with him? What's wrong with me?" And when he cries, I even find myself screaming at this baby to shut up, which seems to make him scream even louder. And it doesn't work. He doesn't stop crying.

Katie: So again we find that it's not his behavior that depresses you. That's not possible. It has to be your own mental behavior that depresses you. This is natural when you believe the thought that he shouldn't scream while he is screaming, and that his screaming means that there is something wrong with him and something wrong with you. That's depressing. We want our children to validate the caring—the love, the nurturing, the acceptance—that we aren't giving ourselves. Otherwise, why do we need them to behave according to our ideal? When you're sane, a screaming child just is what it is: a screaming child. And you're present in your thoughts and in the actions that follow from a clear, loving mind. So how do you treat your baby when you think that he shouldn't scream when he sees people?

Sally: I tell him to be happy. "Let's be happy, happy, happy!"

Katie: So you teach him that he's wrong. If he's screaming and you tell him, "Let's be happy," you teach him that he's wrong. He thinks that he's a failure in your eyes. But if you're sane and calm and happy, even though he's screaming, then through your example, you show him another way to live.

Sally: I'm telling him not to be who he is.

Katie: Yes. You're telling him to be different than he is. That's conditional love. Sweetheart, close your eyes and just for a moment picture him screaming, without your story.

Sally [after a long pause]: It's actually kind of cute! That's just who he is. I just want to hold him and say, "Aw, that's okay."

Katie: You're becoming intimate with your son, and he's not even in the room. Close your eyes now and look at your mother saying to you, "What is the matter with that child? Are you spoiling him again?" Look at her without your story.

Sally [with eyes closed, after a long pause]: That's just my mother telling *her* story, and that's my son screaming his little heart out. They're both just being who they are. Nothing depressing there.

Katie: I hear you say that your son isn't a friendly child. **Can you absolutely know that that's true,** sweetheart?

Sally: No.

Katie: **How do you react when you think that thought?**

Sally: Sad, protective, depressed, frustrated. I want to run, and I want to stay, and I'm miserable, and I feel like a failure as a mom.

Katie: Can you see a reason to drop that thought? And I'm not asking you to drop it. You didn't bring it about, so how can you drop what you didn't cause? In my experience, we don't make thoughts appear, they just appear. One day, I noticed that their appearance just wasn't personal. Noticing that really makes it simpler to inquire. I only want to know if you can see a reason to drop the thought that he isn't a friendly child.

Sally: Yes, I can definitely see several.

Katie: Can you see a sane or stress-free reason to keep this thought, a reason that is not stressful?

Sally: No. I can't find one.

Katie: **Who would you be** at home with your child **without that thought?**

Sally: I see. Without that thought, I would be peaceful and clear. I wouldn't be depressed.

Katie: So what I'm learning from you is that no child can ever cause your depression. Only you can. What I hear from you is that with the thought, there's stress, and without the thought, there's peace. It's no wonder that when we blame others for our insanity, we feel bad. We've been looking outside us for our own peace. We've been looking in the wrong direction.

Sally: I can't believe it's so simple!

Katie: If it weren't so simple, I never could have found it. Good. Welcome to The Work.

I Need My Family's Approval

When Justin sat down to do The Work, he seemed like a misunderstood, idealistic teenager. It's not easy to find your own way when you believe that you need love, approval, appreciation, or anything from your family. It's particularly hard when you want them to see things your way (for their own good, of course). As inquiry progresses, Justin internally rejoins his family, while at the same time he honors his own path.

———

Justin [reading from his Worksheet]: *I'm angry and confused and saddened by my family because they judge me. I'm angry that there is a mold that is placed before me. I'm angry at my family and acquaintances for thinking that their path is the only way. It saddens me that I receive the most love when I assume the predestined pattern and I follow the way they think things should be.*

Katie: Good. And the next statement?

Justin: I want my family to be who they are and not limit their love and attention according to their perception and idea of my progress. I want them to accept me as I learn my own truth in this life and love me for having found parts of my own truth and foundation.

Katie: Good. Read the first one again.

Justin: I'm angry and confused and saddened by my family because they judge me.

Katie: Okay. And not only is it the job of a parent, but it's the job of everyone in this world to judge. That's our job. What else is there? Everything's a judgment. Give me a thought that's not a judgment. "It's a sky"—that's a judgment. That's what we do. So, "Parents shouldn't judge their children"—is that true? What's the reality of it? Do they?

Justin: Yes.

Katie: Yes, honey. That's their job. **How do you react when you think the thought** "My parents aren't supposed to judge me"?

Justin: Well, it weakens me, because I feel that I need to ... I don't know, I disagree with some of the things that I've been taught.

Katie: Let's stay in inquiry. Watch as your mind wants to move into its proof that it's right. When you notice this happening, gently move back to the question. **How do you react when you think that thought?** It weakens you. What else?

Justin: It stops me in my tracks, and I feel terrified.

Katie: How do you treat your parents when you believe the thought "I want you to stop judging me," and they keep judging you?

Justin: I rebel, and I become distant. And that's been my past so far.

Katie: Yes. So can you see a reason to drop this philosophy that would argue with the reality of the ages, that parents shouldn't judge their children?

Justin: Yes.

Katie: Okay. Now what I want you to do after all these years is to give me a reason that is not stressful, just give me one sane or stress-free reason inside you to keep such a ridiculous lie.

Justin: Well, it's a foundation for your life. It's like a religious belief.

Katie: Does that reason feel peaceful?

Justin: No. [Pause] There isn't a peaceful reason.

Katie: This is an insane belief. People should stop judging people? What planet do you think you're on? Make yourself at home here: When you come to planet Earth, you judge us and we judge you. That's it. It's a nice planet to live on, once you get the ground rules straight. But this theory of yours is in direct opposition to what's really happening. It's crazy! **Who would you be without the thought?** Who would you be if you didn't have the ability to think such a crazy thought, "I want my parents to stop judging me"?

Justin: I would have inner peace.

Katie: Yes. It's called playing with a full deck. This is the end of the war inside you. I'm a lover of reality. How do I know I'm better off with what is? It's what is. Parents judge, that's it. You've had a lifetime of proof to know that this is true. So, honey, **turn it around.** Let's see what's possible. Let's see what does work.

Justin: I'm confused and saddened by me because I judge myself.

Katie: Yes. And there's another one. "I'm confused . . ."

Justin: I'm confused and saddened by me because I judge my parents and my family.

Katie: Yes. So I'll strike a deal with you. When *you* stop judging *them* for judging you, then go talk to them about judgment.

Justin: That's so true.

Katie: When you stop doing what you want them to stop doing, then you can talk to them. It may take a while.

Justin: I don't know if I'm ready now.

Katie: Yes, sweetheart. Now, read number 2 on your Worksheet again.

Justin: I want my family to be who they are and not limit their love and attention . . .

Katie: They already *are* who they are. They're people who limit their love and attention and who judge, according to you.

Justin [laughing]: Okay.

Katie: That's who they are, it seems, until they aren't. That's their job, honey. A dog barks, a cat meows, and your parents judge. And they . . . what else did you say they do?

Justin: Well, they limit their love and attention according to . . .

Katie: Yes. That's their job, too.

Justin: But they're my family!

Katie: Yes, they are. And they limit and they judge. Sweetheart, this philosophy of yours is very stressful. Give me one stress-free reason to keep this philosophy that is so off the wall. I mean, we're talking "nuts."

Justin: I did feel nuts for quite some time.

Katie: Well, you would *have* to feel nuts for quite some time. You haven't asked yourself what's true and what's not. So who **would you be** in the presence of your family **without this thought?** Who would you be without the ability to think this thought that opposes reality?

Justin: I'd be fabulous! I'd be so happy!

Katie: Yes. I would go with that. It's also my experience.

Justin: But I want . . .

Katie: You can say "but" all you want, they're still going to do their job.

Justin: Yes.

Katie: Reality doesn't wait for your opinion, vote, or permission, sweetheart. It just keeps being what it is and doing what it does. "No. Wait for my approval." I don't think so! You lose, always. **Turn it around,** let's look at the possibilities. "I want me . . ."

Justin: I want me to be who I am . . .

Katie: Yes.

Justin: . . . and not limit my love and attention for myself according to my perception of the idea of my progress. That's hard to eat.

Katie: Oh, well! I like the part where you thought your parents should eat the same thing all these years. [The audience laughs.] So just sit with it a moment. I realize that I'm coming on strong, but these are great revelations. Without a story, revelations have room to surface from where they have always lived, inside you. There's another turnaround. Be gentle. "I want me . . ."

Justin [after a pause]: I'm not seeing it.

Katie: Read it the way you wrote it.

Justin: *I want my family to be who they are . . .*

Katie: "I want me . . ."

Justin: I want me to be who I am and not limit my love and attention according to . . .

Katie: . . . "their" . . .

Justin: . . . their perception and idea of my progress. Wow! I like that one.

Katie: Yes, it's living what you wanted them to live.

Justin: I just don't want to let it go, it just brings up this turmoil inside me.

Katie: It's supposed to, honey. Tell me more about the turmoil. What are your thoughts?

Justin: There are eleven children in my family, and they're all just going, "You're not doing the right thing."

Katie: Well, they could be right. And you need to live what you need to live. Obviously, you need eleven, twelve, you need thirteen people coming at you so that you can know what's true for yourself. Your path is yours. Theirs is theirs. Let's look at the next statement.

Justin: *I want them to accept me as I learn my own truth in this life.*

Katie: They're going to accept what they accept. Have they made you accept the way they live? Can they do that? Have thirteen people convinced you to follow their path?

Justin: Well, that's my work, right? Because the foundation of their life . . .

Katie: Yes or no. Have they convinced you to walk their path?

Justin: No.

Katie: So if you can't accept theirs, what makes you think that they can accept yours?

Justin: That's true.

Katie: Put it in perspective. Thirteen people can't convince you, and you think you're going to convince all thirteen of them? If this is war, you're outnumbered.

Justin: I know.

Katie: **How do you react when you think the thought** "I want them to accept my way," and they don't?

Justin: It's painful.

Katie: Yes. Lonely?

Justin: Oh, yeah.

Katie: Can you see a reason to drop this theory that anyone in this world needs to accept you at any time?

Justin: I need to drop that.

Katie: I'm not asking you to drop it. I'm just asking if you can see a good reason to. You can't drop concepts. You can only shine a little flashlight on them as you do inquiry, and you see that what you thought was true wasn't. And when the truth is seen, there's nothing you can do to make the lie true for you again. An example we can work on is what you've written: "I want my family to accept my way." It's hopeless. How do you treat them when you believe that thought?

Justin: I get distant.

Katie: **Who would you be** in your family **without this thought,** "I want them to accept my way"?

Justin: Outgoing, loving.

Katie: **Turn it around.**

Justin: I want me to accept myself as I learn my own truth in this life.

Katie: There! If they're not doing it, who does that leave? You. So, sweetheart, can you find another turnaround? "I want me . . ."

Justin: I want me to accept them as they learn their own truth in this life.

Katie: Yes. That's all they're doing. They're just doing what you're doing. We're all doing the best we can. Let's look at the next statement.

Justin: I want them to love me for having found parts of my own truth . . .

Katie: Whose business is it who you love?

Justin: My own.

Katie: Whose business is it who they love?

Justin: Theirs.

Katie: How does it feel when you're mentally over there running their lives, dictating who they should love and why?

Justin: It's not where I should be.

Katie: Is it lonely?

Justin: Yes, very.

Katie: So let's **turn it around.**

Justin: I want me to love them for having found parts of their own truth.

Katie: Bingo! Their truth, not yours. They have a way that is so fabulous that all thirteen of them agree! Give me an example of what they say that is so painful. What's the most painful thing they could say to or about you?

Justin: That I'm lost.

Katie: Can you find the place where you've been lost a while?

Justin: Oh hell, yeah!

Katie: Okay, so they're right. The next time they say, "You're lost," you can say, "You know, I noticed that too one day." Yes?

Justin: Yes.

Katie: So what other terrible thing did they say that might be true? I'll tell you that for me, when someone used to say something that was true, one way I knew it was true was that I immediately felt defensive. I blocked it off, and I went to war with them in my mind and suffered all that goes with it. And they were only saying what was true. As a lover of truth, don't you really want to know what that is? Often it's the very thing that you've been looking for. What else do they say that's painful?

Justin: I feel like they interrupt me when I try to describe what I'm going through. So that's painful.

Katie: Of course it is. You think we're supposed to listen?

Justin: But doesn't a child deserve that?

Katie: No. It's not a matter of deserving. They just don't listen. "There are twelve kids here; give us a break!" **How do you react when you think the thought** "They should listen to me," and they don't?

Justin: Lonely.

Katie: And how do you treat them when you believe that thought?

Justin: I distance myself from them.

Katie: Pretty hard to listen when you're way over there!

Justin: Yes.

Katie: "I want them to listen, so I think I'll go away."

Justin: Yes. I see your point.

Katie: Is it starting to add up a little? **Who would you be** in that amazing family **without that thought?** Who would you be if you didn't have the ability to think the thought "I want them to listen to me"?

Justin: Content and peaceful.

Katie: A listener?

Justin: A listener.

Katie: Let's **turn it around.** Let's hear how *you* should live, sweetheart, not your family.

Justin: I want me to love myself for having found parts of my own truth and foundation. Yes, I do.

Katie: So, just be with it a minute. . . . And the other turnaround.

Justin: I want me to love them for having found parts of their own truth and foundation. Yes. I totally love them for their happiness, but . . . okay, okay. [Justin and the audience laugh.]

Katie: You caught it! That's big. I love how you realized what's more true for you and the judgment stopped. You laughed and stayed real. Okay, the next statement.

Justin: I already know the answer to this one.

Katie: Ah, you are good! Once we get the hang of reality, honey—ah!

Justin: I yearn for them to respect my music that I make and . . .

Katie: Hopeless.

Justin: Yes, it is.

Katie: **Turn it around.**

Justin: I yearn for me to respect my music.

Katie: There's another one. "I yearn for me ..."

Justin: I yearn for me to respect their music?

Katie: Here's what their music is: "We don't want to listen, we don't want to understand. Come on our path, it works for us, we know it will work for you." That's their music. We all have our music, honey. If someone says, "Come walk on my path, it's beautiful," all I hear is that they love me with all their heart and want to give me what they see as beautiful. It just doesn't always happen to be my way. It's certainly equal to mine, though. And I love it that their way works for them and brings them happiness. All these ways! There's no path that's higher than another. Sooner or later, we begin to notice. The communication for that is "I love it that your way makes you happy. Thank you for wanting to share it with me."

Justin: I can handle that when I settle down with everything else. It would be simple to say, "I'm happy for you, and I'm happy for me."

Katie: "Leave yourself out of it; we don't care! We like to hear the part where you're happy for us. Get over it!" Painful stuff. No one wants to hear about you, certainly not at the level that we want you to hear about us. That's how it is for now. Knowing that can be the end of the war in you, and there's such strength in that, and I tell you truly that the truth of what we're speaking of today will flow through your music. Isn't that what you want?

Justin: Yes. I can't believe I never saw this before.

Katie: Oh, honey. I didn't see it for forty years, until I woke up to reality, the way you're doing today. It's always just a beginning. You might go home and ask your mom to sit with you for a while. And if she says, "No, I don't have time," good! Look forward to it. There's always another way to be with her. If she's changing diapers, you might say, "Can I help you?" Or you might sit with her and just listen to what she's saying, just watch what she's doing. Invite her to tell you about her path and listen to her life, watch her light up as she speaks of her God and her way, without letting your story interfere. There are many ways to be with your mother. It might be a whole new world for you. It opens an untapped world when you are

clear about what you really want. No one can deprive me of my family—
no one but me. I love it that you noticed today. There's no family to save.
No family to convert. There's only one, as it turns out—you.

Justin: I like that.

Katie: Let's look at the last statement on your Worksheet.

Justin: I refuse to be left unheard.

Katie: "I'm willing . . ."

Justin: I'm willing to be left unheard.

Katie: "I look forward to . . ."

Justin: I look forward to . . . no, I don't . . . well . . .

Katie: If they don't hear you and it hurts, do The Work again. "They're
supposed to hear me"—is that true?

Justin: No.

Katie: How do you react when you think the thought "They should hear
me," and they don't?

Justin: Terrible.

Katie: So, who would you be without this thought, without this lie,
"They should hear me"?

Justin: Whoa . . . It's such a simple question, but there's . . . Wow! I'd be
happy. Peaceful.

Katie: "They should hear me"—turn it around.

Justin: I should hear me.

Katie: There's another one.

Justin: They shouldn't hear me.

Katie: Yes. Not unless they do. And there's still another one.

Justin: I should hear them.

Katie: Yes. Hear their song. If I want my children to hear me, I'm insane.
They're only going to hear what they hear, not what I say. Let me see,
maybe I'll filter their hearing: "Don't hear anything but what I say." Does
that sound a little crazy to you? "Don't hear anything else, don't hear your

own thoughts, hear what I want you to hear, hear me." Insane. And it just doesn't work.

Justin: You waste so much energy trying to . . . yeah.

Katie: . . . direct their hearing. Hopeless. I want them to hear what they hear. I'm not crazy anymore. I'm a lover of what is. I invite you to go somewhere and be still with yourself this evening. Just be with it. And then you may want to go home and tell your family what you've discovered about yourself. Tell them so that you can hear it. And notice the thought "I want them to hear me." Notice who you are with the thought and who you are without it. Don't expect them to listen. Just say it so you can hear it.

Reality is always kinder

than the stories

we tell about it.

5.
Deepening Inquiry

This chapter offers more ways of working with the four questions and the turnaround and gives you additional perspectives to enable deeper and clearer inquiry. My intention here is to support you as you begin to travel into the infinite mind and begin to realize that there's nothing to fear. There is nowhere you can travel where inquiry won't safely hold you.

The Work always brings us back to who we really are. Each belief investigated to the point of understanding allows the next belief to surface. You undo that one. Then you undo the next, and the next. And then you find that you are actually looking forward to the next belief. At some point, you may notice that you're meeting every thought, feeling, person, and situation as a friend. Until eventually you are looking for a problem. Until, finally, you notice that you haven't had one in years.

Question 1: Is it true?

Sometimes it's immediately evident that the statement you have written is simply not true. If the answer that comes to you is a resounding no, then move on to question 3. Otherwise, let's look at some ways to examine question 1 further.

What's the Reality of It?

If your answer to question 1 is yes, ask yourself this: What's the reality of this situation?

Let's investigate the statement "Paul shouldn't watch so much television." What's the reality of it? In your experience, *does* he watch a lot of television? Yes: The reality is that Paul watches between six and ten hours of television on most days. How do we know that Paul should watch so much television? He does. That's the reality of it; that's what is true. A dog barks, a cat meows, and Paul watches television. That's his job. It may not always be that way, but for now, that's the way it is. Your thought that Paul shouldn't watch so much television is just your way of mentally arguing with what is. It doesn't do you any good, and it doesn't change Paul; its only effect is to cause you stress. Once you accept the reality that he watches so much television, who knows what changes can develop in your life?

Reality, for me, is what is true. The truth is whatever is in front of you, whatever is really happening. Whether you like it or not, it's raining now. "It shouldn't be raining" is just a thought. In reality, there is no such thing as a "should" or a "shouldn't." These are only thoughts that we impose onto reality. The mind is like a carpenter's level. When the bubble is off to one side—"It shouldn't be raining"—we can know that the mind is caught in its thinking. When the bubble is right in the middle—"It's raining"—we can know that the surface is level and the mind is accepting reality as it is. From this position, positive change can take place efficiently, clearly, and sanely. We won't necessarily know how the changes happen, but they happen nonetheless.

Whose Business Is It?

Whose business are you in when you're thinking the thought that you've written? When you think that someone or something other than yourself needs to change, you're mentally out of your business. Of course you feel separate, lonely, and stressed. Ask yourself, "Whose business is it how much television I watch? Whose business is it how much television Paul watches? And can I really know what's best for Paul in the long run?"

Question 2:
Can you absolutely know
that it's true?

If your answer to question 1 is yes, ask yourself, "Can I absolutely know that it's true?" In many cases, the statement *appears* to be true. Of course it does. Your concepts are based on a lifetime of beliefs upheld by uninvestigated evidence.

After I woke up to reality in 1986, I noticed many times how people, in conversations, the media, and books, made statements such as "There isn't enough understanding in the world," "There's too much violence," "We should love one another more." These were stories I used to believe, too. They seemed sensitive, kind, and caring, but as I heard them, I noticed that believing them caused a stress and concern that didn't feel peaceful inside me.

For instance, when I heard the story "People should be more loving," the question would arise in me "Can I absolutely know that that's true? Can I really know for myself, within myself, that people should be more loving? Even if the whole world tells me so, is it really true?" And to my amazement, when I listened within myself, I saw that the world is what it is—nothing more, nothing less. Where reality is concerned, there *is* no "what should be." There is only what is, just the way it is, right now. The truth is prior to every story. And every story, prior to investigation, hides the truth from view.

Now I could finally ask of every potentially uncomfortable story, "Can I absolutely know that it's true?" And the answer, like the question, was an experience: No. I would stand rooted in that answer—solitary, peaceful, free.

How could no be the right answer? Everyone I knew, and all the books, said that the answer should be yes. But I came to see that the truth is itself and will not be dictated to by anyone. In the presence of that inner no, I came to see that the world is always as it should be, whether I opposed it or not. And I came to embrace reality with all my heart. I love the world, without any conditions.

Let's play with the statement "I feel hurt because Paul is angry at me." You may have answered, "Yes, it's true. Paul *is* angry at me. His face is red, his neck is throbbing, and he is shouting at me." So there's the proof. But go inside again. Can you really know that it's you Paul is angry at? Can you really know what's going on inside someone else's mind? Can you know by someone's facial expression or body language what he is really thinking or feeling? Have you felt fear or anger, for example, and observed your own helpless, fearful emotions point the finger of blame at the person nearest you? Can you really know what another person is feeling, even when he tells you? Can you be certain that he is clear about his own thoughts and emotions? Have you ever been confused about, faked, or misrepresented what you were angry about? Can you really know that it's true that Paul is angry at you?

Furthermore, can you really know that you feel hurt because Paul is angry? Is Paul's anger actually *causing* your hurt? Might it be possible for you, in another frame of mind, to stand there in the full blast of Paul's anger and not experience it personally at all? Might it be possible to simply listen, to calmly and lovingly receive what he is saying? After inquiry, that was my experience.

Suppose your statement is "Paul should stop smoking." Of course he should! Everyone knows that smoking diminishes breathing capacity and causes lung cancer and heart disease. Now, go in deeper with the question. Can you really know that it's true that Paul should stop smoking? Can you know that his life would be better or that he would live longer if he stopped smoking? He could be hit by a truck tomorrow. Can you really know that if Paul stopped smoking, it would be best for him or you in the long run? (And I'm not saying that it wouldn't be.) Can you really know what is best for Paul on his life's path? "Paul should stop smoking"—can you absolutely know that it's true?

If your answer is still yes, good. This is as it should be. If you think that what the other person has done or said really is what you have written, and if you think that you can absolutely know that that's true, it's always fine to move right ahead to question 3. Or if you feel a little stuck, try one or more of the exercises offered in the following section.

When You Think That It's True

Sometimes you may not feel comfortable with your yes to questions 1 and 2; they may make you feel that you're grinding to a halt in your inquiry. You want to go deeper, but the statement you've written, or the thought that's torturing you, appears to be an incontrovertible fact. Here are some ways to coax your thoughts out into the open, to prompt new statements that can allow inquiry to go deeper and relieve your stress.

And it means that ____

A powerful way of prompting yourself is to add "and it means that ____" to your original statement. Your suffering may be caused by a thought that interprets what happened, rather than the thought you wrote down. This additional phrase prompts you to reveal your interpretation of the fact. The answer to the prompt, for the purposes of inquiry, is always what *you* think your statement means.

Let's say you wrote, "I am angry at my father because he hit me." Is it true? Yes: you *are* angry, and yes: he *did* hit you, many times, when you were a child. Try writing the statement with your added interpretation. "I am angry at my father because he hit me, and it means that ____." Maybe your addition would be "and it means that he doesn't love me."

Now that you know what your interpretation is, you can take it to inquiry. Write down the new statement, and apply all four questions and the turnaround. You may come to realize that it's your interpretation of the fact that is causing you stress.

What do you think you would have?

Another way of prompting yourself is to read your original statement and ask yourself what you think you would have if reality were (in your opinion) fully cooperating with you. Suppose you originally wrote, "Paul should tell me that he loves me." Your answer to the prompt "What do you think you would have?" might be that if Paul told you that he loves you, you would feel more secure. Write down this new statement—"I would feel more secure if Paul told me that he loves me"—and put it up against inquiry.

What's the worst that could happen?

When your statement is about something that you think you don't want, read it and imagine the worst outcome that reality could hand you. Imagine your worst fears lived out on paper all the way. Be thorough. Take it to the limit.

Your statement might be, for example, "I'm heartbroken because my wife left me." Now ask yourself, "What's the worst that could happen?" Make a list of all the terrible events that you think might happen as a result of your present situation. After each frightening scenario that comes to mind, imagine what could happen next. And then what could happen? And then? Be a frightened child. Be thorough. Don't hold back.

When you've finished writing, start at the top of your list and apply the four questions and turnaround to each "worst that could happen" statement. Inquire into what you have written, statement by statement.

What's the "should"?

A fourth useful prompt is to look for a "should" or "shouldn't" version of your original statement. If your anger arises from the belief that reality should have been different, rewrite the statement "I am angry at my father because he hit me" as "My father shouldn't have hit me." This statement may be easier to investigate. With the first form of this statement, we know the answer—or we think we know it—even before we begin the process of inquiry. "Is it true? Definitely yes." We would stake our lives on it. With the rewritten form, we are not so sure, and we're more open to discovering another, deeper truth.

Where's your proof?

Sometimes you're convinced that your written statement is true and you believe that you can absolutely know that it's true, but you haven't looked at your "proof." If you really want to know the truth, you can bring all your evidence into the open and put it to the test of inquiry. Here's an example:

Original Statement: *I am saddened by Paul because he doesn't love me.*

The proof that Paul doesn't love me:

1. Sometimes he walks by me without speaking.
2. When I enter the room, he doesn't look up.
3. He doesn't acknowledge me. He continues to do what he is interested in.
4. He doesn't call me by name.
5. I ask him to take out the trash, and he pretends not to hear me.
6. I tell him what time dinner is, and sometimes he doesn't show up.
7. When we do talk, he seems distant, as though he has more important things to do.

Investigate each "proof of truth" statement, using all four questions and the turnaround, as in the following example:

1. He sometimes walks by me without speaking. *That proves* that he doesn't love me. Is it true? Can I absolutely know that it's true? (Is it possible that he is mentally absorbed in something else?) Continue with all four questions and the turnaround.

2. When I enter the room, he doesn't look up. *That proves* that he doesn't love me. Is it true? Can I absolutely know that it means he doesn't love me? Continue to test your proof with all four questions and the turnaround.

Test your whole list in this manner, and then return to your original inquiry: "I'm saddened by Paul because he doesn't love me"—is it true?

Finding Your "Proof of Truth"

Think of a person in your life (past or present) who you think doesn't love you. Then make a list of your proof that it's true.

Now investigate each "proof of truth" statement you have written down, using all four questions and the turnaround.

Question 3: How do you react when you think that thought?

With this question, we begin to notice internal cause and effect. You can see that when you believe the thought (and it's okay to believe it), there is an uneasy feeling, a disturbance that can range from mild discomfort to fear or panic. Since you may have realized from question 1 that the thought isn't even true for you, you're looking at the power of a lie. Your nature is truth, and when you oppose it, you don't feel like yourself. Stress never feels as natural as peace does.

After the four questions found me, I would notice thoughts like "People should be more loving," and I would see that they caused a feeling of uneasiness. I noticed that prior to the thought, there was peace. My mind was quiet and serene. There was no stress, no disturbing physical reaction. This is who I am without my story. Then, in the stillness of awareness, I began to notice the feelings that came from believing or attaching to the thought. And in the stillness, I could see that if I were to believe the thought, the result would be a feeling of unease and sadness. From there, it would go to "I should do something about this." From there, it would shift to guilt; I didn't have the slightest idea of how to make people be more loving, because I myself couldn't be any more loving than I in fact was. When I asked, "How do I react when I believe the thought that people should be more loving?" I saw that not only did I have an uncomfortable feeling (this was obvious), but I also reacted with mental pictures—of the wrongs I had once thought I'd suffered, of the terrible things I had once thought people had done to me, of my first husband's unkindness to our children and me—to prove that the thought was true. I flew off into a world that didn't exist. There I was, sitting in a chair with a cup of tea, and mentally I was living in the pictures of an illusory past. I became a character in the pages of a myth of suffering—the heroine of suffering, trapped in a world filled with injustice. I reacted by living in a stressed body, seeing everything through fearful eyes, a sleepwalker, someone in an endless nightmare. The remedy was simply to investigate.

I love question 3. Once you answer it for yourself, once you see the cause and effect of a thought, all your suffering begins to unravel. You may not even realize it at first. You may not even know that you're making progress. But progress is none of your business. Just keep doing The Work. It will continue to take you deeper. The next time the problem you worked on appears, you may laugh in astonishment. You may not feel any stress; you may not even notice the thought at all.

Can you see a reason to drop that thought? (And please don't try to drop it.)

This is an additional question that I often ask as a follow-up to question 3, because it can bring radical shifts in awareness. Along with the next additional question, it goes deeper into an awareness of internal cause and effect. "Can I see a reason to drop the thought? Yes, I can: I was at peace before the thought appeared, and after it appeared I felt contraction and stress."

It's important to realize that inquiry is about noticing, not about dropping the thought. That is not possible. If you think that I'm asking you to drop the thought, hear this: I am not! Inquiry is not about getting rid of thoughts; it's about realizing what's true for you, through awareness and unconditional self-love. Once you see the truth, the thought lets go of *you,* not the other way around.

Can you find one stress-free reason to keep the thought?

The second additional question is "Can you find one stress-free reason to keep the thought?" You may see lots of reasons, but they all cause stress, they all hurt. None of them is peaceful or valid, not if you're interested in putting an end to your suffering. If you find one that seems valid, ask yourself, "Is this reason peaceful, or is it stressful? Does thinking that thought bring peace or stress into my life? And do I operate more efficiently, lovingly, and clearly when I am stressed or when I am free of stress?" (In my experience, all stress is inefficient.)

Question 4: Who would you be without the thought?

This is a very powerful question. Picture yourself standing in the presence of the person you have written about when they aren't doing what you think they should be doing, or when they're doing what you think they shouldn't be doing. Now, just for a minute or two, close your eyes, take a deep breath, and imagine who you would be if you couldn't think this thought. How would your life be different in the same situation without this thought? Keep your eyes closed and watch them without your story. What do you see? How do you feel about them without the story? Which do you prefer—with or without your story? Which feels kinder? Which feels more peaceful?

Many people can barely recognize themselves freed from the limitations of their stories. They have no reference for that. The question reveals a new identity. So "I don't know" is a common answer to this question. People also answer by saying, "I'd be free," "I'd be peaceful," "I'd be a more loving person." You could also say, "I'd be clear enough to understand the situation and act efficiently." Without our stories, we are not only able to act clearly and fearlessly; we are also the friend, the listener. We are people living happy lives. We are appreciation and gratitude that have become as natural as breath itself. Happiness is the natural state for someone who knows that there's nothing to know and that we already have everything we need, right here now.

The answer to question 4 can also leave us without an identity. This is very exciting. You're left with nothing and as nothing other than the reality of the moment: woman sitting in a chair, writing. This can be a little scary, since it leaves no illusion of a past or future. You might ask, "How do I live now? What do I do? Nothing is meaningful." And I would say, "'With no past or future, you won't know how to live'—can you really know that that's true? 'You don't know what to do, and nothing is meaningful'—can you really know that that's true?" Write down your fears and walk yourself through inquiry again on these subtle, intricate concepts. The goal of inquiry is to bring us back to our right mind, so we can realize for ourselves that we live in paradise and haven't even noticed.

"Who would you be without the thought?" is the form of question 4 that I suggest if you're new to The Work. I invite people to phrase the question in another way as well: "Who or what would you be without the thought?" Sit with it. Let any thoughts or pictures come and go as you contemplate this form of the question. It can be an extremely rich experience. You may also want to play with the original form of question 4: "What would you be without the thought?" "Peace" is the answer that people often come to. And again I ask, "What would you be without even that thought?"

The Turnaround

The turnaround is a very powerful part of The Work. It's the part where you take what you have written about others and see if it is as true or truer when it applies to you. Inquiry combined with the turnaround is the fast track to self-realization. As long as you think that the cause of your problem is "out there"—as long as you think that anyone or anything else is responsible for your suffering—the situation is hopeless. It means that you are forever in the role of the victim, that you're suffering in paradise. So bring the truth home to yourself and begin to set yourself free.

For example, the statement "Paul is unkind" turns around to "I am unkind." Go inside and find the situations in your life where this seems true for you. Have you also been unkind to Paul? (Look at your answers to the question "How do you react when you think the thought 'Paul is unkind'? How do you treat him?") Aren't you being unkind in the moment when you are seeing Paul as unkind? Experience what it feels like when you believe that Paul is unkind. Your body may tense, your heart may speed up, you may feel flushed—is that kind to yourself? You may get judgmental and defensive—how does that feel inside you? Those reactions are the results of your uninvestigated thinking.

When Paul insults you, for example, how many times do you replay that scene in your mind? Who is more unkind—Paul (who insulted you once today) or you (who multiplied his insult over and over again in your mind)? Consider this: Were you feeling Paul's action itself or your own judgments about it? If Paul insulted you and you didn't know about it, would you suffer? Be still for a moment. Go deep. Stay vigilantly in your own mental business as you sit with this.

An enemy is the friend you judge on paper in order to clearly see the hidden secrets within yourself. Your perceived enemy is the projection of your thinking. When you work with the projector through inquiry, your enemy becomes your friend.

The Three Types of Turnaround

There are three ways to do the turnaround. A judgment can be turned around to yourself, to the other, and to the opposite. There are many possible combinations of these three. One statement can bring many realizations when it is reversed. The point is not to find the most turnarounds, but to find the ones that bring you the shift to self-realization, the enlightenment that sets you free from the nightmare you're innocently attached to. Turn the original statement around any way you want to until you find the turnarounds that penetrate the most.

Let's play with the statement "Paul should appreciate me."

Turn it around to yourself:
I should appreciate myself. (It's my job, not his.)

Turn it around to the other:
I should appreciate Paul (especially when he doesn't appreciate me).

Turn it around to the opposite:
Paul shouldn't appreciate me (unless he does).

Be willing to go inside with each turnaround you discover, and experience where or how it's as true as or truer than the original statement. How does it apply to you in your life? Own it. If that seems difficult for you, add the word "sometimes" to the turnaround. Can you own that it's true *sometimes,* even if only in the moment that you are thinking that it's true about the other? Watch how you want to leave yourself and fly away mentally into someone else's business.

Wait for an example to appear of how you actually experience the turnaround in your life. How do you do this with Paul? Be specific. Make a list of the many ways and situations where you do not or have not appreciated Paul. Make a list of how you don't appreciate other people and situations in your life. Make a list of things that you do for yourself and for others, and discover how you don't always appreciate yourself.

I suggest that you always use the four questions before applying the turnaround. You may be tempted to take a shortcut and get right to the turnaround without putting your statement up against inquiry first. This is not an effective way of using the turnaround. The feeling of judgment turned back onto yourself can be brutal if it occurs prior to thorough self-education, and the four questions do give you this education. They end the ignorance of what you believe to be true, and the turnaround in the last position feels gentle and makes sense. Without the questions first, the turnarounds can feel harsh and shameful.

The Work is not about shame and blame. It's not about proving that you are the one in the wrong. The power of the turnaround lies in the discovery that everything you think you see on the outside is really a projection of your own mind. Everything is a mirror image of your own thinking. In discovering the innocence of the person you judged, you eventually come to recognize your own innocence.

Sometimes you may not find the turnaround in your behavior or actions. If that's the case, look for it in your thinking. For example, the turnaround for "Paul should stop smoking" is "I should stop smoking." Perhaps you have never smoked a single cigarette in your life. It may be that where you are smoking is in your mind. Over and over, you smoke with anger and frustration as you picture Paul smelling up your house with cigarette smoke. Do you mentally smoke more times in a day than Paul does? Your prescription for peace, then, is for you to stop smoking in your mind and to stop being so smoking angry about Paul's smoking. Should I let myself die of a heart attack from the stress of believing this thought before Paul could die of lung cancer? Let peace begin with me!

Another way of discovery is to substitute something else for the word *smoking*. True, you have never smoked. But is there something that you use in the same way that you think Paul uses cigarettes—food, drugs, credit cards, or relationships? Your turnaround could be a very humbling experience. It could be "I should stop snapping at Paul." Or "I should stop using our credit cards to make myself feel better." Be willing to listen to the advice that you're giving him, the advice that shows you how to live in your own business.

The Turnarounds in Action

The turnarounds bring powerful new awareness. Self-realization is not complete until it lives as action. Live the turnarounds. When you see how you have been preaching to others, go back and make amends, and let them know how difficult it is for you to do what you wanted them to do. Let them know the ways that you manipulated and conned them, how you got angry, used sex, used money, and used guilt to get what you wanted.

I wasn't always able to live the turnarounds that I so generously held out for others to live. When I realized this, I found myself on equal ground with the people I had judged. I saw that my philosophy wasn't so easy for any of us to live. I saw that we're all doing the best we can. This is how a lifetime of humility begins.

Reporting is another powerful way I found to solidify realization. In the first year after I woke up to reality, I often went to the people I had been judging and shared my turnarounds and realizations. I reported only what I had discovered about my part in whatever difficulty I was experiencing. (Under no circumstances did I talk about *their* part.) I did this so that I could hear it in the presence of at least two witnesses—the other person and myself. I gave it, and I received it. If, for example, your statement was "He lied to me," one turnaround would be "I lied to him." Now you list as many of your lies as you can remember and report them to that person, never in any way mentioning his lies to you, which are his business. You are doing this for your own freedom. Humility is the true resting place.

When I wanted to move even faster and more freely, I found that apologizing and making heartfelt amends was a wonderful shortcut. "To make amends" means to right the perceived wrong. What I call "living amends" is more far-reaching. It applies not only to one particular incident but to all future incidents of that kind. When I realized through inquiry that I had hurt someone in my past, I stopped hurting anyone. If, even after this, I hurt someone, I told them immediately why I did it, what I was afraid of losing, or what I wanted to get from them; and I began again, always with a clean slate. This is a powerful way to live freely.

A heartfelt apology is simply a way to undo an error and begin again on an equal and guiltless basis. Apologize and make amends for your own sake. It's all about your own peace. What good is it to be a talking saint? We've got an earth full of them. Peace is who you already are, without a story. Can you just live it?

Go through your list of examples of how the turnaround is true for you, and underline each statement where you feel that you harmed someone in any way. (For those of you who want to end your suffering quickly, your list of answers to the question "How do you react—how do you treat them—when you believe that thought?" could keep you very busy with reporting and apologizing.) Make amends to yourself by making amends to others. Give back in equal measure the opposite of what you believe was taken at their expense in each case.

Honest, nonmanipulative reporting, coupled with living amends, brings real intimacy to otherwise impossible relationships. If any people on your Worksheet are dead, make living amends through the rest of us. Give us what you would have given them, for your own sake.

I knew a man who was very serious about his freedom. He had been a junkie and a thief, had broken into many houses, and had been very good at what he did. After he had been doing The Work for a while, he made a list of everyone he had ever stolen from and what he had taken, as exactly as he could remember. When he finished the list, there were dozens of people and houses on it. And then he began to turn it around. He knew he would end up in jail, and yet he had to do what was right for him. He went house by house and knocked on each door. He was an African-American, and some of the places he returned to were not very comfortable for him, because he had beliefs about prejudice. But he just kept working with them and knocking on the doors. When people opened the doors, he would tell them who he was and what he had stolen, then he would apologize and say, "How can I make this right? I'll do whatever it takes." He went to dozens of houses, and no one ever called the police. And he would say, "I have to do something to make this right. Tell me what to do." So they would say things like, "Okay, fix my car" or "Paint my house." And he would do the job with pleasure and then put a check mark by their name or address on his list. And every stroke of the paintbrush, he said, was God, God, God.

I have a son, Ross, who has been doing The Work for a long time. Eight or nine years ago, I noticed that, as we shopped, he would sometimes say, "Wait for me, Mom, I'll be right back," and leave me for ten minutes or so. On one occasion, I watched him through the store window choose a shirt, take it to the cashier, and pay for it. Then he went back to the shelf, looked around to make sure that no one was watching, put the shirt back, and walked out of the store. I asked him what he was doing. He said, "A while ago, I stole things from five or six stores. It was horrible, Mom. Now when I see a store where I stole something, I walk in, find an item like the one I stole, pay for it, and put it back. I tried turning myself in. I'd say, 'Here's the money for what I stole, and if you want to prosecute, it's okay with me.' And they'd get confused, they'd call in the manager, and the manager wouldn't know what to do with the money, he'd tell me that it was too complicated for the computers. And if they called the police, the police would say that you have to be caught in the act. So they'd end up telling me that there was nothing they could do. But I really needed to turn it around. So I found this way. It works for me."

Ross also likes to play with an exercise that I recommend, which is to do a kind act and not get found out; if you're found out, the act doesn't count, and you start over. I have seen him at amusement parks watch children who don't seem to have enough money. He'll pull out a bill from his wallet, stoop down in front of the child, pretend to pick it up from the ground, and hand it to him, saying, "You dropped this, dude," then quickly walk away without ever looking back. He is a fine teacher of how to practice the turnaround through living amends.

It's generous to bring this practice into everyday life. The results are nothing short of miraculous, realized ever more deeply through further inquiry.

The Turnaround for Number 6

The turnaround for statement number 6 on your Judge-Your-Neighbor Worksheet is a bit different from the others. We change "I don't ever want to . . ." to "I am willing to . . ." and "I look forward to. . . ." For example, "I don't ever want to argue with Paul again" turns around to "I am willing to argue with Paul again" and "I look forward to arguing with Paul again."

Every time you think you're not willing to experience the anger or stress again, be willing to and look forward to it. It could happen again, even if only in your mind. This turnaround is about embracing all of life. Saying —and meaning—"I am willing to . . ." creates openness, creativity, and flexibility. Any resistance that you may have is softened, allowing you to lighten up rather than keep hopelessly applying willpower or force to eradicate the situation from your life. Saying and meaning "I look forward to . . ." actively opens you to life as it unfolds. Inner freedom becomes an expression of love and ease in the world.

For example, "I don't ever want to live with Paul if he doesn't change" turns around to "I am willing to live with Paul if he doesn't change" and "I look forward to living with Paul if he doesn't change." You may as well look forward to it. You could find yourself living with him, if only in your mind. (I have worked with people still bitter even though their mate has been dead for twenty years.) Whether you live with him or not, you will probably have this thought again, and you may feel the resulting stress and depression. Look forward to these feelings, because they are a reminder that it's time to wake yourself up. Uncomfortable feelings will bring you right back to The Work. This doesn't mean that you have to live with Paul. Willingness opens the door to all of life's possibilities.

Here are two more examples from our sample Worksheet.

Original Statement, Number 6: *I refuse to watch Paul ruin his health.*
Turnarounds: *I am willing to watch Paul ruin his health.*
I look forward to watching Paul ruin his health.

Original Statement, Number 6: *I don't ever want to be ignored by Paul again.*
Turnarounds: *I am willing to be ignored by Paul again.*
I look forward to being ignored by Paul again.

It's good to acknowledge that the same feelings or situation may happen again, if only in your thoughts. When you realize that suffering and discomfort are the call to inquiry, you may actually begin to look forward to uncomfortable feelings. You may even experience them as friends coming to show you what you have not yet investigated thoroughly enough. It's no longer necessary to wait for people or situations to change in order to experience peace and harmony. The Work is the direct way to orchestrate your own happiness. You find it within, and The Work takes you there.

No one can hurt me —

that's my job.

6.

Doing The Work on Work and Money

For some of us, life is controlled by our thoughts about work and money. But if our thinking is clear, how could work or money be the problem? Our thinking is all we need to change. It's all we *can* change. This is very good news.

Many of us are motivated by a desire for success. But what is success? What do we want to achieve? We do only three things in life: We stand, we sit, we lie horizontal. Once we've found success, we'll still be sitting somewhere, until we stand, and we'll stand until we lie down or sit again. Success is a concept, an illusion. Do you want the $3900 chair instead of the $39 one? Well, sitting is sitting. Without a story, we're successful wherever we are.

When I work with corporations, I may invite all the employees to judge each other. This turns out to be what employees and bosses have always wanted: to know how they look from the other's point of view. And then they all do The Work and turn it around. Employees and management have to notice and be drawn toward each other's clarity, even if they aren't aware of it. Often, it requires only one person who's willing to take the chance of being honest with the questions—and the whole company begins to match that clarity.

I once did The Work with an executive who said, "My assistant has been with me for ten years. I know she doesn't do the job well, but she has five children." I said, "Good. Keep her here so she can teach the rest of your employees that if they have enough children, they can work for you, whether they do their job well or not." And he said, "Well, I just can't fire her." I said, "I understand that. So put someone qualified in her position, send her home to her five children who need her, and send her a paycheck every month. That's more honest than what you're doing now. Guilt is expensive." And when the executive read his Worksheet to the woman, she agreed with every single thing he had written about her job performance, because it was clear and true. And I said to her, "What do you suggest? What would you do if you were *your* employee?" People usually fire themselves when they realize what's going on, and that's just what she did. She found a similar job in another company, closer to her home, where she was able to be both a good assistant and a good mother. The executive realized that he had never investigated the thoughts that led him to be "loyal" to an assistant who, in reality, had been just as uncomfortable with the situation as he was.

I've never seen a work or money problem that didn't turn out to be a thinking problem. I used to believe that I needed money to be happy. Even when I had a lot, I was often sick with the fear that something terrible would happen and I would lose it. I realize now that no amount of money is worth that kind of stress.

If you live with the uninvestigated thought "I need my money to be safe and secure," you're living in a hopeless state of mind. Banks fail. Stock markets crash. Currencies deflate. Wars break out. People lie, bend contracts, and break their promises. In this confused state of mind, you can make millions of dollars and still be insecure and unhappy.

Look at the energy that stress and fear require. What if every problem were converted into a solution that felt peaceful inside you? Some people believe that fear and stress are what motivate them to make money. But can you really know that that's true? Can you really know that without fear or stress as a motivator, you wouldn't have made the same money, or even more? "I need fear and stress to motivate me"—who would you be if you never believed that story again?

After I found The Work inside myself—after it found me—I began to notice that there was nothing I could do not to have the perfect amount of money for me right now, even when I had little or none. Happiness is a clear mind. A clear and sane mind knows how to live, how to work, what emails to send, what phone calls to make, and what to do to create what it wants without fear. Who would you be without the thought "I need my money to be safe"? You might be a lot easier to be with. You might even begin to notice the laws of generosity, the laws of letting money go out fearlessly and come back fearlessly. You don't ever need more money than you have. When you understand this, you begin to realize that you already have all the security you wanted money to give you in the first place. It's a lot easier to make money from this position.

Just as we often use stress and fear to motivate ourselves to make money, we can find ourselves using anger and frustration to move us to social activism. If I want to act sanely and effectively while I clean up the earth's environment, let me clean up my own environment. All the trash and pollution in my thinking—let me clean that up, by meeting it with love and understanding. Then action can become truly effective. It takes just one person to help the planet. That one is you.

When I work in prisons, there will be maybe two hundred men from a cell block sitting there, looking down at the floor, with their arms folded across their chests. I do The Work with them, and then the guards bring in another two hundred. These are all hard-core violent men—many of them are in prison with life sentences for rape, murder, and other heavy crimes—and I'm the only woman in the room. And I don't say a word until they make eye contact with me. This is not easy for them to do. There is some kind of unspoken code that they have, to keep people like me out of their culture. But I just stand in front of them, waiting for eye contact. I may walk into the rows and pace slowly up and down as I wait for just one man to look me in the eyes. The moment it happens, the moment one man does that, he always looks down, really fast, but it's too late. There was contact. No one but me has seen his glance; it happens so fast that there's no way the others can see that it happened. And yet, immediately, the code begins to break down all over the room. Two or three others look me in the eyes, then another eight, then another dozen, and then everyone is looking at me, laughing, turning red, and saying things to one another like "Sheeeeeeit!" or "Man, she crazy." And it's done. Now I can speak to them and give them The Work, and all because one man dared to look me in the eye.

I love thanking these men for sacrificing their entire lives to teach our children how not to live—and therefore how to live—if they want to be free. I tell them that they are the greatest teachers and that their lives are good and needed. Before I leave, I ask them, "Would you spend the rest of your life in prison if you knew that it would keep one child from having to live what you're living?" And many of these violent men understand, and they just well up with tears like sweet little boys.

There is nothing we can do that doesn't help the planet. That's the way it really is.

He's So Incompetent!

Gary is annoyed by his incompetent employee. Is the person who annoys you someone you work with? Or is it your spouse or your children who didn't do the dishes thoroughly enough or who left toothpaste on the bathroom sink? See if you can find an example in your life, and go inside for your own answers as Gary goes inside for his.

———

Gary: I'm angry at Frank because he is incompetent when he works for me.

Katie: Okay. "Frank should be competent"—is it true?

Gary: I think so.

Katie: Can you absolutely know that it's true? Who ever told you that? His résumé said competent. His recommendation said competent. It's all over the place. You hire him, and he's supposed to be competent. What's the reality of it in your experience? Is he?

Gary: In my experience, he's not.

Katie: So that's the only place you can sanely come from—reality. Is it true that he should be competent? No. He's not. That's it. That's your reality. So we can keep going over this until we get the "Is it true?" thing, because when you understand this, you become a lover of reality and move into balance. How do you react when you believe the lie that he should be competent when he works for you, and he's not?

Gary: It's frustrating and anxiety-producing. I feel like I have to carry his work. I have to clean up behind him every time. I can't leave him alone to do his work.

Katie: Can you see a reason to drop the thought that he should be competent? And I'm not asking you to drop it.

Gary: It would make me feel better if I could drop it.

Katie: That's a very good reason. Can you find one stress-free reason to keep this thought that opposes reality?

Gary: Yes. Well, I don't see what you mean by "opposes reality."

Katie: The reality, as you see it, is that he's not competent. You're saying he should be. That theory is not working for you, because it opposes reality. I hear you say that it causes you frustration and anxiety.

Gary: Okay, I think I'm pulling this apart. The reality is that he's just not competent. What's making me crazy is thinking he's supposed to be, rather than just accepting it.

Katie: He's incompetent whether you accept it or not. Reality doesn't wait for our agreement or approval. It is what it is. You can count on it.

Gary: Reality is what is.

Katie: Yes. Reality is always much kinder than the fantasy. You can have a lot of fun at home with what I refer to as the "proof of truth" exercise. "He should be competent"—where's your proof? Make a list and see if any of it really proves that he should be competent when you put it up against inquiry. It's all a lie. There *is* no proof. The truth is that he should *not* be competent, because he's just not. Not competent for that job.

Gary: The fact is that he's not competent, and I do what I have to do to make up for it. What I don't need to give myself is the extra baggage of "He *should* be yada yada yada."

Katie: Very well said.

Gary: All my job-related angst was about thinking that Frank should be competent. The truth is that he's just not competent. The piece that I added, which made me nuts, was that he should be competent. The fact is that I'm going to do what I have to do. I'm going to backfill until he's not my problem anymore. I'm just going to do it. By adding that he should be competent, I work myself up into a fucking emotional tizzy. Welcome to New York!

Katie: I didn't know you used the f-word in New York. [The audience bursts into laughter.]

Gary: Yeah, we do. Occasionally.

Katie: So who would you be without this insane story that argues with reality?

Gary: I would just be in the flow and do what I have to do in my job.

Katie: Who would you be, standing with this man at work, without the story?

Gary: I would be compassionate and effective.

Katie: Yes. "Frank should be competent"—turn it around.

Gary: Frank should not be competent.

Katie: You've got it. Not until he is. That's reality for now. There's another turnaround.

Gary: I should be competent. That is true.

Katie: Let's look at statement number 2 on your Worksheet.

Gary: I want Frank to take responsibility for his part of the project.

Katie: Turn it around.

Gary: I want me to take responsibility for my part of the project.

Katie: Yes, because until you stop focusing on his incompetence, you're not taking full responsibility for the project.

Gary: And I should take responsibility for his part of the project.

Katie: Yes, if you want the job done with competence and there's no other way. Okay, let's go on to the next statement.

Gary: He should step up to the plate as an expert in his field and as a project leader.

Katie: Is that true? I mean, where would the man even get the ability? "Hey you—the one with no competence—you should step up to the plate!"

Gary: No. It's insanity. I'm with you. He just does what he does.

Katie: How do you treat Frank when you believe that fantasy?

Gary: I turn into a tough guy. I think he has to get it done quicker, and I'm all over him.

Katie: Not very effective. Can you see a reason to drop the thought?

Gary: Absolutely.

Katie: So let's turn it around.

Gary: I should step up to the plate as an expert in my field. I'll just step up. It's got to be done.

Katie: He's the expert who brings you to the highest level of competence in your life. No mistake.

Gary: Yes. He's my teacher. I can feel that.

Katie: Good. Let's move on to your fourth statement.

Gary: I need him to carry his portion of the project. And I see now that I don't really need that.

Katie: Hopeless?

Gary: Absolutely hopeless. I need me to carry his portion and my portion of the project if I want it done.

Katie: Let's look at the next statement.

Gary: Frank is incompetent.

Katie: Turn it around.

Gary: I am incompetent.

Katie: In the moment that you see him as incompetent, you're incompetent. He's perfectly competent for what he was supposed to bring you, and that was clarity. That's what he brought. And he may bring more— who knows?

Gary: I don't really feel that turnaround. I think I'm very competent.

Katie: Just not where *he's* concerned. You weren't competent enough to see that he's not supposed to be competent.

Gary: That I agree with. That's my incompetence. *He needs to be watched even though he is very senior.* I need to watch over myself. That's truer. I can be insane sometimes.

Katie: You've found the internal world. When you see that it's only your thinking that you need to work with, then every problem you experience in the world becomes a joy to bring to inquiry. For people who really want to know the truth, this Work is checkmate.

Gary: I got stuck when I tried to do this myself earlier in the week. I thought I was right. Once I bring it all inside, then all the turnarounds start to make sense.

Katie: The guy walks in, you put your story onto him, and you call your suffering his fault. You believe your story and live in the stressful fantasy that he is the problem. Without the thought that this man should be more competent than he is, it might come to you to fire him. If you fired him, that would free him to get to a job where he *is* competent. Then he could be competent where he's needed. And now there's space for the man or woman who does belong in the position with you. Two weeks later, the guy may call you and say, "Thank you for firing me. I hated working with you. And I love my new job." Anything is possible. Or it could be that because you've done this inner Work and gotten clearer about your thinking, you may look at the guy on Monday morning and see a competence that you never noticed before. Okay, read the last statement of your Worksheet.

Gary: I don't ever want to have him or a person like him on my team.

Katie: Turn it around.

Gary: I am willing to have him or a person like him on my team. And I look forward to having him or a person like him on my team, because it brings me into my inner space to find the solution.

Katie: You do this very well. Welcome to The Work.

Uncle Ralph and His Stock Tips

The following dialogue demonstrates that even though someone is passionately attached to his own story, and therefore to his own suffering, he may still break free if he's willing to go through the whole inquiry with patience. Even if, as Marty points out, the exercise seems "only mental" for a long time, it can suddenly make sense on a far deeper level.

I love not rushing the process. Mind doesn't shift until it does, and when it does shift, it's right on time, not one second too late or too soon. People are just like seeds waiting to sprout. We can't be pushed ahead of our own understanding.

To benefit from this dialogue, you don't need to understand the technical issues Marty is talking about; all you need to know is that his stock went up and then way down, and that his emotions went with it.

Marty: I'm angry at my uncle Ralph for giving me some bum tips on the stock market that cost me all my money. I got indebted to him when he bailed me out on some margin calls—some stocks I borrowed money to buy—and the stocks continued to tumble. And the other stock tip, his big tip, lost 85 percent of its value in two years. And my uncle is in an unconscious pissing contest with me.

Katie: Yes.

Marty: He's always trying to prove that he's better than everyone, by the size of his bank account, and he happens to be a wealthy man, and so he didn't have to borrow anything. I had to borrow when the one stock was going down and the other stock was doing well to have any chance of being able to pay him back all the money that he lent me.

Katie: I hear it.

Marty: And so I kept building up a debt to him, and then recently—this has been going on for two and a half years, it just came to a head—I finally told him, when his other stock went way, way down, I said, "You know, Ralph, now that they've both tanked, I've lost all my money, and some of your money." At which point he said, "Listen, you motherfucker, I *told* you to not borrow and you borrowed. You betrayed me; you went against me; you did this, you did that. . . ." And I only got in one word edgewise, which was, "Ralph, I needed to buy your other stock, and I just didn't have the money." But I didn't say why I needed to buy it, which was to have some hope of paying him back. And I also wanted to make some money, I mean my own fear and greed went in there, too. But . . .

Katie: Sweetheart, just read what you wrote. It's important that you read what you wrote, not narrate a story.

Marty: Okay, okay. I'm sorry. *I want Uncle Ralph to bail me out, give me back the $60,000 I started with plus the other $35,000 that I'm due, to pay off my credit-card debts and take responsibility for having incorrect information and for causing me and my family these financial losses.*

Katie: Good. Keep reading.

Marty: Uncle Ralph should pay off my debts and give me a hundred grand. He shouldn't demand his money from me, because I can't pay. I need Uncle Ralph to bail my ass out from financial ruin. I need him to take responsibility and at least try to get along with me as responsible adults for what we both did. Ralph is a demanding, controlling, possibly vindictive person, who is not interested in the truth as much as he is in proving that he is always right and highly intelligent. Okay, the last one?

Katie: Yes.

Marty: I don't ever want to listen to his stock tips or owe him money again or take his petty, irate, childish shit.

Katie: Yes. Good. Well done. Okay, sweetheart, would you read the first statement again, just the way you wrote it?

Marty: Okay. *I'm angry at my uncle Ralph for giving me some bum tips on the stock market that cost me all my money, some of his, and threatens me with . . .* ah, I can't read my writing.

Katie: Okay, so let's stop there. He gave you the tip?

Marty: Uh-huh.

Katie: Okay. If I offer you this cup, you don't have to take it. It's up to you whether you take it or not. And there's no right or wrong here. "Uncles should not give nephews tips on the stock market"—is it true? What's the reality of it? Do they?

Marty: Well, he wanted me to make money, and that's why he gave me the tips.

Katie: So what's the reality of it? He gave them to you.

Marty: He gave them to me, and I took them, and I played them to the hilt. It got my ass in a sling.

Katie: We all know up-front that stock tips are risky, but knowing that doesn't keep us from acting on them. And realizing what we've done is scary sometimes, at two o'clock in the morning, or at two o'clock in the afternoon. Some of us end up jumping out of buildings. So, "Uncles shouldn't give nephews bum tips"—is it true?

Marty: Yes, right. It's true!

Katie: And what's the reality of it? Do they?

Marty: Yes. My uncle gave me a bum tip, and he doesn't admit that it was a bum tip.

Katie: Okay. "Uncles are supposed to admit their errors"—is that true?

Marty: Yes, you're damn tootin'. Uncles are supposed to admit their errors.

Katie: And what's the reality of it? What's your experience with it?

Marty: He forced all the blame on me, and that . . .

Katie: So your experience is no, they don't admit their errors.

Marty: That's right.

Katie: So is it true that uncles should admit their errors?

Marty: I think it's true that *all* people should admit their errors.

Katie: Oh, well! And what's the reality of it? Do they always? Is it true that uncles should admit their errors?

Marty: Yes.

Katie: And what's the reality of it?

Marty: He's not doing it.

Katie: He's not doing it. So I ask you, on what planet is this supposed to happen? Is it true that people should admit their errors? No. Not until they do. I'm not asking for morality here. I'm just asking for the simple truth.

Marty: But just let me say that I really try to admit my own errors. And what's more, in the action that I'm taking, in sending him all my money and assets, I'm admitting my errors by my actions.

Katie: You are. I live the way you do.

Marty: I hope not.

Katie: I like myself when I take responsibility for my actions. But "People should admit their errors"—is it true? No. How do we know that people are not supposed to admit their errors?

Marty: Because they don't.

Katie: They don't. This is so simple, sweetheart, that we've been missing it for thousands of years. It's the truth that set me free. If you argue with it, you lose. I'm a lover of reality, not because I'm some sort of spiritual being, but because when I argue with it, I lose inside myself. I lose the contact with the place inside that is home. How do you react when you think the thought that he should admit his errors, and he doesn't?

Marty: I feel victimized.

Katie: What else? How does it feel inside?

Marty: I feel pain, sadness, rage, fear . . .

Katie: Separation?

Marty: Yes, all the bad stuff.

Katie: The reason you feel all this turmoil is that you're stuck in the center of a lie. It's not true that he should admit his errors. That's the lie. The world has been teaching this lie for centuries, and if you're tired of the pain, it's time to notice what's true. It's not true that people should admit their errors, yet. This is a tough one for some of us, and I invite you to go there. This Work demands absolute, simple, pure integrity. That's all, and the willingness to hear the truth. "It would be much better for you if he admitted his error and gave your money back. Your highest spiritual path, your greatest freedom, would be if he admitted his error and gave your money back"—can you absolutely know that that's true?

Marty: That that would be my highest spiritual path?

Katie: Yes.

Marty: Umm . . .

Katie: Just a yes or no. Can you absolutely know that it's true?

Marty: I don't know.

Katie: That was my experience too. I can't know if that's true.

Marty: You know, well, let's put it this way . . . I could say yes, and then I'd feel a sense of justice, but I don't know that justice is necessarily the same thing as peace.

Katie: I agree: Justice isn't the same as peace. I don't care about justice. I care about your freedom, the truth inside you that can set you free. This is the ultimate justice.

Marty: No, I know. I'm talking about divine justice. I'm saying that the truthful thing would be to really sit down as two grown men and look where . . . because I made mistakes, too.

Katie: "He should sit down with you"—is that true?

Marty: Yes, definitely true.

Katie: What's the reality of it?

Marty: He ain't.

Katie: He ain't. It's not happening.

Marty: Right.

Katie: So how do you react when you think the thought that he should sit down with you like a grown man, and he doesn't?

Marty: Well, I feel that I've been wronged, and I feel righteous, and I feel like shit.

Katie: Yes, that's the result. So it's not that he's not sitting down with you that hurts; it's your believing the thought that he . . .

Marty: That he should.

Katie: That he should. So just be there a minute. See if you can locate that. Who would you be without the story that he should sit down with you like a grown man or that he should admit his error and apologize? Who would you be without that story? I'm not asking you to drop your story. I'm simply asking who you would be in your daily life today without that story.

Marty: I know I'd be free of any expectations from him.

Katie: Yes.

Marty: Which I guess would make me more whole within myself.

Katie: Yes.

Marty: But you know, I . . .

Katie: Notice how you're about to go into your story when you say "but." Just be still with it.

Marty [after a pause]: I really don't know how it would feel.

Katie: That's right, sweetheart. We're so used to holding on to the lie about what's really happening that we don't know how to live freely. And some of us are learning how, because the pain is just too great not to learn. In my experience, when I don't hold on to the story, I get up, brush my teeth, have breakfast, do what I do all day, come here, and do all the same things, but without the stress—without the hell.

Marty: Sounds great. And, you know, as fleeting as it may have been, I have had a taste of the free state, so I know that state, and I would certainly like to live that way. That's why I'm here.

Katie: So read that part again.

Marty: Okay, the first part. Now I'm able to read my writing. *I'm angry at my uncle Ralph for giving me some bum tips on the stock market that cost me all my money.*

Katie: So now we're going to do what we call a turnaround. The Work is: Judge your neighbor, write it down, ask four questions, turn it around. That's it. Simple stuff. So now we're at the point where we're going to turn it around. "I'm angry at myself . . ."

Marty: I'm angry at myself . . .

Katie: "For taking . . ." He gave, you took.

Marty: For taking his stock tips and believing him.

Katie: Yes, that's close. Keep it very simple. Now read it again, and read it just the way you wrote it. "I'm angry at myself . . ."

Marty: I'm angry at myself for giving me . . . ?

Katie: Yes, honey.

Marty: Oh! I'm angry at myself for giving me some bum tips on the stock market that cost me all my money?

Katie: Yes. You gave them to yourself.

Marty: I see that. I gave the tips to myself by accepting them from him.

Katie: Exactly. He can't give them to you unless you take them. You've been believing your own mythology. I think you're getting this thing.

Marty: That's a hard pill to swallow.

Katie: Well, there's one thing harder to swallow, and that's what you've been living, and how you put yourself at the mercy of other people.

Marty: Yeah. It sure doesn't feel good.

Katie: Let's look at the next one.

Marty: I want Uncle Ralph to bail me out.

Katie: Okay. So, "Uncle Ralph should bail you out"—is it true?

Marty: Yeah, if he were an honorable man. Yeah.

Katie: Why is that? Whose money did you invest?

Marty: Some of his, some of mine.

Katie: Okay, yours and his, but let's look at your money. You invested it in stock tips that you gave yourself after hearing them from your uncle.

Marty: Right.

Katie: And he should bail you out?

Marty: Well, if you put it like that . . . no.

Katie: Good. So what does he have to do with any of it, aside from sharing with you what he believed to be true at the time?

Marty: Nothing.

Katie: Correct. Nothing.

Marty: But the thing is, right at this moment it's very mental to me. It's all in my head. I still feel the anger.

Katie: Just stay with the process. If it seems mental right now, that's the way it's supposed to be. How do you react when you think the thought that he should bail you out? Or that it would even be for your highest spiritual good if he bailed you out?

Marty: I feel all this anxiety and terror, and the bad stuff that I'd rather not have.

Katie: And you can focus on that, and you don't have to bail yourself out.

Marty: Right.

Katie: You just focus on the thought that he's supposed to do it, and you tell yourself why you're right, and you never win, because you *can't* win that. The truth is that he's not supposed to bail you out. He didn't invest your money. You did.

Marty: Right.

Katie: But putting the focus over there on him, rather than on what's true, keeps you from knowing and therefore living your integrity, which is to bail yourself out. You know, there's nothing sweeter than you bailing yourself out. Who got you into this? You did. Whose job is it to get you out when your uncle says that he won't? Yours. If Uncle Ralph does it, then you don't ever get to realize that you can do it.

Marty: That's true.

Katie: And then when Uncle Ralph says no, you resent him and continue to focus on him, and you don't bail yourself out, because you're not in a position to notice that you can do that. And you die yelling, "It's not fair! What did I do to deserve such a heartless uncle?"

Marty: I agree with you. It's true.

Katie: So give me one good reason to hold on to the mythology that he's supposed to bail you out, when the truth is that he hasn't.

Marty: For him, it would be a little bit more than lunch money.

Katie: That's a good one! What I discovered right away was that there were only three kinds of business in the universe—mine, yours, and God's. And if you don't use the G-word, put the word *nature* there or *reality.* So this is a test of discernment. Whose business is his money?

Marty: His business.

Katie: That's it.

Marty: I'm making it my business. That's what hurts.

Katie: Yes. Now here's what I noticed. When I mentally go into your business, I start getting this stress inside me. Doctors call it names like ulcers, high blood pressure, cancer . . . all of it. And then the mind attaches to that, and it creates a whole system to hold up the first lie. Let your feelings tell you when the first lie begins. Then inquire. Otherwise, you get lost in the feelings and in the stories that lead to them, and all you know is that you hurt and that your mind won't stop racing. And if you inquire, you catch the first lie through noticing your feelings. And you can just stop the mind by putting the story you're attached to on paper. There's a portion of your stressful mind stopped, even though it may still be screaming in your head. Now put the statements up against inquiry, ask the four questions, and turn your statements around. That's it. You're the one who sets yourself free, not your uncle. You bail yourself out, or you're not going to get bailed out—haven't you noticed?

Marty: I agree with everything you said. It's right on the beam. It's just that at this point in time, I'm not in touch with my own ability to bail myself out.

Katie: Well, in this country we have bankruptcy. If I put myself in it, I get myself out of it. And if I file for bankruptcy, I eventually pay every debt I owe, because living this way offers me the freedom I'm looking for. I don't care if it's a dime a month. I, too, act as an honorable person, not because I'm spiritual, but because it hurts if I don't. Simple.

Marty: Yes, that's the reason, I agree.

Katie: People think, "When I make a whole lot of money, then I'll be happy." I say, let's skip that part for now and be happy from here. You got yourself into it. Your uncle had nothing to do with it so far.

Marty: I'm with you on that. I'm realizing that he didn't do it. I did it, and in a certain way it's kind of thrilling to sit with, and it's also like "Oh, shit!"

Katie: Yes, welcome to reality. When we begin to live in reality and see it for what it is without our old stories, it's incredible. Look at this for a moment without a story. It's all reality: God. I call it God because it rules, it always is what it is. And the myth of an uncle's responsibility would keep me from the awareness of that. It's so simple. Okay, so whose business is your uncle's money?

Marty: His.

Katie: And whose business is it what he does with his money?

Marty: His.

Katie: I love it!

Marty: I'm clear on those two now. I wasn't before. I really thought it was my business.

Katie: And did you sign your inheritance over to him?

Marty: Yup.

Katie: Okay. Whose money is it now?

Marty: His.

Katie: And whose business is it what he does with his money?

Marty: His.

Katie: Don't you love it? Life is so simple when we move back into our own business.

Marty: I don't feel very good about it now.

Katie: Sweetheart, when we realize something this basic, sometimes we're like a newborn foal. At first our legs won't even work. We just get wobbly and have to sit down. What I suggest is that on the other side of this session, you go somewhere and sit with it for a while and just be still with what you're realizing. It's big. Let's look at the next statement.

Marty: Okay. *Uncle Ralph should pay off my debts and give me a hundred grand.*

Katie: Wonderful! I love it! Now turn it around.

Marty: I should pay my debts and give myself a hundred grand.

Katie: This is very exciting. And if your mind isn't in his business, you would be amazed at the space that opens up for you, the power that opens up to solve your own problems. It's . . . well, it can't be told. It just can't be told. But it's the truth that sets us free to act clearly and lovingly, and there's such excitement in it. Okay, let's do another turnaround. "I . . ."

Marty: I should pay my debts and give myself a hundred grand.

Katie: ". . . and give my uncle a hundred grand." [Marty and the audience laugh.]

Marty: Oh, man!

Katie: Whatever it is that you owe him.

Marty: I should pay my debts . . . You know, I probably do owe him another hundred grand.

Katie: So there it is.

Marty: I should pay my debts and give my uncle a hundred grand. Wow!

Katie: Yes. For your own sake. Even if the man has billions and billions of dollars—it doesn't matter. It's for *your* sake.

Marty: I agree. I absolutely agree with that.

Katie: Yes. So, "He should give you a hundred grand"—what for?

Marty: Well, that would make all of these two and a half years of activity a basic wash.

Katie: And then you'd be happy?

Marty: Well, no.

Katie: How do you react when you believe the thought that he's supposed to give you a hundred grand?

Marty: I'm sore.

Katie: Yes. Who or what would you be without that thought?

Marty: Free.

Katie: Let's look at the next statement.

Marty [laughing]: *I need Uncle Ralph to bail my ass out from financial ruin.* This is hysterical!

Katie: Okay, now turn it around.

Marty: I need myself to bail my ass out from financial ruin.

Katie: You see how you've begun to end your own suffering? People lie on their deathbed at the age of ninety saying, "It's all my uncle's fault." We don't have to do that anymore. And that's the offering here. Judge your uncle, write it down, ask four questions, turn it around. And then send him a thank-you note. How do we know it's for your highest good that your uncle hasn't bailed you out? He hasn't. You're being given a great gift, and when you step into the truth, that gift becomes visible and available. And you end up like a little boy—new.

Marty: I would like that.

Katie: I really appreciate your courage. It would be wonderful to call him and tell him the turnarounds, in your own language. For example, you might say, "Uncle Ralph, every time I call you, I want something from you. And I want you to know that *I* know I do that. I'm clear about it. And in no way do I expect you to bail me out. I've come to see that your money is yours and that I owe you and that I'm working on it, and if you have any suggestions, I'm open. And I'm sincerely sorry for what I've done." And when he says he has some great stock tips, you can say thank you and make your own decisions and not blame him if you do use them and lose money. You gave yourself those stock tips.

Marty: Yes. In fact, I even asked him for them, because I had come into some money and I knew he had a lot, so I wanted to know what he thought I should do with it.

Katie: The greatest stock market you can invest in is yourself. Finding this truth is better than finding a gold mine.

Marty: That thing about calling my uncle with what you just said—as much of it as I can retain —feels incredibly threatening to me.

Katie: Of course. You get to be wrong, and he gets to be right.

Marty: And I don't even know that he'd sit still to listen to it.

Katie: No, you don't. Okay, let's look at the next statement.

Marty: I don't ever want to listen to his stock tips or owe him money again or take his petty, irate, childish shit.

Katie: You might do all this again, if only in your mind. There might also be some residue left in you. And I can tell you that when you let go of one thing, everything falls like dominoes, because concepts are what we are working with—theories that have never been investigated. These concepts may appear again, and this is good news, when you know what to do with them. You may expect something from him again, and it's going to hurt if it's out of alignment with your integrity.

Marty: That's true. Yes, that's actually true. It's hard to admit, but it's true.

Katie: Yes, but it's easier to admit it than not to admit it.

Marty: Yes . . . I don't know . . . I don't know if I'm there yet, but . . .

Katie: You could play the scenario over again in your mind, and if there's something left that you're attached to, if something hurts, it will plunge you back into The Work. So read it just as you wrote it, but say, "I'm willing to . . ."

Marty: Okay. I'm willing to listen to his stock tips and owe him money? [Pause] I guess I am. I am willing to listen to his stock tips and owe him money, and I am willing to take his petty, irate shit.

Katie: Yes. Because if you feel pain around it, it will put you back into The Work, if you want some freedom. Now "I look forward to . . ."

Marty: I look forward to . . . Wait a minute . . . I'm confused now.

Katie: Just do it. Just trust the process. "I look forward to . . ."

Marty: Okay. I look forward to listening to his stock tips and owing him money and taking his petty, irate shit?

Katie: Yes. Because it's possible that you'll play that scenario over again.

Marty: Not likely, because I don't think he'd ever give me a tip again, and I don't think I'll ever have any money to play the market again. Not that I want to anyway.

Katie: You might play this scenario in the middle of the night when you wake up in a cold sweat.

Marty: Oh.

Katie: That's when these things are often done.

Marty: Right.

Katie: And you can just grab your pad and pencil, and judge your uncle again, and clean yourself up. Every concept that has ever existed is inside you. It's not personal. After all these thousands of years, the thoughts are still in each of us, waiting to be met with some friendship and a little understanding finally, rather than with pills and running and hiding and arguing and sexing, because we don't know what else to do with them. When the thoughts arise, just meet them with some integrity. "He owes me"—is it true? Can you absolutely know that it's true? How do you react when you think that thought? Ask yourself. And who would you be without the thought? You would have an uncle you care about, and you would be responsible for yourself. Until you love him unconditionally, your Work's not done. Close your eyes now and look at your uncle trying to help you. *Look* at the guy, without your story.

Marty: Do you want to know what my experience was?

Katie: Yes.

Marty: I'm still feeling the pain of his verbal abuse.

Katie: Okay, verbal abuse—turn it around. "I'm feeling the pain . . ."

Marty: I still am feeling the pain of *my* verbal abuse.

Katie: Toward him in your mind.

Marty: I'm still feeling the pain of my verbal abuse toward him in my mind?

Katie: Yes.

Marty: Maybe everyone else here is getting this. I'm not.

Katie: What's an example of his verbal abuse?

Marty: "Marty, you don't know nothin'. I told you to do it this way, and you did it your own way . . ."

Katie: Okay, let's stop right there. Could it be that he's right and that's what you don't want to hear? That's not verbal abuse. We call it "verbal abuse" when someone tells us the truth about ourselves and we don't want to hear it. That is, we *think* we don't want to hear it. Deep down inside us, we hunger for the truth.

Marty: Okay. I see that. That's true.

Katie: There's no such thing as verbal abuse. There's only someone telling me a truth that I don't want to hear. If I were really able to hear my accuser, I would find my freedom. The "you" you're identified with doesn't want to be discovered, because that is its death. When someone tells me that I lied, for example, I just go inside to see if they're right. If I can't find it in the situation they've mentioned, I can find it in some other situation, maybe twenty years ago. And then I can say, "Sweetheart, I *am* a liar. I see where you're right about me." In this we've found something in common. They know I'm a liar, and now I know it. We join and connect. We both agree. I can find those pieces of who I am from them. This is the beginning of self-love.

Marty: That's right. Oh my God, I never saw that!

Katie: If your uncle says something that hurts, he's just revealed what you haven't wanted to look at yet. The man is a Buddha. [The audience laughs, and Marty laughs with them.] These people that we're close to will give us everything we need, so that we can realize ourselves and be free of the lie. Your uncle knows exactly what to say, because he's you, giving you back to yourself. But you say, "Go away, I don't want to hear it." And you say it mostly in your mind. Because you think that if you got honest with him about it, he might not give you money. Or affection or validation.

Marty: He's never given me any validation.

Katie: Good! I'm *loving* this guy. [Marty and the audience laugh.] He leaves that for you to do, and he just holds his truth.

Marty: If you met him, I don't know if you'd think he was an enlightened being.

Katie: What I know is that he knows the things about you that you haven't wanted to look at yet. And the truth is that he can guide you to the things you really do want to look at. If you go to a friend and say, "Oh, my uncle has treated me so badly," your friend will say, "You poor fellow, that's really a shame." What I say is, find an enemy. They won't give you that sympathy. You go to your friends for refuge, because you can count on them to agree with your stories. But when you go to your enemies, they'll tell you, straight up, anything you want to know, even though you may think you don't want to know it. Your uncle can give you material that's invaluable, if you really want to know the truth. Until you do, you have to resent your uncle.

Marty: You mean that everything I'm defending against is the truth that I don't want to see? Holy shit! No wonder I've been seeing my uncle as an enemy! This is amazing!

Katie: Uncles have never been the problem, and they never will be. It's your uninvestigated thinking about your uncle that's the problem. And as you inquire, you set yourself free. Your uncle is really God in disguise as an uncle. He's giving you everything you need for your freedom.

Angry at Corporate America

A question I often hear is "If I do The Work and I'm no longer fearful for the planet's welfare, why would I get involved in social action? If I felt completely peaceful, why would I bother taking action at all?" My answer is "Because that's what love does."

The fear of not being fearful is one of the biggest stumbling blocks for people beginning inquiry. They believe that without stress, without anger, they wouldn't act, they would just sit around with drool running down their chins. Whoever left the impression that peace isn't active has never known peace the way I know it. I am entirely motivated without anger. The truth sets us free, and freedom acts.

When I take people to the desert, they may see a tin can lying under a cactus and say, "How can anyone do that to this beautiful desert?" But that tin can *is* the desert. It's what is. How can it be out of place? The cactus, the snakes, the scorpions, the sand, the can, and us—all of it. That is nature, not a mental image of the desert without the can. Without any stress or judgment, I notice that I just pick up the can. Or I could tell the story that people are polluting the earth, and that there is no end to human selfishness and greed, and then pick up the can with all the sadness and anger I'd be feeling. Either way, when it's time for the can to move, I notice that I'm there, as nature, picking up the can. Who would I be without my uninvestigated story? Just happily picking up the can. And if someone notices me picking it up, and my action seems right, they may pick up another can. We're already acting as a community, beyond anything that we've planned. Without a story, without an enemy, action is spontaneous, clear, and infinitely kind.

———————

Margaret: I want corporations to start taking responsibility, to start respecting life, care for the future, be in support of the environment and third-world countries, stop abusing animals, and stop thinking about money only.

Katie: So, "They think about money only"—can you really know that that's true? I'm not saying that it's not. I'm not here with a philosophy or the right or wrong of it. Just inquiry.

Margaret: Well, it seems like that.

Katie: How do you react when you believe the thought that they only care about money?

Margaret: I get angry and frustrated, and I don't want to support them as people.

Katie: Yes, even though you do support them. You use the products they put out, their electricity, their oil and gas. You feel guilty as you do it, yet you continue, and maybe, just like them, you find a way to justify your action. So give me a stress-free reason to believe the thought that these people only care about money.

Margaret: Well, that way I make a difference. I at least do what I can do.

Katie: I hear from you that when you believe that thought, you experience anger and frustration. And how do you live when you think that you've made a difference, and they're still cutting down trees? You think that only through further stress can the planet be saved. Now give me a stress-*free* reason to believe that thought.

Margaret: There is no stress-free reason.

Katie: No stress-free reason? So, who would you be without this thought, this philosophy, that they only care about money.

Margaret: Peaceful. Happy. Maybe clearer.

Katie: Yes. And maybe more effective, energized, less confused, and in a position to make a real difference in ways that you haven't even imagined yet. In my experience, clarity moves much more efficiently than violence and stress. It doesn't make enemies along the way, and therefore it can sit comfortably at a peace table, face-to-face with anyone there.

Margaret: That's true.

Katie: When I come at a corporate official, or a logger, pointing my finger and in any way blaming him or his company for destroying the atmosphere, however valid my information is, do you think that he'll be open to what I'm saying? I'm scaring him with my attitude, and the facts can get lost, because I'm coming from fear myself. All he'll hear is that I think he's doing it wrong, it's his fault, and he'll go into denial and resistance. But if I speak to him without any stress, in total confidence that everything is just the way it should be right now, I'm able to express myself kindly and with no fear about the future. "Here are the facts. How can the two of us make it better? Do you see another way? How do you suggest that we proceed?" And when he speaks, I'm able to listen.

Margaret: I understand.

Katie: Sweetheart, let's turn it around and see what you would experience with that. Turn around statement number 2. Say it again with you in all of it. "I . . ."

Margaret: I want to start taking responsibility, I want to start respecting life and care for the future. I want to be in support of the environment and third-world countries, and I want to stop abusing animals. I want to stop thinking about money only.

Katie: Does that ring a bell?

Margaret: Well, I really feel I'm . . . That's what I'm working on all the time.

Katie: And wouldn't you rather work on it without the frustration, stress, and anger? But when you come at us—the corporate people—self-righteously, all we see is the enemy coming. When you come at us clearly, we can hear from you what we already know in our hearts about the welfare of the planet, and we can listen to you and your solutions without feeling threatened and without having to be defensive. We can see you as a loving and attractive person, as someone easy to work with, someone to be trusted. That's my experience.

Margaret: Well, that's true.

Katie: War only teaches war. You clean up your mental environment, and we'll clean up our physical one much more quickly. That's how it works. Let's look at the next statement on your Worksheet.

Margaret: Corporations should be caring and give back to the planet, use their money to support environmental groups, build habitats, support freedom of broadcasting, should wake up and start thinking about tomorrow.

Katie: So, "They don't care"—can you really know that that's true?

Margaret: Well, again, it seems like it, doesn't it?

Katie: Not to me, and I understand where you're coming from. How do you react when you think the thought "They don't care"?

Margaret: Sometimes I get really depressed. But it's good, because I also get very angry. I get very motivated and work very hard at making a difference.

Katie: How does the anger feel inside you?

Margaret: It hurts. I can't stand what they're doing to our planet.

Katie: Doesn't all that anger feel violent inside you?

Margaret: Yes.

Katie: Anger is violent. Feel it.

Margaret: But it motivates me to act, so it's good to have *some* stress. We need it to get things moving.

Katie: So what I hear from you is that violence works, violence is the way to a peaceful solution. That doesn't make sense to me. We humans have been trying to prove this point for eons. What you're saying is that violence is healthy for you, but that corporations shouldn't use it against the planet. "Excuse me, corporations, you should stop your violence and treat the planet peacefully, and by the way, violence really works for me in my life." So, "You need violence to motivate you"—is that true?

Margaret [after a pause]: No. Those bouts of anger leave me depressed and wiped out. Are you saying that without the violence, I would be just as motivated?

Katie: No, sweetheart, that was you. What I would say is that I don't need anger or violence to accomplish things or to motivate myself in any way. If I were to feel anger, I would do The Work on the thought behind it. This leaves love as the motivator. Is there anything more powerful than love? Think of your own experience. And what could be more motivating? I hear from you that fear and anger are depressing. Think of yourself when you love someone—how motivated you become. Who would you be without the thought that you need violence as a motivator?

Margaret: I don't know. That feels very strange.

Katie: So, sweetheart, let's turn it around. "I . . ."

Margaret: I don't care. Yes, that's true. I haven't cared about those people. And I should be caring and give back to the planet. I should use my money to support environmental groups, build habitats, support freedom of broadcasting. I should wake up and start thinking about tomorrow.

Katie: Yes. And if you do that genuinely, without violence in your heart, without anger, without pointing at corporations as the enemy, then people begin to notice. We begin to listen and notice that change through peace is possible. It has to begin with one person, you know. If you're not the one, who is?

Margaret: Well, that's true. That's very true.

Katie: Let's look at the next statement.

Margaret: *I need them to stop hurting and destroying, to start making a difference, and to respect life.*

Katie: So, "You need them to do that"—is that true?

Margaret: Well, that would be a great start.

Katie: "You *need* them to do that"—is that true?

Margaret: Yeah.

Katie: Are you going inside yourself? Are you really asking? "You need them to clean it up"—is that true?

Margaret: Well, I don't need it for my everyday survival, or anything like that, but yeah, that would be great.

Katie: I hear that. And that's what you need to be happy?

Margaret: That's what I want. I know what you mean, but it's so . . .

Katie: You know, this brings about incredible terror inside you. How do you react when you think the thought that this is what you need, and corporations are doing . . . oh my . . . they're doing what they do? They're not listening to you. You're not even on their Board of Advisors. [The audience laughs.] They're not accepting your calls. You just get their answering machines. How do you react when you think the thought that you *need* them to clean it up, and they don't?

Margaret: It feels frustrating. Painful. I become agitated and get very angry, very scared.

Katie: Yes. A lot of people won't even bring children into the world because that thought runs through them without investigation. They live in such fear when they're attached to this belief. Can you see a reason to drop the belief? And I'm not asking you to drop it.

Margaret: Yeah. I can see many reasons, but I'm really afraid that . . .

Katie: If you dropped the belief, what would happen?

Margaret: I wouldn't care anymore.

Katie: And I would ask you: "If you didn't believe this, you wouldn't care, you would lose all caring about the environment" — can you really know that that's true?

Margaret: No.

Katie: If we don't suffer, we won't care: What a thought! How do you react when you think the thought that stress is caring, that fear is caring? How do we react when we believe that thought? We become the champions of suffering. But only for a good cause. Only in the name of humanity. We sacrifice our lives to suffering. The story goes that Jesus suffered for hours on the cross. How many years have you lived with these nails through your body?

Margaret: I understand.

Katie: Let's turn it around, sweetheart.

Margaret: Okay. *I* should stop hurting and destroying.

Katie: Stop hurting and destroying yourself, in the name of cleaning up the planet. "When the planet is cleaned up, then I'll be peaceful." Does that make sense? Your pain—is that how we're going to clean up the planet? Do you think that if you hurt enough, if you suffer enough, someone will hear you and do something about it?

Margaret: Okay. I see it. I need to start making a difference. And I need to start respecting my life.

Katie: Yes, yours. It's a beginning.

Margaret: So I need to start respecting my own life.

Katie: Yes. Take care of yourself, and when you find peace, when your mental environment is balanced, then be the expert who can go out to balance the planet, fearlessly, caringly, and effectively. And in the meantime, do the best you can, just like the rest of us, even us corporate people. How can an internally imbalanced, frustrated woman teach others how to clean up their act? We have to learn that ourselves first, and that begins from within. Violence only teaches violence. Stress teaches stress. And peace teaches peace. And for me, peace is entirely efficient. Well done, honey. Nice Work.

Would you rather be right

or free?

7.
Doing The Work on Self-Judgments

One year, for his birthday, I bought my grandson Race a plastic Darth Vader toy because he had asked for it. He had just turned three; he didn't have a clue about Star Wars, even though he wanted the Darth Vader toy. When you put a coin into Darth Vader, you hear the Star Wars music and Darth Vader's heavy breathing. Then his voice says, "Impressive, but you are not a Jedi yet," and he lifts his sword as if to emphasize the point. After Racey heard the voice, he said, "Grandma, I not a Jedi," and shook his little head. I said, "Honey, you can be Grandma's little Jedi." And he said, "I not," and again shook his head.

A week or so after I gave him the toy, I called him on the phone and asked him, "Sweetheart, are you a Jedi yet? Are you Grandma's little Jedi?" And he said, in a sad little voice, "I not." He didn't even know what a Jedi was, he wasn't even asking, and yet he wanted it. So the little guy was taking orders from a plastic toy and was walking around disappointed at the ripe old age of three.

Racey was visiting me when one of my friends invited me for a flight over the desert in his plane. I told my friend about the Jedi thing and asked if Racey could come with us. He said yes. Racey was very impressed. He loved the instrument panel and all the gadgets. My friend had made an arrangement with the ground crew, and as we landed, we heard a voice over the cabin speakers announcing, "Racey, you are a Jedi! You are a Jedi now!" Racey rolled his little eyes in disbelief. I asked him if he was a Jedi yet. He wouldn't answer me. When we got home, he ran straight to Darth Vader. He dropped in his coin, the music began, with the heavy breathing, the sword rose, and the deep voice said, "Impressive, but you are not a Jedi yet." That seemed to be the way of it. I asked him one more time, and he told me, "Grandma, I not." Most little three-year-olds don't know how to do inquiry yet.

Many of us judge ourselves as relentlessly as that plastic toy played its recording, telling ourselves over and over what we are and what we're not. Once investigated, these self-judgments simply melt away. I have yet to see an inquiry that didn't reveal innocence—innocence in others and innocence in ourselves. If you've been following the instructions up to this point and have done The Work by pointing the finger of blame outward, you will have noticed that your judgments of others always turn back toward you. Sometimes those turned-around judgments can feel uncomfortable. That's how you know that you've hit a belief you have about yourself that you haven't investigated yet. For example, "He should love me" turns around to "I should love myself," and if you experience stress with that thought, you may want to take a look at it. There is much to be found in the inquiry into "I should love myself," and I invite you to take your time when you come to the questions "How do I react when I think I should love myself (and I don't know how)?" and "Who would I be without the thought 'I should love myself'?" There's unlimited self-love to be found there.

As you become fluid with the four questions and turnaround, you'll develop stability. You'll begin to discover for yourself that The Work is equally powerful when the one you're judging is yourself. You'll see that the "you" you judge is no more personal than everyone else turned out to be. The Work deals with concepts, not people.

The four questions are used in exactly the same way when you apply them to self-judgments. For example, let's consider the self-judgment "I am a failure." First, go inside with questions 1 and 2: Is it true? Can I absolutely know that it's true that I'm a failure? My husband or wife may say so, my parents may say so, and I may say so, but can I absolutely know that it's true? Could it be that all along I have lived the life I should have lived and that everything I've done has been what I should have done? Then move on to question 3: Make a list of how you react, how you feel physically, and how you treat yourself and others when you believe the thought "I am a failure." What do you do specifically? What do you say specifically? Do your shoulders slump? Do you snap at people? Do you go to the refrigerator? Continue with your list. Then go inside with question 4: Experience what your life would be like if you never had this thought again. Close your eyes and picture how you would be without the thought "I am a failure." Be still as you watch. What do you see?

The turnaround for self-judgments can be quite radical. When you use the 180-degree turnaround, "I am a failure" becomes "I am not a failure" or "I am a success." Go inside with this turnaround and let it reveal to you how it is as true as or truer than your original judgment. Make a list of the ways in which you are a success. Bring those truths out of the darkness. Some of us find this extremely difficult at first and may be hard-pressed to find even one example. Take your time. If you really want to know the truth, allow the truth to reveal itself to you. Find three successes each day. One could be "I brushed my teeth." Two, "I did the dishes." Three, "I breathed." It's a wonderful thing to be a success at being what you are, whether you realize it or not.

Sometimes replacing the word "I" with "my thinking" will bring a realization or two. "I am a failure" becomes "My thinking is a failure, especially about myself." You can understand this clearly when you go inside to answer question 4. Without the thought "I am a failure," you are perfectly fine. It's the thought that is painful, not your life.

Don't get stuck in the turnarounds, as if there's a right or wrong way of doing them. When you sit with your self-judgments, let the turnarounds find *you*. If a turnaround doesn't work for you, this is as it should be. Don't force it; just move on to the next statement. Remember that The Work is not a method; it's a way of self-discovery.

Afraid of Life

I love this dialogue because it shows that The Work can move fluidly, as a loving conversation. When you facilitate others or yourself, you don't have to use the four questions in a strict order or in a prescribed way. This is particularly helpful when someone—you or the person you're facilitating—is frightened and the painful thoughts are hidden from view.

Marilyn: I kind of didn't follow the rules, because I wrote about myself.

Katie: Yes, you definitely didn't follow the rules. And that's okay. We do that. There are no mistakes. There's no way you can do The Work wrong. What I suggest is that people judge someone else, not themselves yet, and you may find out that you're the someone else. It's all equal. So let's hear what you've written.

Marilyn: Okay. *I'm angry at Marilyn...*

Katie: That's you?

Marilyn: That's me... *because she is the way she is. I want Marilyn to be free. I want her to get over her many fears and her anger.*

Katie: So what are you afraid of, honey?

Marilyn: I think I'm afraid of participating in life.

Katie: What's an example? Tell me more. I want to know.

Marilyn: Well, for example, getting a job, having sex.

Katie: Yes. So, what would be the most frightening thing for you around sex? What's the worst thing that could happen if you were having sex?

Marilyn: Well, that I could freak out. I could just... lose it.

Katie: Okay. Let's say you're having sex and you absolutely lose it. That's what most women want when they have sex. [The audience bursts into loud laughter.]

Marilyn [hiding her face with her Worksheet]: I can't *believe* I'm saying this! I don't think this is going where I want it to! Maybe we should start all over again! I thought we were going to talk about *spiritual* things! [Laughter]

Katie: Oh, God is everything but not sex? Is that true? [Laughter]

Marilyn: I think we should start over! Don't you?

Katie: Hmm. No, that was you thinking that. It wasn't me. [Laughter]

Marilyn: How about if I read some of the other ones?

Katie: Sweetheart, this discussion is part of life, and you're participating *very* well.

Marilyn [moaning and turning her back to the audience]: Oh! I can't believe I said that part! I have all these other things I could have said!

Katie: There's no mistake, angel. So I would like you to look out at the audience. Okay? How many of you are really happy that this woman is participating? [Applause, whistles, and cheers] Look. Look down there at those faces. You see, the very thing that you think won't work *does* work. Maybe it's backward. Maybe you've been participating fully and haven't been aware of it. You are so beautiful. You're so beautiful in your shyness, and you just want to go back to these written words so you can get some control.

Marilyn: Yeah.

Katie: But what's happening now is just like sex. You don't have control. And everyone is falling in love with you. That's the innocence that we're so attracted to. There's no control in it. It's a wonderful thing. It's like an orgasm.

Marilyn [hiding her face with her Worksheet]: I can't *believe* you said that word! I'm so embarrassed! Can't we talk about something else? [Laughter]

Katie: "You can't believe I said that word"—is that true? No! I did say it! I said the word! [Laughter] Losing control can be wonderful, sweetheart.

Marilyn: What about the fear?

Katie: What fear? You mean your embarrassment?

Marilyn: No, it's worse than that. It's terror.

Katie: Sweetheart, "You are in terror"—is that true? "The feelings that you feel now are terror"—can you really know that that's true?

Marilyn: No.

Katie: Who would you be without your story that you are in terror? [Long pause] So let's move back and do one at a time. You're talking about something that you don't want to talk about, in front of a roomful of people, and you're feeling . . .

Marilyn: It's worth it! If it will get me to freedom, I'll do anything.

Katie: Yes, honey. Good. Then let's do inquiry. This is what I know. I am here to give you four questions that are kind enough to leave your freedom to you, not me.

Marilyn: Okay.

Katie: Okay. So are you willing to answer my questions?

Marilyn: Yes.

Katie: I want to know more about your embarrassment. How does being embarrassed *feel?* How does it feel in your chest, in your stomach, in your arms, in your legs? How did it feel, physically, to sit on this couch and feel embarrassed?

Marilyn: I feel heat in my head. And in my tummy there's lots of energy. Kind of going *k-k-k-k,* like that.

Katie: Uh-huh. Good. So that's the worst that can happen. If you talk about the most frightening topic, on stage, the worst that can happen is what you've described. A few fireworks going on in your tummy, and a little heat in your head. Can you handle it?

Marilyn: But what if my mom and dad were here?

Katie: Hmm. You'd feel a little heat in your head, and a little movement here in your . . .

Marilyn: I think I might just faint or black out.

Katie: Okay. Good. You could faint or black out. And then what would happen?

Marilyn: I'd wake up, and then I'd . . . What if I were *still here?*

Katie: What's the worst that could happen? You'd still be here. And notice that you're still here, right now. You're already surviving the worst that could happen.

Marilyn: And life goes on, and I'm still myself, I'm still the way I am.

Katie: And what way is that?

Marilyn: Not free. I'm caught in my stuff.

Katie: Sweetheart, what does freedom look like?

Marilyn [pointing to Katie]: Kind of like . . .

Katie: Hmm. [The audience laughs.] I would take that to inquiry later. Write it out. "Katie is free"—can I absolutely know that that's true? How do I react when I believe that thought? Put it down on paper and follow it through.

Marilyn: I know! I'm really caught up in my stories about this personality and this body, and . . .

Katie: Let's go back to inquiry now, so that you don't avoid realizing what you already know. What you already know can set you free from fear. Answer this: "If your parents were sitting here now . . ."

Marilyn: Oh, God! I know, I know! I'm forty-seven, and I shouldn't even be worried about that!

Katie: Well, of *course* you should be worried about it, because you are. That's reality. You're so beautiful. If your parents were sitting here, what would they be thinking?

Marilyn: Well, they'd probably be mortified that I'm talking about these things out here in public.

Katie: So they'd be mortified.

Marilyn: Uh-huh.

Katie: Can you really know that that's true?

Marilyn: I can guess pretty well.

Katie: You can guess that it's true, yes. And I'm asking you to answer the question. Can you absolutely know that it's true that your parents would be mortified?

Marilyn: Inwardly, on the deepest . . . From the perspective of if they were dead and looking down on me, I can imagine it, but in every other way . . .

Katie: Are you interested in inquiry?

Marilyn: Yes. I'm sorry.

Katie [laughing]: Is it true that you're sorry?

Marilyn: Well, I'm kind of getting off on the track of my drama.

Katie: So just answer the question. Is it true that you're sorry? Yes or no. When you said, "I'm sorry," was it true that you were sorry?

Marilyn: I was more ashamed that I got off track.

Katie: What if you had to answer yes or no? "You were sorry"—is that true?

Marilyn: I think the words just came out. I . . . No! I don't know!

Katie: Sweetheart.

Marilyn: Oh, I'm trying so hard, and I'm just not *getting* this!

Katie: So let's go back a little. Okay? It takes just a yes or no, and please don't worry about giving the right answer. Give the answer that you feel is true for you, even if you think it's wrong. And honey, there isn't anything serious to worry about, ever. This isn't a serious thing. If self-realization didn't make things lighter, who would want it?

Marilyn: Okay.

Katie: This is about asking yourself. "If your parents were in this audience, they would be mortified"—can you absolutely know that that's true?

Marilyn: In the biggest picture I can't. I mean, no.

Katie: Good! [The audience applauds.] You almost gave a straight answer. So you could hear it yourself. It doesn't matter what I think. You gave an answer for *you* to hear. This is *self*-inquiry. Not inquiry for me, or anyone else. How do you react when you think that your parents would be mortified if they were in this audience?

Marilyn: I censor things. I censor my life. And I feel angry about this.

Katie: How do you live your life when you believe that your parents would be mortified about something you did?

Marilyn: Wow! I've been living my whole life in hiding.

Katie: This doesn't sound very peaceful to me. It sounds very stressful.

Marilyn: It is.

Katie: It sounds like living in fear, being very careful all your life so that they won't be mortified.

Marilyn: Yeah.

Katie: Give me a peaceful reason, a reason without stress, to believe that your parents would be mortified if they were in this room.

Marilyn: It doesn't have to do with peace. There's no peaceful reason.

Katie: No peaceful reason. So what would you be, with your parents in the room, if you didn't believe that thought?

Marilyn [laughing, beaming]: Oh! Yeah! Wow!! [The audience laughs.] Thank you!

Katie: What would you be? Freedom? The joy and laughter of just being yourself?

Marilyn: Oh, yeah! Freedom to be. I would be so blissful and happy, right here with you.

Katie: Just as you are now?

Marilyn [looking out at the audience and laughing]: And with all these beautiful people.

Katie: You participate in life very well. So what I'm learning from you is that when you think that thought, you're fearful. And when you don't think it, you're free. What I'm learning from you is that your parents have never been the problem. It's your *thinking* about them that is your problem, your uninvestigated belief about what they think or don't think.

Marilyn: Wow!

Katie: Isn't that amazing? Your parents aren't your problem. That's not a possibility. No one else can be your problem. I like to say that no one can hurt me—that's my job. This is good news.

Marilyn: Oh, I understand! Yes, it *is* good news!

Katie: It leaves you in a position to stop blaming others and to look to yourself for your own freedom, not to them or anyone else.

Marilyn: Yes.

Katie: It leaves *you* responsible for your freedom, not your parents.

Marilyn: Yes.

Katie: Thank you. I look forward to our friendship.

Marilyn: There's great liberation in this.

Katie: Yes, sweetheart. Yes, there is.

When I argue with reality,

I lose —

but only 100 percent of the time.

8.

Doing The Work
with Children

I am often asked if children and teenagers can do The Work. My answer
is "Of course they can." In this process of inquiry, we're not dealing with
people; we're dealing with thoughts and concepts, and people of all ages
—eight or eighty—have the same concepts. "I want my mother to love
me." "I need my friend to listen to me." "Mommy and Daddy shouldn't
fight." "People shouldn't be mean." Young or old, we believe concepts that
through inquiry are seen to be nothing more than superstitions.

I have found that even young children are very receptive to The Work
and that it changes their lives. During one children's workshop, a six-year-
old girl got so excited that she said, "This Work is amazing! Why didn't
anyone ever tell me about it?" Another child, a seven-year-old boy, said
to his mother, "The Work is the best thing in the whole wide world!"
Curious, she asked, "What is it that you like so much about The Work,
Daniel?" "When I'm scared and we do The Work," he said, "then afterward I'm not scared anymore."

When I do The Work with young children, the only difference I'm
aware of is that I draw from a simpler vocabulary. If I use a word that I
think might be beyond them, I ask them if they understand it. If I feel that
they really don't understand, then I say what I mean in another way. But I
never use baby talk. Children know when they are being talked down to.

The following excerpt is from a dialogue I had with a five-year-old girl:

Becky [frightened, not looking at me]: There's a monster under my bed at night.

Katie: "There's a monster under your bed"—sweetheart, is that true?

Becky: Yes.

Katie: Sweetheart, look at me. Can you absolutely know that that's true?

Becky: Yes.

Katie: Give me your proof. Have you ever seen the monster?

Becky: Yes.

Katie: Is that true?

Becky: Yes.

Now the child is beginning to laugh and warm up to the questions, beginning to trust that I'm not going to force her to believe or not to believe, and we can have fun with this monster of hers. Eventually, the monster has a personality, and before the end of the session, I'll ask the child to close her eyes, talk to the monster face-to-face, and let the monster tell her what he's doing under the bed and what he really wants from her. I'll ask her just to let the monster talk, and to listen and tell me what the monster said. I've done this with a dozen children afraid of monsters or ghosts. They always report something kind, such as, "He says he's lonely" or "He just wants to play" or "He wants to be with me." At this point, I can ask them, "Sweetheart, 'There's a monster under your bed'—is that true?" And they usually look at me with a kind of knowing amusement that I would believe such a ridiculous thing. There's a lot of laughter. This is the end of the child's nightmare.

It's so simple to move to the next question at any point. For example: "How do you react at night in your room alone when you think the thought that there is a monster under your bed? How does it feel when you think that thought?" "Scary. I get scared." Here they often begin to squirm and fidget. "Sweetheart, who would you be, lying in bed at night, if you couldn't think the thought 'There's a monster under my bed'?" "I'd be okay" is what they usually answer.

Parents report that after the session, the nightmares stop occurring. This always happens. I also hear that parents don't have to talk their children into coming back to see me. We share an understanding together as a result of inquiry. I love at this point to say to children, "What I learned from you is that without the thought, you're not afraid, and with the thought, you are afraid. What I learned from you is that it's not the monster that you're afraid of, it's the *thought*. This is such good news. Whenever I'm frightened, I know that I'm just frightened of a thought."

I once worked with a four-year-old boy, David, at his parents' request. They had been taking him to a psychiatrist, because he seemed so intent on hurting his baby sister. They always had to keep track of him; whenever he had the chance, he would attack her, even in front of the parents. He would poke her, pull her, try to push her off surfaces, and he was surely old enough to know that she would fall. They saw him as seriously disturbed. He was getting angrier and angrier. The parents were at their wits' end.

In our session, I asked him some of the questions on the Judge-Your-Neighbor Worksheet, and the mother's therapist wrote down his answers. The parents had been doing The Work in another room. When they returned, I had them read their Worksheets on each other in front of the child, so that he could understand that there would be no punishment for expressing his feelings honestly.

Mother: I'm angry at the new baby because I have to change her diapers all day long and can't spend more time with my David. I'm angry at Dad because he works all day and can't help me change diapers for the new baby.

Both Mother and Father continued to judge each other and the baby in front of the little boy. Then it was David's turn to hear his statements read out loud. *"I'm angry at Mommy because she spends all her time with Kathy." "I'm angry at Daddy because he's not home enough."* Finally, we heard his statements about his little sister.

David: I'm angry at Kathy because she doesn't want to play games with me. I want her to play ball with me. She should play with me. She shouldn't just lie there all the time. She should want to get up and play with me. I need her to play with me.
Katie: "She should play with you"—honey, is that true?
David: Yes.

Katie: David, sweetheart, how does it feel when you think that thought?

David: I'm mad. I want her to play with me.

Katie: How did you learn that babies should play ball with you?

David: My mommy and daddy.

We had heard the answer, and we knew what was happening. His parents explained that throughout the entire pregnancy, they had told this little fellow that soon he would have a brother or sister who would play games with him and be there as his playmate. What they had failed to tell him was that the baby would have to grow before she could run or hold a ball. When they explained this to David and apologized to him, he of course understood. He left her alone after that. They later informed me that the troubling behavior had stopped, that they were all working on clear communication, and that he was beginning to trust them again.

I love working with children. They come to inquiry so easily, just as we all do when we really want to be free.

"I don't know"

is my favorite position.

9.

Doing The Work on Underlying Beliefs

Often beneath the judgments we've written lie other thoughts. These may be thoughts that we've believed for years and that we use as our fundamental judgments of life. In most cases, we haven't ever questioned them. I call these thoughts "underlying beliefs." These beliefs are broader or more general versions of our stories. Some underlying beliefs may expand a judgment of an individual to include an entire group of people. Some are judgments about life that may not sound like judgments at all. But if you notice that you feel stress when you become aware of these beliefs, they may be worth investigating.

Underlying beliefs are the religion we actually live. They can sometimes be found just beneath the most commonplace, everyday judgments. Suppose you have written down a trivial-sounding, uncomfortable thought like "George should hurry up so we can go for a walk." Inquiry might bring to your awareness various unexamined thoughts that may be linked to "George should hurry up":

> The present is not as good as the future.
> I'd be happy if I had my way.
> It's possible to waste time.
> If I slow down, I'll notice my suffering and
>   won't be able to stand it.

Attachment to these underlying beliefs will make life painful for you in situations where you're waiting or where you perceive other people as moving too slowly. If any of these beliefs seem familiar to you, the next time you're waiting for someone, I invite you to write down the thoughts that underlie your impatience and see if they're really true for you. (You'll find suggestions below for doing this.) Wouldn't it be wonderful never to have to wait for anything, to feel that what you want is what you already have?

Underlying beliefs are the building blocks of your concept of heaven and your concept of hell. They show exactly how you think you would improve reality if you had your way, and how bad reality could look if your fears came true. All of this is liberating information when you bring it to inquiry. To watch it all collapse—to discover that those painful beliefs that we've carried around for years are not true for us, that we've never needed them at all—is an incredibly freeing experience. There's a flow to inquiry at this point, a steady flow of self-revelation. Here are some examples of the kind of statements you may find yourself working with:

> It's possible to be in the wrong place
>   at the wrong time.
> Life is unfair.
> It's necessary to know what to do.
> I can feel your pain.
> Death is sad.
> It's possible to miss out on something.
> If I don't suffer, it means that I don't care.
> God will punish me if I'm not good.
> There is life after death.
> Children are supposed to like their parents.
> Survival is necessary.
> Something terrible could happen to me.
> Parents are responsible for their children's choices.
> I need to remember.
> It's possible to make a mistake.
> There is a right way to do The Work.
> There is evil in the world.

You may want to do The Work on any of these statements that seem like obstacles to your freedom.

Whenever you notice that you're feeling defensive in conversations with your friends or family, or whenever you're sure that you're right, you may want to jot down your own underlying belief and do The Work on it later. This is wonderful material for inquiry, if you really want to know the truth and to live without the suffering these beliefs cause.

One of the best ways of discovering your underlying beliefs is to write out your "proof of truth" for question 1. Rather than moving immediately to the awareness that you can't really know anything, allow yourself to stay in the story. Stay in the place where you really do believe that what you have written is true. Then write down all the reasons that prove it's true. From this list, a wealth of underlying beliefs will become evident. The following is an example of using the "proof of truth" exercise to discover underlying beliefs.

Using "Proof of Truth" to Discover Underlying Beliefs

Original Statement: *I am angry at Bobby, Ross, and Roxann because they don't really respect me.*

Proof of Truth:
1. They ignore me when I ask them to put their things away.
2. They fight noisily when I am on the telephone with a client.
3. They make fun of things I care about.
4. They walk in unannounced and expect immediate attention when I am working or even in the bathroom.
5. They don't eat or appreciate the food I prepare for them.
6. They don't remove their wet shoes before they come into the house.
7. If I correct one of them, they tease that one and fight.
8. They don't want me to be with their friends.

Underlying Beliefs:
1. *They ignore me when I ask them to put their things away.*
   Children should respect adults.
   People should respect me.
   People should follow my directions.
   My direction is best for other people.
   If someone ignores me, that means they don't respect me.

2. *They fight noisily when I am on the telephone with a client.*
   There is a time and a place for everything.
   Children have the self-control to be quiet when the phone rings.
   Clients are more important than children.
   What people think about my children matters to me.
   It's possible to gain respect through control.
3. *They make fun of things I care about.*
   People shouldn't have fun or be happy at my expense.
   Children should care about what their parents care about.
4. *They walk in unannounced and expect immediate attention when I am working or even in the bathroom.*
   There are appropriate times to ask for what you want.
   Children should wait for attention.
   The bathroom is sacred ground.
   Other people are responsible for my happiness.
5. *They don't eat or appreciate the food I prepare for them.*
   Children shouldn't make their own decisions about what to eat.
   I need to be appreciated.
   People's tastes should shift when I say so.
6. *They don't remove their wet shoes before they come into the house.*
   I am overworked and not appreciated.
   Children should care about the house.
7. *If I correct one of them, they tease that one and fight.*
   I have the power to cause war.
   War is my fault.
   Parents are responsible for their children's behavior.
8. *They don't want me to be with their friends.*
   Children should see their parents the way they see their friends.
   Children are ungrateful.

When you discover an underlying belief, apply the four questions to it and then turn it around. As with self-judgments, the most pertinent turn-around is often the one to the opposite polarity, the 180-degree turn-around. The undoing of one underlying belief allows whole families of related beliefs to surface and therefore to become available for inquiry.

Now let's walk through an underlying belief. Take your time and listen as you ask yourself the questions.

My Life Should Have a Purpose

"My life should have a purpose" might at first seem like an odd subject for inquiry. You might think that this underlying belief couldn't possibly cause people pain or problems, that a statement like "My life *doesn't* have a purpose" might be painful enough to warrant inquiry, but not this one. It turns out, though, that this apparently positive belief is just as painful as an apparently negative belief. And that the turnaround, in its apparently negative form, is a statement of great relief and freedom.

Underlying Belief: My life should have a purpose.

Is it true? Yes.

Can I absolutely know that it's true? No.

How do I react when I think the thought? I feel fear, because I don't know what my purpose is, and I think I should know. I feel stress in my chest and head. At this point, I may snap at my husband and children, and this eventually takes me to the refrigerator and the television in my bedroom, often for hours or days. I feel as if I'm wasting my life. I think that what I actually do is unimportant and that I need to do something big. This is stressful and confusing. When I believe this thought, I feel great internal pressure to complete my purpose before I die. Since I can't know when that is, I think that I have to quickly accomplish this purpose (which I don't have a clue about). I feel a sense of stupidity and failure, and this leaves me depressed.

Do I see a reason to drop this story? Yes. It's very painful to live this way. Also, when I believe this story, I envy some people. I think they have found their purpose and are clear about it. I imitate these people. I even take on their purpose as my purpose. I come at them in a phony way and keep myself emotionally distant from them.

Can I find one stress-free reason to keep this story? No.

Who would I be without the belief that my life should have a purpose? I have no way of knowing. I know I'm more peaceful without it, less crazed. I would settle for that! Without the fear and stress around this thought, maybe I'd be freed and energized enough to be happy just doing the thing in front of me.

The turnaround: My life should *not* have a purpose. That would mean that what I've lived has always been enough, and I just haven't recognized it. Maybe my life shouldn't have a purpose other than what it is. That feels odd, yet it somehow rings truer. Could it be that my life as it's already lived is the purpose? That seems a lot less stressful.

Applying Inquiry to an Underlying Belief

Now write down a stressful underlying belief of your own and put it up against inquiry:

Is it true? Can you really know that it's true?

How do you react when you believe that thought? (How much of your life is based on it? What do you do and say when you believe it?)

Can you see a reason to drop the thought? (And please don't try to drop it.)

Can you find one stress-free reason to keep the thought?

Who would you be without the thought?

Turn the underlying belief around.

The dialogues that follow could have been included in chapter 4 ("Doing The Work on Couples and Family Life") and chapter 6 ("Doing

The Work on Work and Money"). They have been placed here because they are good examples of doing The Work on underlying beliefs that can affect you in many areas of your life. If you believe that your happiness depends on someone else, as Charles did before inquiry, that belief will undermine all your relationships, including the relationship with yourself. If, like Ruth in the second dialogue, you believe that you need to make a decision when you're not ready to, life will seem like a succession of bewildering responsibilities. Charles thinks that the problem is his wife; Ruth thinks that it's her money. But, as these experts will teach us, the problem is always our uninvestigated thinking.

She Was Supposed to Make Me Happy

Charles is sure that his happiness depends on his wife. Watch as this amazing man discovers that even his worst nightmare—his wife's affair—turns out to be what he really wants for her and for himself. In an hour or so, by investigating his own thinking, he changes his whole world. Happiness may look entirely different from the way you imagine it.

Notice also how in this dialogue, I sometimes use the turnaround without the four questions. I don't recommend that people new to The Work do it this way, because they could experience shame and guilt if they turn statements around without inquiring first. But I didn't see Charles experiencing the turnaround that way, and I wanted to walk with him through as many statements as possible in our limited time together, knowing that after the session he could go back and give himself as intricate a surgery as he wanted in any areas that may have been missed.

Charles: I'm angry at Deborah because she told me the night before she left for a month that I repulse her—I repulse her when I'm snoring, and I repulse her because of my overweight body.

Katie: Yes. So, have you ever been repulsed? Have you experienced that?

Charles: I've been repulsed by myself.

Katie: Yes, and what else? Someone in your past, maybe: a friend, your parents at some time or other?

Charles: By people who beat children in airports, and things like that.

Katie: Yes. So, could you stop feeling repulsed at the time?

Charles: No.

Katie: Okay. Feel it. Look at yourself in that situation. Whose business was your repulsion?

Charles: Obviously mine.

Katie: Whose business is it what repulses Deborah . . . is she your wife?

Charles: Yes.

Katie: Whose business is it what repulses her?

Charles: I get into some heavy "shoulds" about what a beloved soul mate should think and feel about me.

Katie: Oh, well! That's a good one! [The audience laughs.] I love how you don't answer the question.

Charles: It's not my business.

Katie: Whose business is her repulsion?

Charles: Hers.

Katie: And what happens when you're mentally in her business? Separation. Could you stop being repulsed when you witnessed the child abuse at the airport?

Charles: No.

Katie: But *she's* supposed to stop being repulsed? Because of the soul-mate mythology you have going?

Charles: I've been carrying this "should" about how she should be with me for my whole life, and right now I'm at the point where I'm losing that "should."

Katie: Okay, sweetheart. How do you treat her when you believe the thought that wives are supposed to see their husbands as not repulsive?

Charles: I put her in a prison. I two-dimensionalize her.

Katie: How do you treat her *physically?* How does it look? How does it sound? Close your eyes and look at yourself. Look at how you treat her when you believe the thought that she's supposed to stop being repulsed, and she doesn't stop. What do you say? What do you do?

Charles: "Why are you being that way with me? Don't you see who I am? How can you not see?"

Katie: So when you're doing that, how does it feel?

Charles: It's a prison.

Katie: Can you see a reason to drop the story that your wife shouldn't be repulsed by you?

Charles: Absolutely.

Katie: Can you see a stress-free reason to keep the story?

Charles: No, not anymore. When it comes to keeping our family together, and honoring what I know to be true, for us as souls . . .

Katie: Oh. Is it the soul-mate thing?

Charles: Yeah. I'm really caught there.

Katie: Yes. So read the part about her being your soul mate.

Charles: You're not ridiculing me now, are you?

Katie: I'm doing whatever you say I'm doing. I am your story of me—no more and no less.

Charles: Okay. Fascinating.

Katie: Yes. When you sit on this couch, your concepts are meat in the grinder, if you really want to know the truth. [The audience laughs.]

Charles [laughing]: Okay. Ground round, here I am. [More laughter]

Katie: I'm a lover of truth. And when someone sits on this couch with me, I am clear that he is, too. I love you. I want what you want. If you want to keep your story, that's what I want. If you want to answer the questions and realize what's really true for you, that's what I want. So, sweetheart, let's continue. Read the part about soul mates.

Charles: I don't have that written down. It would be like "She doesn't accept me for who I am."

Katie: "She doesn't accept me for who I am"—turn it around.

Charles: I don't accept me for who I am. That's true. I don't.

Katie: There's another turnaround.

Charles: I don't accept her for who she is.

Katie: Yes. She is a woman who tells herself a story about you that she hasn't investigated and who repulses herself. Nothing else is possible.

Charles: Ahhh. I've been holding her to that for years. Yes. And myself.

Katie: You tell a story about her, and you repulse yourself.

Charles: I do.

Katie: Or you make yourself happy. You tell one story of your wife, and you turn yourself on. You tell another story of your wife, and you turn yourself off. She tells a story of you, and she turns herself on. She tells another story of you, and she repulses herself. Uninvestigated stories often leave chaos and resentment and hatred within our own families. Until we investigate, nothing else is possible. So read the first one again.

Charles: Okay. *I'm angry at Deborah because she told me that I repulse her because of my snoring and my overweight body.*

Katie: Yes. So turn it around. "I'm angry at myself . . ."

Charles: I'm angry at myself because . . .

Katie: "I told Deborah . . ."

Charles: I told Deborah . . .

Katie: "That she . . ."

Charles: That she repulses me.

Katie: Yes. For her what?

Charles: For her willingness to dispose of the relationship so easily.

Katie: Yes. So you have everything in common with her. You snore, she's repulsed. She leaves, you're repulsed. What's the difference?

Charles: I *am* repulsed by that. [There are tears in his eyes.] Oh, my God!

Katie: There's no way she can't be a mirror image of your thinking. There is no way. There's no one out there but your story. Let's look at the next one. "I'm angry at myself for" ... what?

Charles: For being self-righteous, for thinking that she should be the way I want her to be.

Katie: Whose business is it who you live with?

Charles: Mine.

Katie: Yes. You want to live with her. It's your business who you want to live with.

Charles: Right.

Katie: So this is exactly a turnaround. She wants to live with someone else. You want to live with someone else.

Charles: Oh, I see. I want to be with someone else—someone who doesn't exist, the woman I want her to be. [Charles bursts into tears.]

Katie: Good, sweetheart. [She passes Charles a box of tissues.]

Charles: That's true. That's true. I've been doing that for a long time.

Katie: Let's look at the next statement.

Charles: I want Deborah to be grateful for life as it is.

Katie: She is or she's not. Whose business is it?

Charles: It's her business.

Katie: Turn it around.

Charles: I want me to be grateful for life as it is.

Katie: Yes. You know that thing you preach to her? You know that thing you preach to your children? *You* live it.

Charles: Yeah.

Katie: But as long as you're trying to teach us, there's no hope. Because you're teaching what you don't know how to live yet. How can a person who doesn't know how to be happy teach someone how to be happy? There's no teacher there of anything but pain. How can I end my spouse's pain or my child's pain if I can't end my own? Hopeless. Who would you be without your story of pain? You might be someone without pain, selfless, a listener, and then there would be a teacher in the house. A Buddha in the house—the one that lives it.

Charles: I hear you.

Katie: This is actually the sweetest thing to know. It gives you an internal responsibility. And that's where realization is born into the world and how we find our freedom. Rather than being Deborah-realized, you can be self-realized. Let's look at the next one.

Charles: I want her to own her own power. I mean, this is just such bullshit!

Katie: You've come a long way since you wrote this statement, angel. Can you hear the arrogance? "Excuse me, dear, but you should own your own power." [The audience laughs.]

Charles: But it's so ironic, because she's the one who *has* the power in the family. I've given her that. I've abdicated my own power.

Katie: Yes. So turn it around.

Charles: I want me to own my own power.

Katie: And stay out of her business and experience the power of that. Yes?

Charles: Mmm. *I want her to understand that there are consequences to her temper.*

Katie: Oh! My, my, my!

Charles: So much self-righteousness here I can't even believe it.

Katie: Honey, are you good! This is self-realization. We are so clear about our partners, but when it hits here, it's like "Whoa!" [The audience laughs.] We begin now. This now is the beginning. It's where you can meet yourself with new understanding. So, let's look at the next statement of mind on paper.

Charles: Deborah shouldn't . . . Oh, my God!

Katie: There are some people in the audience saying, "Read it anyway." Obviously they're the ones who need it. So "read it anyway" means "I want some freedom here."

Charles: Deborah shouldn't fall in love with a fantasy. She's meeting another man in Europe right now.

Katie: Oh. She's doing everything *you* wanted to do. [The audience laughs.]

Charles: It's everything I *have* done. I've been in love with a fantasy. And fighting, and hitting my head against Deborah, and being repulsed that she doesn't match the fantasy.

Katie: Yes. Welcome home.

Charles: And every single one of the things I wrote here is . . . I'm rubbing my face in self-righteousness. *Deborah should see how incredibly thoughtful, considerate, and loving I am.* I've been hanging myself on that story my whole life. And I've coupled that with beating myself up for not being better. That self-importance / self-rejection thing has been dancing right through my life.

Katie: Yes, sweetheart.

Charles: So, I want myself to see how thoughtful and considerate and loving I am.

Katie: Yes.

Charles: And how thoughtful and considerate and loving she is.

Katie: Yes.

Charles: Because she *is*.

Katie: Yes. And you love her with all your heart. That's the bottom line. There's nothing you can do about that. No condemning is going to move that in you. You love her.

Charles: I do.

Katie: Yes. So let's continue.

Charles: Deborah should . . . it's all self-righteousness . . . *be grateful for all the years I've been the sole breadwinner.*

Katie: So you gave her your money because you wanted something from her.

Charles: Absolutely.

Katie: What was it?

Charles: Her love. Her approval. Her appreciation. Her acceptance of me as is. Because I couldn't give it to myself . . .

Katie: So you gave her nothing. You gave her a price tag.

Charles: Right.

Katie: Yes. And that's what you feel.

Charles: And I'm repulsed by that.

Katie: Yes, angel. Yes.

Charles: I really did feel I could buy that.

Katie: Yes. Isn't it *fine* that you're seeing that now? So the next time you try to buy your children, or her, or anyone else, you have this wonderful life experience. You can call on the expert: you. The next time you give your children money, or give her money, you can know that the receiving is in the moment you give it. That's it!

Charles: Can you say that another way?

Katie: The getting, the receiving, is experienced in the moment you give something away. The transaction is complete. That's it. It's all about you. One day, when my grandson Travis was two years old, he pointed to a huge cookie in a store window. I said, "Honey, are you sure that's the one you want?" He was sure. I asked him if we could share it, and he said yes. I bought it and took his little sweet hand, and we walked to a table. I took the cookie out of the bag and broke off a small piece, and I held up both pieces. He reached for the small one and looked very shocked as I moved it away and put the large piece in his hand, and his face lit up as he began to move the cookie to his mouth. Then his eyes caught mine. I felt so much love that I thought my heart would burst. He smiled and took his huge cookie from his lips, gave it to me, and took the small piece. It's natural in us. The giving is how we receive.

Charles: I see.

Katie: Giving is spontaneous, and only the story of a future, a story about what they owe you for it, would keep you from knowing your own generosity. What comes back is none of your business. It's over. So, sweetheart, let's look at the next statement.

Charles: I need Deborah to love me as I am, warts and all. To love my strengths and weaknesses, to understand my need to actualize myself as an artist and spiritual being, to give me room to go through this major midlife passage and try to find more meaning in what I'm doing. So with all that, I should just focus on one, shouldn't I?

Katie: Yes. Keep it simple, and just turn it around.

Charles: I need Deborah to . . .

Katie: "I need me . . ."

Charles: I need me to love myself as I am, warts and all. I haven't been loving myself that way. But I'm starting to.

Katie: And it's the story you tell of the wart that keeps you from loving it. The wart just waits for a sane mind to see it clearly. It doesn't do any harm. It's just there like . . . like a leaf on a tree. You don't argue with a leaf and say, "Yo! Let's talk. Look at your shape. You need to do something about it." [Charles and the audience laugh.] You don't do that. But you focus here [pointing to her hand], on a wart, you tell a story about it, and you repulse yourself. A wart is . . . God. It is reality. It is what is. Argue with that.

Charles: I've been feeling so needy. Needing her to stay at home for the children's sake, too.

Katie: "Your children would be much better off with her at home"—can you absolutely know that that's true?

Charles: No, I don't know that it's true.

Katie: Isn't that amazing?

Charles: And that's the thing that's caused the most pain—the thought of not living together.

Katie: Yes.

Charles: But I don't know that it's true, that my daughter wouldn't thrive without us being together.

Katie: Yes. "Your daughter's path would be much richer with her mother at home"—can you absolutely know that that's true? [Charles begins to cry.] Sweetheart, take all the time you need. What's the sound of it?

Charles [bursting out]: I don't want to be separated from my kids! I want to be a twenty-four-hour, seven-days-a-week dad!

Katie: Yes. That's the truth of it, isn't it?

Charles: But my devotion to my work and being in the studio has taken me away a lot. So there's a contradiction in that. I want to wake up with my daughter, you know?

Katie: Yes, I do.

Charles: And I have the picture of a family together. That picture is really imbedded.

Katie: Yes, you do.

Charles [crying and laughing]: *Donna Reed* was my favorite TV show. [Katie and the audience laugh.] It really was!

Katie: So her leaving is not the problem. It's the death of your mythology.

Charles: Oh, God! Yes. Absolutely. I've been lying about that.

Katie: Yes. She's messing with your dream.

Charles: Big time! And I'm so grateful to her for this.

Katie: Yes, sweetheart. So what I'm hearing is that she really did give you a gift.

Charles: Yes, she did.

Katie: Good. Let's look at the next one.

Charles: Okay. *I need Deborah to hold our relationship and family sacred so she won't fall in love or sleep with another man.*

Katie: Is it true that that's what you need?

Charles: It's my myth. I don't need her to do anything that isn't her truth. And I love her a lot. I want her to do her truth.

Katie: And how do you treat her and how do you talk to her and how are you with your daughter when you believe this story—the one you just read?

Charles: Selfish, needy, wanting her to give me, give me, give me.

Katie: To give you a phony her that doesn't exist other than in your myth. You want her to be a lie for you. So, angel, close your eyes. Look at her. Watch how you treat her when you believe that story.

Charles: Ahhhhh.

Katie: Okay, now look at her and tell me who you would be, in her presence, if you didn't believe your story?

Charles: A strong, talented, sexy, powerful man.

Katie: Whoa! [Laughter, whistles, and applause] Oh, my goodness!

Charles: That's my secret. That's what I've been . . .

Katie: Yes, honey, welcome to the power of ownership. No one can touch that. Not even you. This is your role. You've just been pretending not to see these qualities in you. It didn't work.

Charles: Forty-five years of it.

Katie: Yes, sweetheart. Did you feel the shift from repulsive to sexy and powerful? [To audience] How many felt the shift? [Applause] And nothing happened but awareness.

Charles: I closed my eyes and saw it.

Katie: Teach *that* by the way you live.

Charles: I want to.

Katie: Yes. Let it come through your music, and live it with your daughter. And when she says something about her mother that you have taught her, you can let her know that you used to feel that way, too.

Charles: You mean in a negative way?

Katie: Yes.

Charles: I don't do that to my daughter.

Katie: Not in words.

Charles: Ahhh.

Katie: The opposite of this empowered, sexy man, this empowered composer. You've taught her the opposite by the way that you live. You've taught her how to react, how to think, how to be.

Charles: I've been a total wuss.

Katie: That's what you've been teaching her about how to react when someone leaves her. You can tell her what your experience has been, and you can begin to live what you know now. And watch as she learns to live the way you live. That's how it shifts in our families, and we don't have to give them The Work unless they ask. We *live* it. That's where the power is. You *live* the turnarounds. "She's wrong to leave"—the turnaround is "I'm wrong to leave," especially in this moment. I left my own life to mentally travel to Europe. Let me come back to my life here now.

Charles: Good.

Katie: There's a story I like to tell. Roxann, my daughter, called me one day and said she wanted me to attend my grandson's birthday party. I told her that I had a commitment that day to be doing a public event in another city. She was so hurt and angry that she hung up on me. Then, maybe ten minutes later, she called me back and said, "I am so excited, Momma. I just did The Work on you, and I saw that there is nothing you can do to keep me from loving you."

Charles: Wow!

Katie: Okay, let's look at the next statement.

Charles: I don't ever want to have her light into me with verbal abuse.

Katie: Yes. So, "I'm willing. . . ." Because you may have that picture in your mind again. Or it may be someone else.

Charles: How do you turn it around?

Katie: "I'm willing . . . ," and you read it just the way you wrote it.

Charles: I'm willing to be abused. Oh. Because it's what happens. Okay.

Katie: All of a sudden, there's nothing unexpected.

Charles: I'm willing to have her light into me with verbal abuse. Oh my! Okay.

Katie: "I look forward to . . ."

Charles: I look forward to having her light into me . . . Oh . . . I look forward to her verbal abuse. Wow! *That* is a turnaround. Especially for self-righteous stuff. That's a big one.

Katie: Yes.

Charles: Okay. *I don't ever want to hear her say that she's in love with some-one she hasn't seen but one day in fourteen years.* All right. So . . .

Katie: "I'm willing . . ."

Charles: I'm willing to hear her say that she's in love with someone she hasn't seen in fourteen years except one day.

Katie: "I look forward to . . ."

Charles: I look forward to it. Wow! Okay.

Katie: And if it still hurts . . .

Charles: Then I've got more work to do.

Katie: Yes. Isn't that fine?

Charles: Because I'm arguing with the truth—with reality.

Katie: Yes.

Charles: So, Katie, I have a question about this. I've been wanting to stay, rather than leave the house, probably because of my investment in the Donna Reed myth.

Katie: I would drop the word *probably.*

Charles: Okay, definitely. So, I have a feeling she's going to come back, wanting to actually try it again. And I have the thought that if I stay and continue to be willing to face somebody that I can't trust, then I'm not the strong, powerful, sexy man with integrity.

Katie: So, sweetheart, do The Work. There's nothing else to do. If she comes back—do The Work. If she stays away—do The Work. This is about you.

Charles: But I don't want to be a doormat anymore.

Katie: Oh, really! Do The Work. Have it for breakfast. You eat The Work, or the thought will eat you.

Charles: But if I leave from a place of self-love, because I choose to leave, because I don't want to do that anymore, I don't want to . . .

Katie: Sweetheart, there's nothing you can do to keep yourself from

coming or going. You just tell the story about how you have something to do with it.

Charles: You mean that's my habit? Is that what you're saying?

Katie: If a story arises and you believe it, you may think you have to decide. Investigate and be free.

Charles: So if I find and notice that I'm still there, even though I'm telling myself that the path of integrity would be to finally walk away and start a new life with somebody else, that's okay.

Katie: Honey, the decisions will make themselves for you as you inquire.

Charles: So either I will do it or I won't.

Katie: Yes.

Charles: And I should just trust that.

Katie: It happens whether you trust it or not—haven't you noticed? Again, life is a very nice place to be, once you understand it. Nothing ever goes wrong in life. Life is heaven, except for our attachment to a story that we haven't investigated.

Charles: That's *really* being in the moment.

Katie: What is is. I am not running this show. I don't belong to myself, and you don't belong to yourself. We are not ours. We are the "is." And we tell the story of "Oh, I have to leave my wife." It's just not true. You don't have to leave her, until you do. You are the "is." You flow with that, as that. There's nothing you can do to not let her in. And there's nothing you can do to not leave her. This isn't our show, in my experience.

Charles: Wow!

Katie: She comes, and you tell a story, and the effect is that you get to be a martyr. Or she comes, and you tell the story of how you're grateful, and you get to be a happy guy. You are the effect of your story, that's all. And this is hard to hear unless you inquire. That's why I say, "Have The Work for breakfast." Come to know for yourself what's true for you, not for me. My words are of no value to you. You're the one you've been waiting for. Be married to your*self*. You're the one you've been waiting for all your life.

I Need to Make a Decision

When you become a lover of what is, there are no more decisions to make. In my life, I just wait and watch. I know that the decision will be made in its own time, so I let go of when, where, and how. I like to say I'm a woman with no future. When there are no decisions to make, there's no planned future. All my decisions are made for me, just as they're all made for you. When you mentally tell yourself the story that you have something to do with it, you're attaching to an underlying belief.

For forty-three years, I was always buying in to my stories about the future, buying in to my insanity. After I came back from the halfway house with a new understanding of reality, I would often return from a long trip to find the house full of dirty laundry, piles of mail on my desk, the dog dish crusted, the bathrooms a mess, and the sink piled high with dishes. The first time this happened, I heard a voice that said, "Do the dishes." It was like coming upon the burning bush, and the voice from the bush said, "Do the dishes." It didn't sound very spiritual to me, but I just followed its directions. I would stand at the sink and just wash the next dish, or sit with the piles of bills and pay the one on top. Just one at a time. Nothing else was required. At the end of the day, everything would be done, and I didn't need to understand who or what did it.

When a thought appears such as "Do the dishes" and you don't do them, notice how an internal war breaks out. It sounds like this: "I'll do them later. I should have done them by now. My roommate should have done them. It's not my turn. It's not fair. People will think less of me if I don't do them now." The stress and weariness you feel are really mental combat fatigue.

What I call "doing the dishes" is the practice of loving the task in front of you. Your inner voice guides you all day long to do simple things such as brush your teeth, drive to work, call your friend, or do the dishes. Even though it's just another story, it's a very short story, and when you follow the direction of the voice, that story ends. We are really alive when we live as simply as that—open, waiting, trusting, and loving to do what appears in front of us now.

What we need to do unfolds before us, always—doing the dishes, paying the bills, picking up the children's socks, brushing our teeth. We never receive more than we can handle, and there is always just one thing to do. Life never gets more difficult than that.

Ruth: I am frightened and panicked to the point of paralysis about making decisions about my money, about whether to stay in the market or get out because of the current volatility and my future depending upon it.

Katie: "Your future depends on your money"—can you really know that that's true?

Ruth: No, but a lot of me gets frantic about it.

Katie: Yes, a lot of you would *have* to be frantic about it, because you believe it's true and you haven't asked yourself. "Your future depends on the money you have invested"— how do you react, how do you live, when you believe that thought, whether or not it's true?

Ruth: In a panicky state. In a high state of anxiety. When there was more of it, I was much more calm, but when it fluctuates, I get into a horrible state.

Katie: Who would you be without the thought "My future depends on the money I have invested in the market"?

Ruth: A much more relaxed person. My body wouldn't be so tense.

Katie: Give me a reason to keep the thought that isn't stressful and doesn't make you panic.

Ruth: There isn't one that's not stressful, but *not* thinking about money is a different kind of stress . . . like I'm being irresponsible then. So either way, I lose.

Katie: How can you *not* think about something? *It's* thinking *you.* Thought appears. How can not thinking about it be irresponsible? You either think about it or you don't. Thought either appears or it doesn't. It's just amazing that, after how many years, you think you can control your thinking. Can you control the wind too?

Ruth: No, I can't control it.

Katie: What about the ocean?

Ruth: No.

Katie: "Let's stop the waves." Not likely. Except they stop when you're asleep.

Ruth: The thoughts?

Katie: The waves. No thought, no ocean. No stock market. How irresponsible of you to go to sleep at night! [The audience laughs.]

Ruth: I don't sleep very well! I've been up since five.

Katie: Yes, it's irresponsible. "Thinking and worrying will solve all my problems"—has that been your experience?

Ruth: No.

Katie: So, let's stay awake and get some more of that. [Ruth and the audience laugh.]

Ruth: I can't control my thinking. I've been trying for years.

Katie: This is a very interesting discovery. Meeting thought with understanding is as good as it's going to get. It will work. And there's a lot of humor in it, as well as a good night's rest.

Ruth: I need some humor around this. I definitely need some humor around this.

Katie: So, "Without this stressful thinking, you wouldn't make the right decision"—can you really know that that's true?

Ruth: It seems that quite the opposite would be true.

Katie: Let's experience how it feels to do a 180-degree turnaround. "My future depends on the money I have invested in the stock market"—how would you turn that around?

Ruth: My future does not depend on the money I have invested in the stock market.

Katie: Feel it. That could be just as true. When you get all this money, and you're an absolute success in the market and have more money than you could ever spend, what are you going to have? Happiness? Isn't that why you want the money? Let's take a shortcut that can last a lifetime. Answer this question: Who would you be without the story "My future depends on the money in the stock market"?

Ruth: I would be much happier. I'd be more relaxed. I'd be more fun to be around.

Katie: Yes. With or without the money from the stock-market success. You'd have everything you wanted money for in the first place.

Ruth: That's . . . Yes!

Katie: Give me a stress-free reason to keep the thought "My future depends on the money I have invested in the stock market."

Ruth: There isn't one.

Katie: The only future you want is peace and happiness. Rich or poor—who cares, when we're secure in our happiness? This is true freedom: a mind that is no longer deceived by itself.

Ruth: That was my childhood prayer—peace and happiness.

Katie: So the very thing you seek keeps you from the awareness of what you already have.

Ruth: Yes, I've always been trying to live in the future, to fix it, to make it safe and secure.

Katie: Yes, like an innocent child. We're either attaching to the nightmare or we're investigating it. There's no other choice. Thoughts appear. How are you going to meet them? That's all we're talking about here.

Ruth: We're either attaching to the problem or we're inquiring?

Katie: Yes, and I love it that the stock market is not going to cooperate with you. [Ruth laughs.] If that's what it takes to bring peace and true happiness into your life. That's what everything is for. It leaves you to your own solution. So when you get all this money, and you're happy, totally happy, what are you going to do? You're going to sit, stand, or lie horizontal. That's about it. And you're going to witness the internal story you're telling now if you haven't taken care of it in the way that it deserves, and that is to meet it with understanding, the way a loving mother would meet her child.

Ruth: I get the sense that's all there is to do.

Katie: Yes. Sit, stand, or lie horizontal—that's about it. But take a look at the story you're telling as you're doing these simple things. Because when you get all this money, and you have everything you ever wanted, what appears is what appears in this chair now. This is the story you're telling. There's no happiness in it. Okay. Let's look at the next statement, honey.

Ruth: I don't want to have to be deciding where to invest, and I don't trust others to do it.

Katie: "You have to decide where to invest"—can you absolutely know that that's true?

Ruth: No. I could just leave the money alone. And see what it does. Just leave it alone totally. A lot of me says that's the best way.

Katie: "You need to make decisions in life"—can you really know that that's true?

Ruth: It feels like I need to, but as you say it, I'm not sure.

Katie: It would have to feel that way, because you believe the thought and therefore you're attached to it.

Ruth: Yes.

Katie: That's where all terrorism comes from. You didn't ask yourself what you really believe. It has all been a misunderstanding.

Ruth: The thought of not having to make decisions sounds glorious.

Katie: That's my experience. I don't make decisions. I don't bother with them, because I know they'll be made for me right on time. My job is to be happy and wait. Decisions are easy. It's the story you tell about them that isn't easy. When you jump out of a plane and you pull the parachute cord and it doesn't open, you feel fear, because you have the next cord to pull. So you pull that one, and it doesn't open. And that's the last cord. Now there's no decision to make. When there's no decision, there's no fear, so just enjoy the trip! And that's my position—I'm a lover of what is. What is: no cord to pull. It's already happening. Free fall. I have nothing to do with it.

Ruth: It was real clear to come here. I didn't have to think, "Should I, shouldn't I, should I?" It was "Mmm, yes. You're available then. Go."

Katie: So how was that decision made? Maybe it just made itself. A moment ago, you moved your head like that. Did you make that decision?

Ruth: No.

Katie: You just moved your hand. Did you make that decision?

Ruth: No.

Katie: No. "You need to make decisions"—is that true? Maybe things are just moving right along, without our help.

Ruth: That's my insanity, the need to control.

Katie: Yes. Who needs God when *you* are running the show? [Ruth laughs.]

Ruth: I don't want to do that, I just don't know how not to.

Katie: Thinking this way, and therefore living this way, is in direct opposition to reality, and it's fatal. It feels like stress, because everyone is a lover of what is, no matter what horror story they believe in. I say, let's have peace now, within this apparent chaos. So, sweetheart, how do you react when you believe the thought "I need to make a decision," and the decision doesn't come?

Ruth: Horrible. Just horrible.

Katie: That's a very interesting place to attempt to make a decision from. From that place, we can't even decide to stop or go. That will tell you something. And when you're convinced that you did it, where's your proof? Give me a stress-free reason to keep the thought "I need to make a decision." I'm not asking you to stop thinking that you make decisions. This Work has the gentleness of a flower opening to itself. Be gentle with your beautiful self. This Work is about the end of your suffering. We're just taking a look at possibilities here.

Ruth: Would it work as an experiment to try not to decide anything for a period of time? Is that craziness, or . . .

Katie: Well, you just made a decision, and it may change by itself. And then you can say "I" changed my mind.

Ruth: And I'll still be caught in the same ugly loop.

Katie: I don't know. But it's interesting to watch. If I say I won't make a decision, then I've just made a decision. Watch. That's what inquiry is for, to break through stressful mythology. These four questions take us into a world of such beauty that it can't be told. Some of us haven't even begun to explore it yet, even though that's the only world that exists. And we're the last to know.

Ruth: I get glimpses of what it means not to make a decision, and it's feeling like that now against a background of control, trying to do it as an experiment.

Katie: Give me a stress-free reason to keep the thought "I need to make a decision about the stock market."

Ruth: I can't come up with any. I just can't come up with any.

Katie: Who or what would you be without the thought "I need to make a decision"?

Ruth: I wouldn't be like my anxious mother. I wouldn't be becoming more and more insane. I wouldn't feel like I had to isolate myself from people because I was too awful to be around.

Katie: Oh, sweetheart. I love it that you've discovered inquiry.

Ruth: I've been trying so hard at something that doesn't work.

Katie: "I need to make decisions"—turn it around.

Ruth: I don't need to make decisions.

Katie: Yes. Believe me, they will be made. In the peace of that, everything is clear. Life will give you everything you need to go deeper. A decision will be made. If you act, the worst that can happen is a story. If you don't act, the worst that can happen is a story. It makes its own decisions—when to eat, when to sleep, when to act. It just moves along on its own. And it's very calm and entirely successful.

Ruth: Mmm.

Katie: Feel where your hands are. And your feet. This is good. Without a story, it's always good, everywhere you sit. Let's look at the next statement.

Ruth: I don't want money in the stock market to be so irrational. Hopeless! Hopeless!

Katie: "Money in the stock market is irrational"—turn it around, sweetheart. "My thinking . . ."

Ruth: My thinking is irrational.

Katie: Yes. When you see money that way, your thinking is irrational and frightening. "Money's irrational, the stock market is irrational"—can you really know that that's true?

Ruth: No.

Katie: How do you react when you think that thought?

Ruth: With fear. I get so scared that I leave my body.

Katie: Can you see a reason to drop the thought? And I'm not asking you to drop it. For those of you new to The Work, you *can't* drop it. You may think you can, and then the thought reappears and brings the same fear with it that it did before, possibly even more, because you're a little more attached. So what I'm asking is simply, "Can you see a reason to drop the thought that the stock market is irrational?"

Ruth: I can see a reason to drop it, but that doesn't mean that I have to drop it.

Katie: Exactly so. This is about realization, not about changing anything. The world is as you perceive it to be. For me, clarity is a word for beauty. It's what I am. And when I'm clear, I see only beauty. Nothing else is possible. I am mind perceiving my thoughts, and everything unfolds from that, as if it were a new solar system pouring itself out in its delight. If I'm not clear, then I'm going to project all my craziness out onto the world, *as* the world, and I'll perceive a crazy world and think that it is the problem. We've been working on the projected image for thousands of years and not on the projector. That's why life seems to be chaotic. It's chaos telling chaos how to live differently, and never noticing that it has always lived that way and that we have been going about it backward, absolutely backward. So you don't drop your thoughts of chaos and suffering out there in the apparent world. You *can't* drop them, because you didn't make them in the first place. But when you meet your thoughts with understanding, the world changes. It has to change, because the projector of the entire world is you. You're it! Let's look at the next statement.

Ruth: Decisions shouldn't be so difficult or frightening.

Katie: When you're trying to make them ahead of their time, it's hopeless, as you said. You can't make yourself make a decision ahead of its time. A decision is made when it's made, and not one breath sooner. Don't you love it?

Ruth: It sounds wonderful.

Katie: Yes. You can sit there and feel, "Oh, I need to do something with my stocks," and then you can inquire. "Is it true? I can't really know that." So you just let it have you. You just sit there with what your passion is, and read, and watch the Internet, and let it educate you. And the decision will come from that, when it's time. It's a beautiful thing. You'll lose money because of that decision, or you'll make money. As it should be. But when you think you're supposed to do something with it and imagine that you're the doer, that's pure delusion. Just follow your passion. Do what you love. Inquire, and have a happy life while you're doing it.

Ruth: Sometimes I can't read. I'm losing pieces of memory and losing the ability to track and . . .

Katie: Oh, honey, you've been spared! [Ruth and the audience laugh.] Have you heard me say that anytime I lose someone or something, I've been spared? Well, that's how it really is. Let's look at your last statement.

Ruth: I don't ever want to panic over money in the stock market again.

Katie: "I'm willing . . ."

Ruth: I'm willing to panic over money in the stock market.

Katie: "I look forward to . . ." It could happen.

Ruth [laughing]: I look forward to panicking over money in the stock market.

Katie: Yes, because that will put you back into The Work.

Ruth: That's where I want to be.

Katie: That's the purpose of stress. It's a friend. It's an alarm clock, built in to let you know that it's time to do The Work. You've simply lost the awareness that you're free. So you investigate, and you return to what you are. This is what's waiting to be recognized, what is always real.

I don't let go of my concepts—

I meet them with understanding.

Then *they* let go of *me.*

10.
Doing The Work on Any Thought or Situation

There is no thought or situation that you can't put up against inquiry. Every thought, every person, every apparent problem is here for the sake of your freedom. When you experience anything as separate or unacceptable, inquiry can bring you back to the peace you felt before you believed that thought.

If you aren't completely comfortable in the world, do The Work. That's what every uncomfortable feeling is for—that's what pain is for, what money is for, what walls and clouds and dogs and cats and trees are for, what everything in the world is for: your self-realization. It's all a mirror image of your own thinking. Judge it, investigate it, turn it around, and set yourself free, if freedom is what you want. It's good that you experience anger, fear, or sadness. Sit down, identify the story, and do The Work. Until you can see everything in the world as a friend, your Work is not done.

The Turnaround to "My Thinking"

Once you feel competent in doing The Work on people, you can inquire into issues like world hunger, fundamentalism, bureaucracy, government, sex, terrorism, or any uncomfortable thought that appears in your mind.

As you inquire into issues and turn your judgments around, you come to know that every perceived problem appearing "out there" is really nothing more than a misperception within your own thinking.

When your writing on the Worksheet is pointed at an issue, first inquire with the four questions as usual. Then, when you get to the turnaround, substitute the words "my thinking" for the issue, wherever that seems appropriate. For example, "I don't like war because it frightens me" turns around to "I don't like my thinking because it frightens me" or "I don't like my thinking—especially about war—because it frightens me." Is that as true or truer for you?

Here are a few more examples of the turnaround to "my thinking":

Original Statement: *I'm angry at bureaucrats for making my life complicated.*
Turnaround: *I'm angry at my thinking for making my life complicated.*

Original Statement: *I don't like my handicap because it makes people avoid me.*
Turnarounds: *I don't like my thinking because it makes me avoid people. I don't like my thinking because it makes me avoid myself.*

Original Statement: *I want sex to be gentle and loving.*
Turnaround: *I want my thinking to be gentle and loving.*

When the Story Is Hard to Find

Sometimes when you feel disturbed, you may find it difficult to identify the thought behind your uncomfortable feeling. If you're having trouble sorting out exactly what thoughts are disturbing you, you might want to try the following exercise:

Start with six blank sheets of paper and somewhere to spread them out.

Number the first page "1," and write across the top: *sad, disappointed, ashamed, embarrassed, afraid, irritated, angry.* Below that, write *because* _____. About halfway down the page, write *and it means that* _____.

Number the next page "2," and write at the top the word *want.*

Number the next page "3," and write at the top the word *should.*

Number the next page "4," and write at the top the word *need*.
Number the next page "5," and write at the top the word *judge*.
Number the next page "6," and write at the top the words *never again*.

Spread out the six pages, and let your mind run wild over the upset. Use your thoughts to fan the flame of your upset, and note which ones do the best job. If no thought works particularly well, try out new or exaggerated thoughts. Write down the thoughts as simply as you can. It helps to be blunt. There's no need to follow a particular sequence. Here is a guide for using the six pages:

Page 1 is where you write down what appears as a "fact": for example, "she didn't show up for our lunch date, kept me waiting in the restaurant, never even called." Write "facts" down in the space after the *because*. Then circle the relevant emotions—sad, angry, etc. Then, after *and it means that*, write your interpretation of the "fact." Try to include your worst-case thoughts: for example, "she doesn't love me anymore" or "she's seeing someone else."

If you catch yourself thinking, "I want_____," write it down on page 2. Otherwise, use that page to prompt yourself by focusing on exactly how you would improve the situation or person. What would make it perfect for you? Write in the form "I want_____." Play God and create your perfection—for example, *want* her to unfailingly appear on time no matter what, *want* to know exactly what she's doing all the time, etc. (When you've almost filled this page, ask yourself if you've written what you *really want*, and if not, write that down at the bottom of the page.)

Thoughts in the form of "So-and-so should or shouldn't" go on page 3. If you are unaware of any "shoulds," think about what would restore to the situation your sense of justice and order. Write down all the "shoulds" that would make it "right."

Page 4 is the "I need" page, where you can bring the situation back in line with your sense of comfort and security. Write down your requirements for a happy life. Write down the adjustments that would make things be the way they are supposed to be: for example, "I need her to love me" or "I need to succeed at my job." When you've written a few statements on this page, it can be helpful to ask yourself what you would have then, after all your needs are filled. Write that at the bottom of the page.

On page 5, write your merciless evaluation of the person or situation.

Make a list of their qualities as they have become apparent to you through this upset.

On page 6, write down the aspect of the situation that you vow or hope you will never have to live through again.

Now underline all the statements that have the highest emotional charge, and do The Work on them, one by one. When you have finished, go back and do The Work on the rest of your statements.

If, after completing the above, you find that you can't look forward to what you wrote on page 6, or that the troublesome story still seems to elude you, another exercise can be very effective. Take several blank sheets of paper and a watch or timer. Focus on the upset and write about it free-form for five minutes *without stopping*. When you want to stop, write the last phrase you wrote, over and over, until you're ready to continue. Afterward, review what you wrote and underline the phrases that are most painful or embarrassing. Transfer the underlined statements to whichever of the six pages they best fit on. Walk away from your pages for a while, perhaps overnight, and then reread them, underlining all the statements that seem most highly charged. Now you know where to begin doing The Work.

Nothing outside you

can ever

give you what you're looking for.

11.

Doing The Work
on the Body and
Addictions

Bodies don't think, care, or have any problem with themselves. They never beat themselves up or shame themselves. They simply try to keep themselves balanced and to heal themselves. They are entirely efficient, intelligent, kind, and resourceful. Where there's no thought, there's no problem. It's the story we believe, prior to investigation, that leaves us confused. My pain can't be my body's fault. I tell the story of my body, and because I haven't inquired, I believe that my body is the problem and that if only this or that changed, I would be happy.

The body is never our problem. Our problem is always a thought that we innocently believe. The Work deals with our thinking, not with the object that we think we're addicted to. There *is* no such thing as an addiction to an object; there is only an attachment to the uninvestigated concept arising in the moment.

For example, I don't care if I smoke or if I don't smoke; it's not about a right or a wrong for me. I smoked heavily, even chain-smoked, for many years. Then, in 1986, after the experience in the halfway house, all at once it was over. When I went to Turkey in 1997, I hadn't smoked a cigarette in eleven years. I got into a taxi, and the driver had some wild Turkish music playing on his radio very loud, and he was honking constantly (honking is what they do there, it's the sound of God, and the two lanes are really six lanes merging, and everyone drives around honking at one another, and it's all happening in a perfect flow), and he turned around and with a big smile offered me a cigarette. I didn't think twice. I took it, and he lit a match for me. The music was going full blast, the horns were going full blast, and I sat in the backseat, smoking and loving each moment. It's okay if I do smoke, I noticed, and it's okay if I don't, and I notice that I haven't smoked since that one wonderful taxi ride.

But here's addiction: A concept arises that says that I should or I shouldn't smoke, I believe it, and I move from the reality of the present. Without inquiry, we believe thoughts that aren't true for us, and these thoughts are the reasons that we smoke or drink. Who would you be without your "should" or "shouldn't"?

If you think that alcohol makes you sick or confused or angry, then when you drink it, it's as if you are drinking your own disease. You're meeting alcohol where it is, and it does exactly what you know it will do. So we investigate the thinking, not in order to stop drinking, but simply to end any confusion about what alcohol will do. And if you believe that you really want to keep drinking, just notice what it does to you. There's no pity in it. There's no victim in it. And eventually there's no fun in it— only a hangover.

If my body gets sick, I go to the doctor. My body is his business. My thinking is my business, and in the peace of that, I'm very clear about what to do and where to go. And then the body becomes a lot of fun, because you're not invested in whether it lives or dies. It's a projected image, a metaphor of your thinking, mirrored back to you.

On one occasion in 1986, while I was getting a massage, I began to experience a sudden paralysis. It was as if all the ligaments, tendons, and muscles had tightened to an extreme. It was like rigor mortis; I couldn't make even the slightest movement. Throughout the experience, I was perfectly calm and joyful, because I didn't have a story that the body should look a certain way or move fluidly. Thoughts moved through, like "Oh my God, I can't move. Something terrible is happening." But the inquiry that was alive within me wouldn't allow any attachment to these thoughts. If that process were slowed down and given words, it would sound like this: "'You're never going to be able to walk again'—sweetheart, can you really know that that's true?" They're so fast, these four questions. Eventually, they meet a thought at the instant of its arising. At some point, after about an hour, the body began to relax and go back to what people would call its normal state.

An Unhealthy Heart?

How do you live when you believe the thought that your body should be different? How does that feel? "I'll be happy later, when my body is healed." "I should be thinner, healthier, prettier, younger." This is a very old religion. If I think my body should be different from what it is now, I'm out of my business. I'm out of my mind!

I'm not asking you to let go of your body, as if such a thing were possible. I'm asking you to own your body, to care for it, to take a look at your beliefs about it, to put them on paper, inquire, and turn them around.

———

Harriet: I'm angry at my heart because it is diseased and weak. It restricts all my physical activities, and I could easily die at any time.

Katie: Is it true that your heart is diseased and weak?

Harriet: Well, yes, it's hereditary. Both my parents and three grandparents died of heart disease.

Katie: Your parents had heart disease, and it sounds as though you've inherited a belief system that terrifies you. The doctors have told you that you have heart disease. And I'm inviting you to ask yourself today, "Can you really know that it's true?"

Harriet: Well . . . no. I can't really know that. It could have changed in the last four minutes.

Katie: That's right. We can't ever really know. How do I know that my heart should be like this? That's the way it is. Reality always shows me. How do you react when you believe the thought that your heart is diseased and weak?

Harriet: I get frightened. I limit my activities. I stay inside and become very inactive. I get depressed that I can't do what I want to do. I imagine the pain and terror of a heart attack. I feel hopeless.

Katie: The result is that you stay focused on the hopelessness and don't look at your thinking. That's where the fear comes from—from your uninvestigated thoughts. As long as you see your heart as the problem and look outside your own mind for solutions, you can't know anything but fear. Who or what would you be if you never had the thought that your heart is diseased and weak?

Harriet: I think I'd be more peaceful and also freer to do what I want to do.

Katie: Let's turn around what you wrote, replacing the word *heart* with "thinking."

Harriet: I'm angry at my thinking because it is diseased and weak.

Katie: Your mind is diseased and weak when it names your heart as the problem. You're quite insane in that moment. Your mind is diseased when you believe that your heart isn't exactly as it should be now. How do you know that? If you have one belief that opposes what is, you feel out of harmony and your heart begins to race. Your body is the loving reflection of your mind. Until you understand that, your heart will continue to be your teacher, always showing you the kinder way. Read your next statement.

Harriet: I want my heart to be healed completely.

Katie: Is that true? Is that really true?

Harriet: What a question! [Pause] Hmmm.

Katie: Interesting, isn't it? Can you absolutely know that your heart needs to heal completely?

Harriet: It sure seems that way. [Pause] No, I can't absolutely know that.

Katie: How do you react when you believe the thought that your heart isn't normal for you and needs to be healed?

Harriet: I think about it all the time. I think about dying, and I scare myself. I try to consider all the medical options and natural healing options, and I get really confused. I'm desperate to figure it out, and I can't.

Katie: Who or what would you be without the story "I want my heart to be healed completely"?

Harriet: I would just be living my life. I wouldn't be so afraid. I'd be more present when my doctor is talking to me. I see myself just enjoying what I'm doing, whether I'm active or not. And I wouldn't be so focused on the future, on dying.

Katie: That makes sense to me. Let's turn it around.

Harriet: I want my thinking to be healed completely.

Katie: Isn't that as true or truer? We've been attempting to heal bodies for thousands of years, and they still get sick and old, and they die. Bodies come to pass, not to stay. No body has ever been healed ultimately. There is only the mind to heal if it's peace that you want, whether you're sick or well. Read the next statement.

Harriet: My heart is weak, diseased, not dependable, restrictive, confining, and prone to pain.

Katie: Is that true?

Harriet: No, not really. It's just as true to say my mind is weak, diseased, not dependable, restrictive, confining, and prone to pain when it sees my heart as that.

Katie: How does it feel when you think that your heart is insufficient? Everyone's heart is perfect as it is right now. Everyone's heart should be exactly as healthy as it is now—even someone whose heart is stopping.

Harriet: If I think my heart is perfect and I have pain, will I still take action?

Katie: Absolutely. I call it doing the dishes and loving it. When you have some understanding of your thoughts through inquiry, then you can call 911 consciously, without fear or panic. You're more able to describe your situation and answer questions clearly. You've always known what to do; that doesn't change. Let's look at the next statement.

Harriet: I am not willing to give up on my heart or let it cease to function or preclude my living a normal, active life.

Katie: Yes, you are, sweetheart. If your heart stops, you die. Dying, like everything else, isn't a choice, even though it can appear that way. Can you see a way to turn that last one around?

Harriet: I am willing to give up on my heart.

Katie: Good for you! Give up on your heart. Turn that over to your doctor. Work with your thinking. That's where it will count. Your heart will love you for it. Continue with the turnaround.

Harriet: I am willing to let it cease to function. I am willing to let my heart preclude my living a normal life.

Katie: Now read these last statements again. Read each one as "I look forward to."

Harriet: I look forward to giving up on my heart. I look forward to letting my heart cease to function. I look forward to letting it preclude me from living a normal life.

Katie: Sounds like freedom to me. Follow your doctor's advice and watch what happens from a sane and loving position. Eventually, you may come to know that your body is not your business, it's your doctor's business. The only thing for you to heal is an erroneous belief appearing now. Thank you, sweetheart.

My Daughter's Addiction

I have worked with hundreds of alcoholics, and I've always found that they were drunk with their thinking before they were drunk with their drinking. Many of them have told me that The Work includes all the twelve steps of Alcoholics Anonymous. For example, it gives a very clear form to the fourth and fifth steps—"taking a fearless inventory of ourselves, and admitting the exact nature of our wrongs"—that thousands have wanted to do and haven't known how to.

"Don't necessarily do The Work on drinking," I tell them. "Go back to the thought just prior to the thought that you need a drink, and do The Work on that, on that man or woman again, on that situation. The prior thought is what you're trying to shut down with alcohol. Apply The Work to that. Your uninvestigated thinking is the problem, not alcohol. Alcohol is honest and true: It promises to get you drunk, and it does; it promises to make things worse, and it does. It's always true to its word. It's a great teacher of integrity. It doesn't say, 'Drink me.' It just sits there, true to itself, being what it is and waiting to do its job.

"Do The Work on these thoughts and also go to twelve-step meetings; give away your experience and strength at meetings so that you can hear it yourself. You are always the one you're working with. It's your truth, not ours, that will set you free."

When my own daughter, Roxann, was sixteen, she drank very heavily and also did drugs. This had begun to happen before I woke up with the questions in 1986, but I was so depressed then that I was totally unaware of it. After inquiry was alive in me, though, I began to notice her actions as well as my thoughts about them.

She used to drive off every night in her new red Camaro. If I asked her where she was going, she would give me a furious look and slam the door on her way out. It was a look I understood well. I'd taught her to see me that way. I myself had worn that look on my face for many years.

Through inquiry, I learned to become very quiet around her, around everyone. I learned how to be a listener. I would often sit and wait up for her far past midnight, for the pure privilege of seeing her—just for that privilege. I knew she was drinking, and I knew I couldn't do a thing about it. The thoughts that would appear in my mind were thoughts like these: "She's probably drunk and driving, and she'll be killed in a crash, and I'll never see her again. I'm her mother, I bought her the car, I'm responsible. I should take her car from her (but it wasn't mine to take; I'd given it to her; it was hers), she'll drive while she's drunk, and she'll kill someone, she'll crash into another car or drive into a lamppost and kill herself and her passengers." As the thoughts appeared, each one would be met with wordless, thoughtless inquiry. And inquiry instantly brought me back to reality. Here is what was true: woman sitting in chair waiting for her beloved daughter.

One evening, after being gone for a three-day weekend, Roxann came through the door with a look of great misery on her face and, it seemed to me, without any defenses. She saw me sitting there, and she just fell into my arms and said, "Mom, I can't do this anymore. Please help me. Whatever this thing is that you're giving to all these people who come to our house, I want it." So we did The Work. That was the last time she did alcohol or drugs. Whenever she had a problem after that, she didn't need to drink or drug, and she didn't need me. She just wrote the problem down, asked four questions, and turned it around.

When there's peace here, there's peace there. To have a way to see beyond the illusion of suffering is the greatest gift. I love that all my children have taken advantage of it.

———

Charlotte: I'm afraid of my daughter's drug addiction because it's killing her.

Katie: Can you absolutely know that that's true? And I'm not saying that it's not. This is just a question. "Her drug addiction is killing her"—can you absolutely know that that's true?

Charlotte: No.

Katie: How do you react when you think the thought "Her drug addiction is killing her"?

Charlotte: I get very angry.

Katie: And what do you say to her? What do you do?

Charlotte: I judge her, and I push her away. I'm afraid of her. I don't want her around.

Katie: Who would you be, in the presence of your daughter, without the thought "Her drug addiction is killing her"?

Charlotte: I'd be more relaxed, and I'd be more myself, and less mean to her, less reactive.

Katie: When this Work found me, my daughter was, in her words, an alcoholic and doing drugs. And the questions were alive in me. "Her addiction is killing her"—can I absolutely know that that's true? No. And who would I be without this story? I would be totally there for her, loving her with all my heart, as long as she lasts. Maybe she'll die tomorrow of an overdose, but she's in my arms now. How do you treat her when you think the thought "Her drug addiction is killing her"?

Charlotte: I don't want to see her. I don't want her around.

Katie: That's fear, and fear is what we experience when we're attached to the nightmare. "Drug addiction is killing her"—turn it around. When you're turning around an issue like drugs, put the words "my thinking" in place of the issue. "My thinking . . ."

Charlotte: My thinking is killing her.

Katie: There's another turnaround. "My thinking is . . ."

Charlotte: Killing me.

Katie: Yes.

Charlotte: It's killing our relationship.

Katie: She's dying of a drug overdose, and you're dying of a thinking overdose. She could last a lot longer than you.

Charlotte: Yes, that's true. The stress is really wearing me down.

Katie: She's stoned, you're stoned. I've been through this one.

Charlotte: Yeah, I get really toxic when it comes up in my face again that she's using drugs.

Katie: "She's using"—turn it around.

Charlotte: I'm using?

Katie: Yes, you're using her to stay toxic. She uses drugs, you use her— what's the difference?

Charlotte: Hmm.

Katie: Let's look at your next statement.

Charlotte: I'm angry and saddened by Linda's drug addiction because I feel that it's endangering my granddaughter Debbie's life.

Katie: So you think that something will happen, and your granddaughter will die.

Charlotte: Or be molested or . . .

Katie: So because of your daughter's addiction, something terrible can happen to your granddaughter.

Charlotte: Yeah.

Katie: Is that true? And I'm not saying it's not true. These are just questions; there's no motive here. This is about the end of your suffering. Can you absolutely know that that's true?

Charlotte: No. I can't know that.

Katie: How do you react when you think that thought?

Charlotte: Well, I've been crying for most of the last two days. I haven't slept in forty-eight hours. I've been feeling terror.

Katie: Give me a stress-free reason to believe this.

Charlotte: There is none.

Katie: "My daughter's drug addiction is endangering my granddaughter's life"—turn it around. "My thinking addiction . . ."

Charlotte: My thinking addiction is endangering my life. Yeah. I can see that. That's true.

Katie: Now read it saying, "My drug addiction . . ."

Charlotte: My drug addiction is endangering my life?

Katie: Yes, and your drug addiction is her.

Charlotte: Oh. Well, I can see that. My drug addiction is her. I'm so much in her business.

Katie: That's it. She's addicted to drugs, and you're addicted to mentally running her life. She's your drug.

Charlotte: Okay.

Katie: It's insane to mentally be in my children's business.

Charlotte: Even with the baby?

Katie: "She should take care of the baby"—turn it around.

Charlotte: I should take care of the baby?

Katie: Yes. *You* do it.

Charlotte: Oh God! I should do that?

Katie: What do you think? According to you, she's not available.

Charlotte: Well, I'm already raising three of my other daughter's babies from birth, so . . .

Katie: Well, raise four, raise five, raise a thousand. There are children hungry all over the world! What are you doing sitting here?

Charlotte: I guess my question about that is if I raise the child for her, then I'm enabling her to use drugs. I could be the one to kill her.

Katie: So taking care of the baby is a problem for you? It's the same way for her. This just puts us in a place of humility. Are you doing the best you can?

Charlotte: Yes.

Katie: I believe you. When you think, "My daughter should do something about it," turn it around. "*I* should do something about it." And if you can't, you're just like your daughter. When she says, "I can't," you can understand. But when you get furious at her, because you haven't investigated your own thinking, you're both stoned, and you teach your daughter craziness.

Charlotte: Ah.

Katie: "Drug addiction is endangering Debbie's life"—turn it around.

Charlotte: My thinking about Linda's drug addiction is endangering my life.

Katie: Yes.

Charlotte: That's absolutely true.

Katie: Whose business is her drug addiction?

Charlotte: Hers.

Katie: Whose business is your drug addiction?

Charlotte: Mine.

Katie: Take care of that. Let's look at the next one.

Charlotte: My daughter's drug addiction is ruining her life.

Katie: Can you absolutely know that it's true that your daughter's drug addiction is ruining her life in the long run?

Charlotte: No.

Katie: It all begins to make sense. I love that you answered that question. What I found when I did The Work on my daughter in 1986 was that I had to go deep to find the same thing. And it turned out that because of that addiction, her life today is very rich. The bottom line is that I just can't know anything. I watch the way things are in reality. This leaves me in a position to act sanely and lovingly, and life is always perfectly beautiful. And if she died, I'd still be able to see that. But I can't fool myself. I really have to know the truth. If this path were your only way to God, would you choose it?

Charlotte: Yes.

Katie: Well, that seems to be the case. No mistake. We've been daughter-realized forever; now let's be self-realized. Read the statement again.

Charlotte: My daughter's drug addiction is ruining her life.

Katie: How do you react when you think that thought?

Charlotte: I feel hopeless.

Katie: And how do you live when you feel hopeless?

Charlotte: I don't live at all.

Katie: Can you see a reason to drop this thought?

Charlotte: Yes.

Katie: Who would you be, living your life, without this thought?

Charlotte: Well, I'd certainly be a better mother.

Katie: Good. You're the expert, and here's what I'm learning from you. With the thought, suffering; without the thought, no suffering and you'd be a better mother. So what does your daughter have to do with your problem? Zero. If you think that your daughter is your problem, welcome to The Work. Your daughter is the perfect daughter for you, because she's going to bring up every uninvestigated concept you have until you get a clue about reality. That's her job. Everything has its job. This candle's job is to burn, this rose's job is to blossom, your daughter's job is to use drugs, my job is to drink my tea now. [Takes a sip of tea] And when you understand, she'll follow you, she'll understand. It's a law, because she's your projection. When you move into the polarity of truth, so will she. Hell here, hell there. Peace here, peace there. Let's look at the next one.

Charlotte: It almost seems silly now. Should I read what I wrote anyway?

Katie: You may as well. Thought appears.

Charlotte: I'm angry, confused, saddened, and afraid—all of it—*at my daughter Linda's drug addiction because it brings me excruciating pain.*

Katie: Turn it around.

Charlotte: Obviously, my thinking about her is what brings me excruciating pain. Yeah.

Katie: Yes. Your daughter has nothing to do with your pain.

Charlotte: Mmm. That's absolutely true. I can see that. I can feel it.

Katie: I love it when people realize this, because when they see the innocence of their children and their parents and their partners, they come to see their own innocence. This Work is about 100 percent forgiveness, because that's what you want. That's what you are. Let's look at the next one.

Charlotte: I'm afraid of Linda's drug addiction because it changes her personality.

Katie: Turn it around. "I'm afraid of my thinking . . ."

Charlotte: I'm afraid of my thinking because it changes Linda's personality?

Katie: Interesting. Now try "It changes my . . ."

Charlotte: It changes my personality. Yeah, okay.

Katie: And therefore Linda's.

Charlotte: And therefore Linda's.

Katie: Isn't it funny how we're the last place we look? Always trying to change the projected rather than clear the projector. We haven't known a way to do this until now.

Charlotte: Yeah.

Katie: So read it just like that.

Charlotte: I'm afraid of my thinking because it changes my personality.

Katie: Feel it.

Charlotte: Wow! And I can't see her then. That's it! I'm afraid of my thinking because it changes my personality, and then I can't see myself or her. Yeah.

Katie: Have you ever been angry at her and thought, "How can I say that to her? Why am I hurting her? She's my whole life, I love her, and I just treat her like . . ."

Charlotte: Like shit. It's like I become someone else. I'm so mean to her when she's using.

Katie: Because you're a drug user, and she's your drug. How else can you be a champion of suffering? Parents call me and say, "My child's a drug addict, she's in trouble," and they don't see that *they're* the ones in trouble. Their child is often doing fine, or at least as well as the parent. And when you get clear, your daughter will follow. You are the way. Let's look at the next one.

Charlotte: I'm angry at Linda's drug addiction because when she uses, I'm afraid of her.

Katie: Turn it around.

Charlotte: I'm angry at my drug addiction because then I'm afraid of myself. That's exactly what happens when she shows up and she's using. I'm afraid of my own behavior around her.

Katie: "You're afraid of her"—is that true?

Charlotte: No.

Katie: How do you react, how do you treat her, when you think that thought?

Charlotte: I get angry, volatile, aggressive, and especially I shut her out.

Katie: Like some kind of poison walked into the house.

Charlotte: Yeah, that's exactly what I do.

Katie: And she's your baby.

Charlotte: Yeah.

Katie: And you treat her like some bug that just crawled in.

Charlotte: Right. That's exactly right.

Katie: She's your dearest child, and you treat her like an enemy. That's the power of uninvestigated thinking. That's the power of the nightmare. It has to live itself out. You think, "I'm afraid of her," and you have to live that out. But if you investigate that thought ("'I'm afraid of her'—is it true?"), the nightmare disappears. When she walks into the house and you have the thought "I'm afraid of her," laughter replaces fear. You just put your arms around her, and you can hear how she's afraid of herself. She'll sit there and tell you. There's no listener in your home now; there's just a teacher of fear. That's understandable, because up until now, you haven't asked yourself if your thoughts are true. Let's look at the next statement.

Charlotte: I need Linda to stay away from me when she's on drugs.

Katie: Is that true? And I'm not saying it's not.

Charlotte: I feel like it is.

Katie: And does she come to you when she's on drugs?

Charlotte: No, not anymore.

Katie: So that's what you need, because that's what you have. No mistake. If my daughter doesn't come to me, that's how I know I don't need her. If she comes, that's how I know I need her.

Charlotte: And when she does come, I treat her in this horrible way.

Katie: So turn the statement around.

Charlotte: I need myself to stay away from me when I'm on drugs. That's really true.

Katie: One way you can stay away from yourself when you're on drugs, the drug of Linda, is to judge your daughter, write it down, ask four questions, and turn it around. And stay away from who you think you are—this fearful, angry woman—and come back to your beautiful self. It's what you wanted her to do, so I know that you can. This is a life's work. You have much more energy when you're just working on yourself.

Charlotte: Yeah, then I would want her around, whether she was using or not.

Katie: I don't know.

Charlotte: At least I would be available to her when she's using, instead of shutting off.

Katie: That could be a lot less painful for both of you.

Charlotte: Yeah.

Katie: It's wonderful to realize that. Nice Work, sweetheart.

Everything happens

for me,

not *to* me.

12.

Making Friends with the Worst That Can Happen

I have helped people do The Work on rape, war in Vietnam and Bosnia, torture, internment in Nazi concentration camps, the death of a child, and the prolonged pain of illnesses like cancer. Many of us think that it's not humanly possible to accept extreme experiences like these, much less meet them with unconditional love. But not only is that possible, it's our true nature.

Nothing terrible has ever happened except in our thinking. Reality is always good, even in situations that seem like nightmares. The story we tell is the only nightmare that we have lived. When I say that the worst that can happen is a belief, I am being literal. The worst that can happen to you is your uninvestigated belief system.

Afraid of Death

In The School for The Work, I love to use inquiry to walk people through the thing they fear most, the worst that could possibly happen. For many of them, the worst thing is death: They often believe that they'll suffer terribly not only during the process of dying, but also after they die. I take them deep enough into these waking nightmares to dispel the illusion of fear, pain, and suffering.

I have sat with many people on their deathbeds, and after we do The Work, they always tell me that they're fine. I remember one very frightened woman who was dying of cancer. She had requested that I sit with her, so I came. I sat down beside her and said, "I don't see a problem." She said, "No? Well, I'll show you a problem!" and she pulled off the sheet. One of her legs was so swollen that it was at least twice the size of the normal leg. I looked and I looked, and I still couldn't find a problem. She said, "You must be blind! Look at this leg. Now look at the other one." And I said, "Oh, now I see the problem. You're suffering from the belief that that leg should look like this one. Who would you be without that thought?" And she got it. She began to laugh, and the fear just poured out through her laughter. She said that this was the happiest she had ever been in her entire life.

I once went to visit a woman who was dying in a hospice. When I walked in, she was napping, so I just sat by her bed until she opened her eyes. I took her hand, and we talked for a few minutes, and she said, "I'm so frightened. I don't know how to die." And I said, "Sweetheart, is that true?" She said, "Yes. I just don't know what to do." I said, "When I walked in, you were taking a nap. Do you know how to take a nap?" She said, "Of course." And I said, "You close your eyes every night, and you go to sleep. People look forward to sleeping. That's all death is. That's as bad as it gets, except for your belief system that says there's something else." She told me she believed in the after-death thing and said, "I won't know what to do when I get there." I said, "Can you really know that there's something to do?" She said, "I guess not." I said, "There's nothing you have to know, and it's always all right. Everything you need is already there for you; you don't have to give it a thought. All you have to do is take a nap when you need to, and when you wake up, you'll know what to do." I was describing life to her, of course, not death. Then we went into the second question, "Can you absolutely know that it's true that you don't know how to die?" She began to laugh and said that she preferred being with me to being with her story. What fun, having nowhere to go but where we really are now.

When the mind thinks of death, it looks at nothing and calls it something, to keep from experiencing what it—the mind—really is. Until you know that death is equal to life, you'll always try to control what happens, and it's always going to hurt. There's no sadness without a story that opposes reality.

The fear of death is the last smokescreen for the fear of love. We think that we're afraid of the death of our body, though what we're really afraid of is the death of our identity. But through inquiry, as we understand that death is just a concept and that our identity is a concept too, we come to realize who we are. This is the end of fear.

Loss is another concept. I was in the delivery room when my grandson Race was born. I loved him at first sight. Then I realized that he wasn't breathing. The doctor had a troubled look on his face and immediately started to do something with the baby. The nurses realized that the procedures weren't working, and you could see the stress and panic begin to take over the room. Nothing they did was working—the baby wouldn't breathe. At a certain moment, Roxann looked into my eyes, and I smiled. She later told me, "You know that smile you often have on your face, Mom? When I saw you look at me like that, a wave of peace came over me. And even though the baby wasn't breathing, it was okay with me." Soon afterward, breath entered my grandson, and I heard him cry.

I love that my grandson didn't have to breathe for me to love him. Whose business was his breathing? Not mine. I wasn't going to miss one moment of him, whether he was breathing or not. I knew that even without a single breath, he had lived a full life. I love reality, not the way a fantasy would dictate, but just the way it is, right now.

––––––––

Henry: I'm angry at death because it destroys me. I'm afraid of dying. I can't accept death. Death should let me be reincarnated. Death is painful. Death is the end. I never want to experience the fear of death again.

Katie: Let's start at the top. Read your first statement again.

Henry: I'm angry at death because it destroys me.

Katie: If you want to live in terror, get a future. That's quite a future you've planned, sweetheart. Let's hear the next statement.

Henry: I'm afraid of dying.

Katie: What's the worst that could happen when you die? Let's play with that.

Henry: The death of my body.

Katie: And then what will happen?

Henry: I don't know.

Katie: Well, what do you think is the worst that could happen? You think that something terrible could happen. What is it?

Henry: That death is the end, and I'm not born again. And that there is no soul.

Katie: And then? You're not born again. There is no soul. So far, there's nothing. So far, the worst that can happen to you is nothing. And then?

Henry: Yes, but it's painful.

Katie: So the nothing is painful.

Henry: Yes.

Katie: Can you really know that that's true? How can nothing be painful? How can it be anything? Nothing is nothing.

Henry: I imagine this nothing as a black hole that is very uncomfortable.

Katie: So nothing is a black hole. Can you really know that that's true? I'm not saying it's not true. I know how you love your stories. It's the old black-hole story.

Henry: I think that's the worst thing that could happen.

Katie: Okay. So when you die, you would go into a big, black hole forever.

Henry: Or to hell. I call this black hole hell.

Katie: A big, black hell-hole forever.

Henry: And it is a hell fire.

Katie: A big, black hell-hole fire forever.

Henry: Yes, and it's turned away from God.

Katie: Totally away from God. Fire and darkness in this big, black hell-hole forever. I want to ask you, can you absolutely know that that's true?

Henry: No. I can't.

Katie: How does it feel when you believe that thought?

Henry [crying]: It's painful. It's horrible.

Katie: Sweetheart, look at me. Are you in touch with what you're feeling right now? Look at yourself. *This* is the dark hole of hell. You're in it. It doesn't come later; you're living your story of your future death right now. This terror is as bad as it gets. Can you see a reason to drop this story? And I'm not asking you to drop it.

Henry: Yes.

Katie: Give me a reason to keep this story that doesn't feel like being in a dark fire from hell.

Henry: I can't.

Katie: Who or what would you be without this story? You've already been living the worst that could happen. Imagination without investigation. Lost in hell. No way out.

Henry: Pushed away from God.

Katie: Yes, angel, pushed away from the awareness of God in your life. You can't push yourself away from God; that's not a possibility. You can only push yourself away from the awareness of God within you, for a while. As long as you worship this old idol, this old black-hole story of yours, there's no room for any awareness of God in you. This story is what you've been worshiping like a child, in pure innocence. Let's look at the next statement.

Henry: I'm afraid of dying.

Katie: I understand that. But no one is afraid of dying; they're just afraid of their story about dying. Look at what you think death is. You've been describing your life, not death. This is the story of your life.

Henry: Hmmm. Yes.

Katie: Let's look at the next statement.

Henry: I can't accept death.

Katie: Is that true?

Henry: Well, yes. I have a lot of trouble accepting it.

Katie: Can you absolutely know that it's true that you can't accept death?

Henry: It's hard to believe that that's possible.

Katie: When you're not thinking about death, you fully accept it. You're not worrying about it at all. Think of your foot.

Henry: Okay.

Katie: Did you have a foot before you thought of it? Where was it? When there's no thought, there's no foot. When there's no thought of death, there's no death.

Henry: Really? I can't believe it's that simple.

Katie: How do you react, how do you feel, when you believe the thought "I can't accept death"?

Henry: Helpless. Frightened.

Katie: What would you be in your life without this story "I can't accept death"?

Henry: What would my life be without that thought? It would be beautiful.

Katie: "I can't accept death" — turn it around.

Henry: I can accept death.

Katie: Everyone can. Everyone *does*. There's no decision in death. People who know that there's no hope are free. The decision's out of their hands. It has always been that way, but some people have to die bodily to find out. No wonder they smile on their deathbeds. Dying is everything they were looking for in life. Their delusion of being in charge is over. When there's no choice, there's no fear. And in that, there is peace. They realize that they're home and that they've never left.

Henry: This fear of losing control is very strong. And also this fear of love. It's all connected.

Katie: It's terrifying to think you could lose control, even though the truth is that you never had it in the first place. That's the death of fantasy and the birth of reality. Let's look at the next statement.

Henry: Death should let me be reincarnated.

Katie: "You should be reincarnated"—can you really know that that's true? Welcome to the story of a future.

Henry: No. I can't know if that's true.

Katie: You don't even like it *this* time around. Why do you want to do it again? [Henry laughs.] "Boy, what a dark hole *this* is. Hmm, I think I'll come back again." [The audience laughs.] "You want to come back again"—is that true?

Henry [laughing]: No, it's not. I don't want to be reincarnated. It was a mistake.

Katie: "We reincarnate"—can you absolutely know that that's true?

Henry: No, I've just heard and read that we do.

Katie: How do you react when you think that thought?

Henry: I feel anxious about what I'm doing now, because I think I may have to make up for it later and I may even be punished for it or at least have to suffer for many lifetimes because I've hurt so many people in my life. I'm afraid that I've piled up a lot of bad karma and maybe I've blown it this lifetime and I'll have to start over again and again in lower forms of life.

Katie: Who would you be without the thought that we reincarnate?

Henry: Less fearful. Freer.

Katie: Reincarnation may be a useful concept for some people, but in my experience, nothing reincarnates but a thought. "I. I am. I am woman. I am woman with children." And so on, ad infinitum. Do you want to end karma? It's simple. I. "I am"—is it true? Who would I be without this story? No karma whatsoever. And I look forward to the next life, and here it comes. It's called "now." Let's look at the next statement.

Henry: Death is painful.

Katie: Can you really know that that's true?

Henry: I can't.

Katie: How does it feel when you believe the thought that death is painful?

Henry: It feels stupid now.

Katie: "Death is painful"—turn it around. "My thinking . . ."

Henry: My thinking is painful.

Katie: Isn't that truer?

Henry: Yes. Yes.

Katie: Death was never that unkind. Death is simply the end of thought. Fantasy without investigation is painful, sometimes. Let's look at the next.

Henry: Death is the end.

Katie [laughing]: That's a good one! Can you really know that that's true?

Henry: I can't.

Katie: Isn't that one of your personal favorites? [The audience laughs.] How do you react when you think that thought?

Henry: Up to now, I've always been afraid.

Katie: "Death is the end"—turn it around.

Henry: My thinking is the end.

Katie: The beginning, the middle, the end. [Henry and the audience laugh.] All of it. You know how to die really well. Have you ever just gone to sleep at night?

Henry: Yes.

Katie: That's it. Dreamless sleep. You do it really well. You sleep at night, then you open your eyes, and there's still nothing, there's no one awake. There's never anyone alive until the story begins with "I." And that's where life begins, with the first word you think. Prior to that, there's no you, no world. You do this every day of your life. Identification as an "I" wakes up. "I" am Henry. "I" need to brush my teeth. "I" am late for work. "I" have so much to do today. Before that, there's no one, nothing, no black hell-hole, only peace that doesn't even recognize itself as peace. You die very well, sweetheart. And you're born very well. And if things get rough, you have inquiry. Let's look at your last statement.

Henry: I never want to experience the fear of death again.

Katie: "I'm willing . . ."

Henry: I'm willing to experience the fear of death again.

Katie: Now you know what to do with it. So give it a shot. "I look forward to ..."

Henry [laughing]: I look forward to experiencing the fear of death again. I'll try my best.

Katie: Good. There's no place, there's no dark hole you can go into, where inquiry won't follow. Inquiry lives inside you if you nurture it for a while. Then it takes on its own life and automatically nurtures you. And you're never given more pain than you can handle. You never, ever get more than you can take. That's a promise. Death experiences are just mental experiences. And when people die, it's so wonderful that they never come back to tell you. It's so wonderful, they're not going to bother. [Laughter] That's what investigation is for. So, sweetheart, look forward to the fear of death. If you're a lover of truth, set yourself free.

Bombs Are Falling

The next dialogue, with a sixty-seven-year-old Dutch man, shows the power of an uninvestigated story, which can control our thoughts and actions for almost a whole lifetime.

Bombs also fell on a German man who participated in one of my European Schools for The Work. He was six years old when Soviet troops occupied Berlin in 1945. The soldiers took him, along with many other children, women, and old people who had survived the bombing, and put him in a shelter. He remembers playing with one of the live hand grenades that the soldiers had given the children as toys. He watched as another of the little boys pulled the pin; the grenade exploded, and the boy's arm was blown off. Many of the children were maimed, and he remembers their screams, faces wounded, skin and limbs flying. He also remembers a girl of six who slept near him being raped by a soldier, and he told me that he could still hear the screams of the women being raped night after night in the barracks. His whole life had been dominated by the experience of a six-year-old, he said, and he had come to The School to go deeper into himself and his nightmares and to find his way back home.

At the same School, there was a Jewish woman whose parents had survived Dachau. When she was a child, her nights too were filled with screams. Her father would often wake up in the middle of the night screaming and spend hours pacing back and forth, crying and moaning. Most nights, her mother would wake up too and join her father in his moans. Her parents' nightmare became her nightmare. She was taught that if people didn't have a number tattooed on their arm, they were not to be trusted. She was as traumatized as the German man.

A few days into The School, after I'd heard their stories, I put these two people together for an exercise. The Worksheets they had written out were judgments on the enemy soldiers in World War II, from opposite sides. Each one in turn gave inquiry to the other. I loved watching these two survivors of thought as they became friends.

In the following dialogue, Willem investigates childhood terrors that have been with him for more than fifty years. Although he isn't yet ready to look forward to the worst that can happen, he does have some important insights. We can never know how much we have received when we've finished a piece of honest inquiry or what effect it will have on us. We may never even be aware of the effect. It's none of our business.

Willem: I don't like war because it has brought me a lot of fear and terror. It showed me that my existence is very insecure. I was hungry all the time. My father wasn't there when I needed him. I had to spend many nights in the bomb shelter.

Katie: Good. And how old were you?

Willem: At the beginning of the war I was six, and at the end, twelve.

Katie: Let's look at "It has brought me a lot of fear and terror." So go to the worst time, to the very worst time you had, with all the hunger and the fear and no father. How old were you then?

Willem: Twelve.

Katie: And where are you? I'll talk to the twelve-year-old.

Willem: I'm coming home from school, I hear the bombs, so I go into a house and then the house falls down on me. The roof hits me on the head.

Katie: And then what happens?

Willem: First, I thought I was dead, then I realized that I was alive, and I crawled out of the ruins and ran away.

Katie: So you ran away, and then what happened?

Willem: I ran down the street and into a bakery. And then I left the bakery and went into a church, into the crypt, thinking, "Maybe I'll be safer here." And later, I was put onto a truck with other wounded people.

Katie: Was your body okay?

Willem: Yes, but I had a concussion.

Katie: Okay. I'd like to ask the little twelve-year-old boy, What is the worst moment? When you hear the bombs? When the house falls in on you?

Willem: When the house is falling down.

Katie: Yes. And while the house is falling, apart from your thinking, little boy, is it okay? Except for your thoughts, is it okay? In reality?

Willem: Now, as an adult, I can say it's okay, because I know I survived it. But as a child, it was not okay.

Katie: I understand. And I'm asking the twelve-year-old boy. I'm asking you to look at the house falling down. It's coming down. Are you okay?

Willem: Yes. I'm still alive.

Katie: And then when the house falls on you, are you okay? In reality?

Willem: I'm still alive.

Katie: Now you're crawling out of the house. Tell me the truth, little boy. Are you okay?

Willem [after a long pause]: I'm alive.

Katie: And again, I'm asking the little boy, is anything not okay?

Willem: I don't know whether my stepmother or my brothers are still alive.

Katie: Good. Now except for that thought, are you okay?

Willem [after a pause]: I'm alive, and that's okay, given the situation.

Katie: Without the story of your mother and your family, are you okay? I don't mean just alive. Look at the twelve-year-old.

Willem: Although I was in panic, I can say this is okay. I was alive and happy that I came out of the house.

Katie: So close your eyes. Now move aside from the little boy. Just watch the little twelve-year-old. Watch him with the house falling in on him. Now watch him crawling out. Look at him without your story, without the story of bombs and parents. Just look at him without your story. You can have your story back later. Just for now, look at him without your story. Just be with him. Can you find the place in you where you knew it was okay?

Willem: Hmm.

Katie: Yes, sweetheart, you tell the story of how the bomb is going to wipe out your family and you, and you scare yourself with that story. Little boys don't understand how the mind works. They can't know that it's just a story that's scaring them.

Willem: I didn't know.

Katie: So the house fell, the roof hit you on the head, you got a concussion, you crawled out, you went to a bakery, you went to a church. Reality is much kinder than our stories. "I need my father. Did a bomb hit my family? Are my parents alive? Will I ever see them again? How will I survive without them?"

Willem: Hmm.

Katie: I'd like to go back and be with that little boy again, because he's still sitting here today. The story "It's going to fall down and kill my family" causes much more terror and pain than the house actually falling on you. Did you even feel it falling on you?

Willem: Probably not, because I was in so much fear.

Katie: So, sweetheart, how many times have you experienced the story? For how many years?

Willem: Very often.

Katie: How many more bombs did you hear?

Willem: Just two more weeks of bombing.

Katie: So you experienced that for two weeks, and you've lived it in your mind for how many years?

Willem: Fifty-five.

Katie: So the bombs have been falling inside you for fifty-five years. And in reality, only for part of six years.

Willem: Yes.

Katie: So who is kinder, war or you?

Willem: Hmm.

Katie: Who is making war unceasingly? How do you react when you believe this story?

Willem: With fear.

Katie: And look at how you live when you believe this story. For fifty-five years, you've been feeling fear with no bombs and no houses falling. Can you see a reason to drop this little boy's story?

Willem: Oh, yes.

Katie: Who would you be without it?

Willem: I would be free, free of fear probably, especially free of fear.

Katie: Yes, that's my experience. I want to talk to the little twelve-year-old again. Is it true that you need your father? Is it really true?

Willem: I know that I missed him.

Katie: I understand that fully. And is it true you need your father? I'm asking you for the truth.

Willem: I've grown up without a father.

Katie: So, is it really true you needed him? Is it true you needed your mother until you met her again? In reality?

Willem: No.

Katie: Is it true that you needed food when you were hungry?

Willem: No. I didn't starve.

Katie: Can you find a stress-free reason to keep the story that you needed your mother, you needed your father, you needed a house, you needed food?

Willem: So I can feel like a victim.

Katie: That's very stressful. And stress is the only effect of this old, old story, which isn't even true. "I needed my mother." It's not true. "I needed my father." It's not true. Can you hear it? How would you live if you weren't a victim?

Willem: I would be much freer.

Katie: Little twelve-year-old boy in the shelter, can you see a reason to drop the story "I need my mother, I need my father, I need a house, I need food"?

Willem: Yes.

Katie: It's only our story that keeps us from knowing that we always have everything we need. Can you turn your statement around? Read the statement again.

Willem: I don't like war because it has brought me a lot of fear and terror.

Katie: "I don't like my thinking . . ."

Willem: I don't like my thinking about war because it has brought me a lot of fear and terror.

Katie: Yes. The worst that happened to you in reality was a concussion. So let's move gently to the next statement.

Willem: There should only be discussions, instead of war.

Katie: Can you really know that that's true? You've been having a mental discussion for fifty-five years! [Willem laughs.] And it hasn't settled any war—inside you.

Willem: Hmm.

Katie: How do you react when you think the thought "There should be no war"? How have you lived your life, for fifty-five years, when you think that thought and you read about war in the newspaper?

Willem: It makes me frustrated, disappointed, and angry, and sometimes desperate. I struggle to resolve conflicts in a peaceful manner, and I'm not very successful at it.

Katie: So in reality, war keeps breaking out in you and in the world, and in your mind there's a war against reality with the story "There should be no war." Who would you be without that story?

Willem: I could deal more freely with conflicts if I didn't have that idea.

Katie: Yes. You would experience the end of war with reality. You would be someone we could hear, a man of peace, telling the truth about how to end war—someone to be trusted. Let's look at the next statement.

Willem: International conflicts should be resolved in a peaceful way. Should I turn it around?

Katie: Yes.

Willem: My inner conflicts should be resolved in a peaceful way.

Katie: Yes, through inquiry. You learn to resolve problems peacefully within yourself, and now we have a teacher. Fear teaches fear. Only peace can teach peace. Let's look at the next statement.

Willem: War destroys a lot of human lives and wastes huge amounts of material resources. It brings great sorrow and suffering to families. It's cruel, brutal, and terrible.

Katie: Can you hear the turnaround as you're saying it? Are you experiencing it? Let's see what it sounds like. Turn it around and put yourself on all of it.

Willem: Put me . . . ?

Katie: "My thinking destroys . . ."

Willem: My thinking destroys a lot of my human life and wastes huge amounts of my own material resources.

Katie: Yes. Every time you tell the story of war inside you, it diminishes your own favorite resources: peace and happiness. And the next one? Turn it around.

Willem: I bring great sorrow and suffering to my own family.

Katie: Yes. How much sorrow do you bring when you come home to your family with this story inside you?

Willem: That's hard to accept.

Katie: I don't see any bombs falling. No bombs have fallen around you for fifty-five years, except in your mind. There's only one thing harder than accepting this, and that is *not* accepting it. Reality rules, whether we're aware of it or not. The story is how you keep yourself from experiencing peace right now. "You needed your mother" — is that true?

Willem: I survived without her.

Katie: Let's work with a yes or no and see what that feels like. "You needed your mother" — is it true in reality?

Willem: No.

Katie: "You needed your father" — is it true?

Willem: No.

Katie: Feel it. Close your eyes. Look at that little guy taking care of himself. Look at him without your story. [Long pause. Finally, Willem smiles.] Me, too. I lost my story, I lost my old pain-filled life. And I found a wonderful life on the other side of terror and internal war. The war that I made against my family and against myself was as brutal as any bomb that could be dropped. And at a certain point, I stopped bombing myself. I began to do this Work. I answered the questions with a simple yes or no. I sat in the answers, I let them sink in, and I found freedom. Let's look at the next statement.

Willem: I don't ever want to experience again the bombs falling on my head, or being a hostage, or feeling hunger.

Katie: You may experience the story again. And if you don't feel peace or laughter when you hear yourself telling the story of the poor little boy who needed his parents, then it's time to do The Work again. This story is your gift. When you can experience it without fear, then your Work is done. There is only one person who can end your internal war, and that's you. You're the one the internal bombs are falling on. So let's turn it around. "I'm willing . . ."

Willem: I'm willing for the bombs to be falling on my head again.

Katie: If only in your thinking. The bombs aren't coming from out there; they can only come from inside you. So "I look forward to . . ."

Willem: It's hard to say this.

Katie: I look forward to the worst that can happen, only because it shows me what I haven't yet met with understanding. I know the power of truth.

Willem: I look forward to the bombs falling again and feeling hunger. Hunger is not so bad. [Pause] I don't feel it yet. Maybe I will later.

Katie: You're not supposed to feel it now. It's okay. It's good that you can't quite look forward to the bombs falling; there's some freedom in that admission. The next time the story arises, you may experience something that delights you. The processing that you did today can take you over, days or weeks from now. It may hit you like a sledgehammer, or you may not even feel it. And just in case, look forward to it. Sit down and write out what's left. It's not easy doing mental surgery on a fifty-five-year-old phantom. Thank you for your courage, sweetheart.

Mom Didn't Stop the Incest

I have worked with hundreds of people (mostly women) who are hope-lessly trapped by their own tormented thinking about their rape or incest. Many of them still suffer, every day of their lives, from their thoughts of the past. Again and again, I have seen inquiry help them overcome any obstacle that they have innocently used to prevent their healing. Through the four questions and turnaround, they come to see what no one but they can realize for themselves: that their present pain is self-inflicted. And as they watch this realization unfold, they begin to set themselves free.

Notice how each statement in the following dialogue appears to be about a past event. In reality, the pain we feel about a past event is created in the present, whatever our past pain might have been. Inquiry looks at this present pain. Even though I lead Diane back to the scene where the event took place, and she answers the questions as if she were in that fear-ful time, she never leaves the perfect safety of the present.

I invite those of you who have had a similar experience to be gentle with yourselves as you read this dialogue and as you consider the answers that can free you from your pain. If at some point you find it difficult to continue, just leave the dialogue for a while. You'll know when to come back to it.

Please be aware that when I ask these questions, in no way am I condoning cruelty or even the smallest unkindness. The perpetrator is not the issue here. My sole focus is the person sitting with me, and I am concerned solely with her freedom.

If you feel that you are a victim of a similar past event, I invite you to take some extra time with two parts of your inquiry. First, after you ask yourself question 3 and realize the pain that results from your thought, ask the additional questions I ask Diane: How many times did it happen? How many times have you relived it in your mind? Second, when you discover your own part in the event, however small—your innocent compliance with the act, for the sake of love or in order to escape worse harm— let yourself feel the power of owning that part, and feel how painful it is to deny it. Then take the time to forgive yourself for any pain you've inflicted on yourself. The identity that's left after that may not feel like the identity of a victim at all.

———

Diane: I am angry at my mother because she allowed me to be abused by my stepfather and never did anything to stop it even though she knew it was going on.

Katie: So, "She knew it was going on"—is that true?

Diane: Yes.

Katie: Is that really true? Did you ask her? Let's do a yes or a no.

Diane: No.

Katie: Did she see the abuse?

Diane: No.

Katie: Did he tell her?

Diane: No, but three other girls did, who were also being abused.

Katie: They told her that he was abusing you?

Diane: No. That he was abusing them.

Katie: So, "She knew that he was abusing you"—is that true? Can you absolutely know that that's true? I don't want to play around here. Where I go with it is: Yes, she probably made that assumption, and yes, she was informed by them, and yes, she probably knew that he was capable of this. I'm not missing this part; I want you to know that. But "She knew that he was abusing you"—can you absolutely know that that's true?

Diane: No.

Katie: I'm not asking if she could easily have guessed it. But sometimes you think something is going on and you're not quite sure, so you just don't mentally go there, because you don't really want to find out, you think it would be too horrible. Have you ever experienced that?

Diane: Yes. I have.

Katie: I have, too. So that puts us in the position of understanding. I can see how someone could live that way, because I used to live like that in so many ways. How do you react when you think the thought "She knew what was going on, and she did nothing"?

Diane: I get angry.

Katie: And how do you treat her when you think that thought?

Diane: I don't talk to her. I see her as a co-conspirator. I see her as using me to do her job. I hate her, and I want nothing to do with her.

Katie: And how does it feel to see her that way? To be motherless?

Diane: Very sad. Lonely.

Katie: Who would you be without the thought "She knew what was going on, and she did nothing"?

Diane: At peace.

Katie: "She knew what was going on, and she did nothing"—turn it around. "I . . ."

Diane: I knew what was going on, and I did nothing.

Katie: Is that as true or truer? Did you tell her? Did you tell anyone?

Diane: No.

Katie: There was a reason for that. What were your thoughts when you wanted to tell her and you didn't say anything?

Diane: I kept seeing my older sister being beaten.

Katie: By your stepfather?

Diane: Yes. She had the courage to stand up and say, "This abuse is going on." And my mother just sat there.

Katie: While your sister was being beaten.

Diane [sobbing]: And I don't know how to let it go. I don't know how . . .

Katie: Honey, isn't that what you're doing in this chair today—learning how to inquire and allow the pain to let go of you? Let's keep moving through this surgery. How old were you when you saw your sister being beaten for telling?

Diane: Eight.

Katie: Okay, I'll talk to the eight-year-old you. So answer from that place. Little eight-year-old, "If you tell your mother, you'll be beaten, too"—can you really know that that's true? And I'm not saying that it's not true. This is just a question.

Diane: Yes.

Katie: That's how it looks, little girl; you have the proof. And I'm asking you to go deeper inside. Can you absolutely know that if you tell the truth, you'll be beaten? And let's go with a yes if you need to; that's your answer for now, and I love that we respect it. You seem to have the evidence that would lead you to believe that it's true. And, little girl, can you really know that that would happen to you, too? [There is a long pause.] Both answers are equal, honey.

Diane: That's the only thing that I can see happening. Either he'd beat me or I'd be sent away.

Katie: So the answer is no. I hear from you that there might have been another option. Let's look at it, okay? So, little girl, "If you tell, you'll be sent away"—can you really know that that's true?

Diane: I don't know which would be worse, though—the staying or leaving.

Katie: Being beaten or leaving. How do you react when you think that thought "I'll either be beaten or sent away if I tell"?

Diane: Scared. And I don't tell anyone.

Katie: And then what happens?

Diane: I withdraw into myself. I can't make up my mind what I want to do. I don't say anything.

Katie: Yes, and then what happens when you don't say anything?

Diane: He comes into my room, and I still don't say anything.

Katie: And then what happens?

Diane: He just continues.

Katie: Yes, honey, it continues. This isn't about a right or wrong. We're just taking a look here. The abuse continues. What was going on, sweetheart?

Diane: It was sexual abuse.

Katie: Was there penetration?

Diane: Yes.

Katie: So, little girl, can you see a reason to drop the thought "If I tell, I'll either be beaten or sent away"? And I'm not asking you to drop the thought. Your decision not to tell could have saved your life. We're just investigating here.

Diane: I can't see a reason. I don't know how to make that decision. He just kept coming into my room. He wouldn't stop.

Katie: Okay, angel, I see that. So he just kept coming into your room. Let's go back again. How often did he come into your room?

Diane: Whenever my mother wasn't there.

Katie: Yes. So, once a month? Once a week? And I realize there's no way you could know accurately. But what does it seem like to you?

Diane: Sometimes it was every night. She was at school. Sometimes it could go on for weeks.

Katie: Yes, sweetheart. So that's a reason to drop the thought "If I tell, I'll either be beaten or sent away." The abuse continued and continued.

Diane: Oh.

Katie: This is not about making a right decision or a wrong decision. The abuse continued. How do you react when you believe the thought that you'll be beaten or sent away? Night after night, he came into your room when your mother went to school. Give me a reason to keep this story that is not stressful inside you, or rape-making.

Diane: There is none. Every thought of it is . . .

Katie: A torture chamber? How many times did you see your sister beaten for telling?

Diane: Just that once.

Katie: How many times did your stepfather come into your room? Many times, yes? Which would be less painful, that or the beating?

Diane: The beating would be much less painful.

Katie: Little girls, even big girls, don't realize these things. We're just taking a look inside the fear today. What was the worst that happened? Can you go into the sexual act, sweetheart? The sexual act with him, and your experience of it? Go to the time that was the most painful, the very worst time. How old are you?

Diane: Nine.

Katie: Okay, so tell me, little girl, what's going on?

Diane [crying]: We had met my grandfather at an ice-cream parlor because it was my birthday. And when we left, my mother told me to ride with my stepfather. And he made me sit on his lap while he was driving. He grabbed my arm and pulled me over.

Katie: Yes. Okay. So, what was the most painful part?

Diane: It was my birthday, and I just wanted to be loved.

Katie: Yes, honey. Yes. What we do for love. . . . That's what you are. And when you're confused, it takes interesting directions, doesn't it? So tell me about that. Tell me about seeking love. What happened? What were your thoughts? He pulled you over. What was your part?

Diane: I just let it happen.

Katie: Yes. Was there a part there where you pretended it was okay... for love? What was your part? [To audience] If any of you have had a similar experience, go inside now, if you can, and answer the question. "What was your part? What is your part?" This is not about blame. Be gentle with yourself. This is about your freedom. [To Diane] What was your part? You just let it happen and ...

Diane [crying]: I loved him.

Katie: Yes. That's how that is. Yes, honey. So what was the most painful part?

Diane: It wasn't the sex. It was that he just left. He just left me in the car, got out, and started walking.

Katie: That he left. So the sitting on his lap wasn't the worst. It's not getting what you were seeking that was the worst. You were just left there. No payoff for the sacrifice. No payoff for seeking what we can never really find from another. Have you heard my prayer, if I had one? I once experienced what you did. I got just a taste of it. But my prayer—if I had one—would be: "God, spare me from seeking love, approval, or appreciation. Amen."

Diane: So that makes me just as guilty as him?

Katie: No, sweetheart: just as innocent. How could you have known another way? If you had known another way, wouldn't you have gone for it?

Diane: Yes.

Katie: Yes. So where's the guilt in that? We're all looking for love, in our confusion, until we find our way back to the realization that love is what we already are. That's all. We're looking for what we already have. Little eight-year-olds, little nine-year-olds. Little forty- and fifty- and eighty-year-olds. We're guilty of seeking love, that's all. Always looking for what we already have. It's a very painful search. Were you doing the best you could?

Diane: Yes.

Katie: Yes. Maybe he was too. "He abused me"—turn it around. "I ..."

Diane: I abused me?

Katie: Yes. Can you see that? Again, this is not about right or wrong.

Diane: Yes, I can see that. I can see that.

Katie: This is a great insight on your part, angel. So just be with that little girl a moment. You might eventually want to shut your eyes and imagine that you are holding her in your arms. And you might want to make a few gentle amends to her. Let her know that you'll always be there for her if she needs someone. She didn't know what you're learning today, that's all. She lived that for your education now, today. There is no greater teacher for you than she is. She's the one who has lived through what you need to know now. She's the one you can believe. She lived it so that you don't have to live it. She is where your wisdom lies. We're just getting a taste of this beautiful little girl who would live that way for the sake of your freedom today. Sweetheart, there's another turnaround. "He abused me." "I abused me." There's another turnaround. "I . . ."

Diane: I . . .

Katie: ". . . abused . . ."

Diane: . . . abused . . . [There is a long pause.] I abused . . . him? That's a hard one.

Katie: Tell me about that. Sweetheart, he did this much [holds her hands wide apart]. You did this much [holds her hands almost touching]. That's what you need to know—this little bit—to set yourself free. This is yours. And this little bit could hurt as much as that huge amount. Tell me. "He abused me"—turn it around. "I . . ."

Diane: I abused him.

Katie: Yes, sweetheart. Tell me about it. Let's go in for the surgery.

Diane: After it happened . . . I could basically get anything I wanted from him.

Katie: Yes, honey. Yes. What we'll do for love, approval, or appreciation, huh? This is self-realization. What else?

Diane: I sometimes think that if I'd said something sooner, the end of it would have been so much different.

Katie: We can't know that either, can we, honey? What I know is that I am a respecter of your path, because I know the value of my own. Whatever it takes for you to find your freedom, that's what you've lived. Not one ingredient more or less. That's what that little girl has lived for you. All of it. She holds the key to your freedom today. So, sweetheart, of the two positions, which role would be the most painful for you, his role or yours? A man who would penetrate a little eight- or nine-year-old, or the eight- or nine-year-old? Which would be the most painful position for you to live? If you had to choose one.

Diane: I would think his.

Katie: Yes? So your answer tells me that you know the pain he was living, through your own eyes, and what it feels like—the hell that it is—to do harm. Sweetheart, let's look at the next one. You're doing very well. You walk through yourself very sweetly. Quite a surgery you're doing here. I see you're tired of the pain.

Diane: Yes. I don't want to pass it on to my son.

Katie: Yes, your son doesn't need this kind of pain. But he'll have to wear it as long as you hold on to it. That's not a choice. He is the world as you perceive it to be. And he'll mirror that back to you as long as you hold on to it. You're doing this surgery for him, too. He'll follow you—he has to, just as the hand in the mirror moves when your hand moves.

Diane: My mother blamed me for it happening and asked me to lie about it to the courts, so she wouldn't lose her alimony and child support.

Katie: And did you lie?

Diane: No.

Katie: And then what happened?

Diane: Nobody believed me.

Katie: And then what happened?

Diane: I was sent away.

Katie: Yes. How old were you?

Diane: Fourteen.

Katie: And have you had contact with her since?

Diane: Off and on over the years. Not recently, though. Not for two years.

Katie: You love her, don't you?

Diane: Yes.

Katie: There's nothing you can do about that.

Diane: I know I can't get rid of it.

Katie: So, you may want to call her today and let her know, just for your sake. Tell her what you've found here about yourself, not what you've found out about her or your sister or your stepfather or anything that would cause her pain. Call her when you really know that your call is about your own freedom and has nothing to do with her. What I hear from you is that you love her and there's nothing she or you can do to change that. Tell her because you love to hear yourself sing your song. This is about your happiness, sweetheart. Read your statement again.

Diane: I am angry at my mother because she allowed me to be abused by my stepfather and never did anything to stop it even though she knew it was going on.

Katie: Turn it around.

Diane: I am angry at myself because I allowed me to be abused by my stepfather and never did anything to stop it.

Katie: Yes. You know that song "Looking for Love in All the Wrong Places"? We're children, sweetheart, we're babies just learning how to live out our love. We keep trying to meet love in everything and everyone, because we haven't noticed that we already have it, that we *are* it. Let's look at the next one.

Diane: She never loved me like she loved her natural son.

Katie: Can you really know that that's true? It's a tough one, hmm?

Diane: I hear myself saying it, and I know it's not true.

Katie: You're amazing. Good. So how do you treat her when you believe that thought? How did you treat her growing up in that house?

Diane: I gave her hell.

Katie: Yes. How did it feel to give hell to this mother you love so much?

Diane: I hated myself for it.

Katie: Yes, angel. Can you see a reason to drop the thought "She loves her natural son more than she loves me"?

Diane: Yes.

Katie: Yes, hell is a reason. [Katie and Diane laugh.] Give me a stress-free reason to keep this thought.

Diane: I haven't found one yet. I can't imagine that I'm going to find it.

Katie: Who or what would you be without this story?

Diane: I'd be better to myself, I'd be better to my son. I wouldn't be so angry.

Katie: Yes. How would you turn that around?

Diane: I never loved myself like I loved her natural son.

Katie: Does that make sense to you?

Diane: I did love him and treated him the way I wanted to be taken care of.

Katie: Oh, honey . . . Why does that not surprise me?

Diane: He was lovable, you know?

Katie: I do. I can see him through your sweet eyes. It's visible. After you've been doing inquiry for a while, if you have the thought "She doesn't love me," you just get the immediate turnaround with a smile: "Oh, I'm not loving myself in this moment." "She doesn't care about me": "Oh, I'm not caring about myself in the moment I think that thought." Feel it, feel what it's like to think that thought, how unkind you're being to yourself when you believe it. That's how you know that you're not caring about yourself. Just keep mothering yourself, sweetheart. That's what this Work does—it holds us, it mothers and fathers us. In the realization of love, of who we really are, from that place we've been looking for, that knows its true self and knows what's true. Let's look at the next statement.

Diane: I want Mom to admit she was wrong and to apologize to me.

Katie: Whose business is it if she was wrong, and whose business is it whether or not she apologizes?

Diane: Hers.

Katie: So turn it around.

Diane: I want me to admit I was wrong and to apologize to me.

Katie: And there's another one.

Diane: I want me to apologize to Mom. And to admit that I was wrong.

Katie: Just in those areas that you know weren't right for you. Apologize for what you see as your small part in this, and apologize for your own sake. Again, her part could be like this [hands extended wide]. That's not your business. Let's get your part cleaned up. You sit with it, make your list, and call her, for your own freedom's sake.

Diane: I've wanted to.

Katie: I say, call her with specifics. Tell her your part in this. We want to apologize, but we don't even know why or how. This Work can not only show you, but it can take you into all the hidden corners of it and flood them with light as you go. It's a thorough housecleaning. And until it's done, there's no peace. This Work is the key to your heart. It makes it all so simple. The truth, I hear from you today, is that you love her.

Diane: Yes.

Katie: Okay, read this one again.

Diane: I want Mom to admit that she was wrong and to apologize to me.

Katie: Is that true? Is that really true?

Diane: I think so.

Katie: And if you think it would hurt her, if it's a little more than she can deal with now, do you still want her to apologize?

Diane: I don't want to hurt her.

Katie: No. That's usually why people don't apologize, it's just too painful to face what they've done. They're not ready yet. And you're one who knows about that kind of thing. In that, you discover who you are.

Diane: That's what I want. I just want to be at peace.

Katie: Well, honey, that little nine-year-old girl who would sit on a man's lap and be penetrated for his love—that's a big one. That's like love to the death. So we're learning who and what we are under the confusion. Let's look at the next statement.

Diane: Mom should love me and know that I love her.

Katie: Is that true? Isn't this starting to sound like a dictatorship? [Diane and the audience laugh.] And have you also noticed that it's hopeless to dictate people's awareness or behavior? So let's turn it around. She loves you, but she may not know it yet, and that lack of awareness is very painful. I am very clear that the whole world loves me. I just don't expect them to realize it yet. [The audience laughs.] So, let's turn it around and see where some awareness will work in your life now.

Diane: I should love me and know that I love me.

Katie: Yes, it's not her job. It's no one's job but yours.

Diane: I'm getting there.

Katie: Yes, you are. There's another turnaround. See if you can find it.

Diane: I should love Mom and know that I love her.

Katie: And you do. There are just a few little uninvestigated thoughts here and there to interrupt the awareness of this fact. And now you know how to meet them. It's a beginning. All right, let's look at the next statement.

Diane: I need Mom to tell the family that she was wrong.

Katie: Is that true?

Diane [laughing]: No.

Katie: No. The nightmare always becomes laughter, once it's understood. Turn it around and see what real understanding is possible.

Diane: I need me to tell the family that I was wrong.

Katie: How sweet it is.

Diane: I could have stopped it earlier by speaking up. I was wrong. But now I'm right . . .

Katie: Yes.

Diane [in a whisper, crying]: I'm right.

Katie: It's obviously time that you know that. Isn't it marvelous to discover that you're the one you've been waiting for? That you are your own freedom? You go with inquiry into the darkness and find only light. And now you can see, even when you've been to the depths of hell, that that's all that was ever there—ever. We just haven't known how to go in, sweetheart. Now we do. What a trip! Let's look at the next statement.

Diane: Mom is a repressed asshole. [Laughing] I might as well just do the turnaround right here and now. I'm a repressed asshole. [Diane and everyone else laugh even harder. The audience breaks into applause.]

Katie: Sometimes. I like to say about myself, "But only for forty-three years"—which is when I woke up to reality. So, you can put that on your list of amends. What was it like for you to live as a repressed . . .

Diane [laughing]: Very tight. [Loud laughter from the audience] Wow! I understand now. It has nothing to do with her! Nothing! It's all me! It's all me! [A long silence. There is a look of wonderment on Diane's face.]

Katie: So, sweetheart, I suggest that you gently take yourself to the back of the room and just lie down with your beautiful self. Just let everything you've realized in this session have you. Let it take you over and make the changes it will make. Just be still and let the realization unfold.

I'm Angry at Sam for Dying

It takes a great deal of courage to see through the story of a death. Parents and relatives of children who have died are especially attached to their stories, for reasons that we all understand. Leaving our sadness behind, or even inquiring into it, may seem like a betrayal of our child. Many of us aren't ready to see things another way yet, and that's as it should be.

Who thinks that death is sad? Who thinks that a child shouldn't die? Who thinks that they know what death is? Who tries to teach God, in story after story, thought after thought? Is it you? I say, let's investigate, if you're up for it, and see if it's possible to end the war with reality.

———

Gail: This is about my nephew, Sam, who recently died. I was very close to him. I helped bring him up.

Katie: Good, sweetheart. Read what you've written.

Gail: I'm angry at Sam for dying. I'm angry that Sam is gone. I'm angry that Sam took such stupid risks. I'm angry that at twenty he's gone in a blink. I'm angry that Sam slipped and fell sixty feet off the mountain. I want Sam back. I want Sam to be more careful. I want Sam to let me know that he's fine. I want the image of his body falling sixty feet off the cliff, landing on his head, to go away. Sam should have stuck around.

Katie: "Sam should have stuck around"—is that true? This is our religion, the kind of belief that we live by but haven't known how to examine. [To audience] You may want to go inside and ask for yourself, about the one who divorced you, or who died and left you, or about your children who moved away, "That person should have stuck around"—is that really true? [To Gail] Read it again.

Gail: Sam should have stuck around.

Katie: Is that true? What's the reality of it? Did he?

Gail: No. He left. He died.

Katie: How do you react when you think this thought, this concept, that argues with reality?

Gail: I feel tired and sad, and I feel separate.

Katie: That's how it feels to argue with what is. It's very stressful. I'm a lover of reality, not because I'm a spiritual woman, but because it hurts when I argue with what is. And I notice that I lose, 100 percent of the time. It's hopeless. We take these concepts to the grave with us, if they're not examined. Concepts *are* the grave we bury ourselves in.

Gail: Yes. It's always stressful when I think that.

Katie: So, angel, who would you be without that thought?

Gail: I'd feel happy again.

Katie: Which is why you want him to live. "If he were alive, then I'd be happy." This is using him for your happiness.

Gail: Right.

Katie: We live; we die. Always right on time, not one moment sooner or later than we do. Who would you be without your story?

Gail: I'd be here, present in my own life, and I'd let Sam do his thing.

Katie: You'd even let him die in his own time?

Gail: Yes. As if I had any choice. I would be here instead of . . .

Katie: In the grave. Or falling off the mountain with Sam, over and over again in your mind.

Gail: Yes.

Katie: So, your story is "Sam should stick around." Turn it around.

Gail: I should stick around.

Katie: Yes. Your story that Sam shouldn't have died is yourself mentally falling off that cliff he falls off. *You* should stick around instead and mentally stay out of his business. This is possible.

Gail: I understand.

Katie: Sticking around would look like this: woman sitting in chair with friends, present, living her life, not mentally returning to that cliff to watch Sam fall, over and over. There's another turnaround to "Sam should stick around." Can you find it?

Gail: Sam should *not* stick around.

Katie: Yes, angel. He's gone in the way that you knew him. Reality rules. It doesn't wait for our vote, our permission, or our opinion—have you noticed? What I love most about reality is that it's always the story of a past. And what I love most about the past is that it's over. And because I'm no longer insane, I don't argue with it. Arguing with it feels unkind inside me. Just to notice what is is love. And how do I personally know that Sam lived a full life? It's over. He lived it to the end—*his* end, not the end you think he should have had. That's reality. It hurts to fight what is. And doesn't it feel more honest to open your arms wide to it? This is the end of war.

Gail: I can see that.

Katie: Okay, let's look at the next statement.

Gail: I need Sam back.

Katie: That's a good one. Is it true?

Gail: No.

Katie: No. It's just a story, a lie. [To audience] The reason I call it a lie is that I asked her, "Is it true?" and she said no. [To Gail] How do you react when you believe the story "I need Sam back," and he's not back?

Gail: Shut down inside. Anxious. Depressed.

Katie: Who would you be without the thought "I need Sam back"?

Gail: I'd be back. I'd be alive again, connecting with what's in front of me.

Katie: Yes. Just as you felt when he was here.

Gail: Right. If I let him go, I'd have what I wanted. Thinking I need him now keeps me from having what I've been wanting ever since he died.

Katie: So, "I need Sam back"—turn it around.

Gail: I need *myself* back.

Katie: And another turnaround?

Gail: I *don't* need Sam back.

Katie: Yes. You keep going back to that cliff and falling off with Sam. So come back yourself. You keep thinking, "Oh, I wish he hadn't done that." But *you* keep doing it, over and over, in your mind. You just keep falling off that cliff. So if you need help, turn it around, see how you can help yourself. Let's look at the next statement.

Gail: I need to know that Sam is totally fine and at peace.

Katie: "He's not fine"—can you absolutely know that that's true?

Gail: No. I can't know that he's not fine.

Katie: Turn that one around.

Gail: I need to know that *I'm* totally fine and at peace, with or without Sam's body here.

Katie: Yes. *That's* possible. So how are your toes and your knees and your legs and your arms? How are you, sitting here in this moment?

Gail: They're good. I'm fine.

Katie: Are you in any better or worse shape now than when Sam was here?

Gail: No.

Katie: Sitting here right now, in this moment, do you *need* Sam to come back?

Gail: No. That's just a story.

Katie: Good. You investigated. You wanted to know. Now you do.

Gail: Right.

Katie: So let's look at the next statement.

Gail: I need God, or someone, to show me the perfection of Sam's dying.

Katie: Turn it around.

Gail: I need me to show me the perfection of Sam's dying.

Katie: Yes. You don't grieve when the lawnmower cuts the grass. You don't look for the perfection in the grass dying, because it's visible to you. In fact, when the grass grows, you cut it. In the fall, you don't grieve because the leaves are falling and dying. You say, "Isn't it beautiful!" Well, we're the same way. There are seasons. We all fall sooner or later. It's all so beautiful. And our concepts, without investigation, keep us from knowing this. It's beautiful to be a leaf, to be born, to fall, to give way to the next, to become food for the roots. It's life, always changing its form and always giving itself completely. We all do our part. No mistake. [Gail begins to cry.] What are your thoughts, sweetheart?

Gail: I really like what you're saying, talking about it as beauty, as part of the seasons. It makes me feel glad and appreciative. I can see it in a bigger way, and I can appreciate life and death and the cycles. It's like a window I can look through and see it differently, see how I could hold it in that way, and how I could appreciate Sam and the way he died.

Katie: Do you realize that he's given you life?

Gail: Yes. He's like the fertilizer, or the soil that's growing me right now.

Katie: So that you can give it back and live as appreciation, fully nourished, as you understand our pain and give us the new life you're realizing. Whatever happens, that's what's needed. There is no mistake in nature. Look how painful it is to have a story that won't embrace such beauty, such perfection. Lack of understanding is always painful.

Gail: Until now, I couldn't really see it as beauty. I mean, I've seen beauty come to me from Sam's death, but I couldn't see the actual death—him dying—as beauty. I only saw it as him being a twenty-year-old doing stupid things. But he was just doing it his way.

Katie: Oh, my . . . Who would you be without that story?

Gail: I'd appreciate his death, the way you appreciate the leaves. I could appreciate him going out that way, instead of thinking it was wrong.

Katie: Yes, honey. Through self-inquiry, we see that only love remains. Without an uninvestigated story, there's only the perfection of life appearing as itself. You can always go inside and find the beauty that's revealed after the pain and fear are understood. Let's look at the next statement.

Gail: Sam is gone, dead. Sam is the beloved boy I got to mother. Sam is exquisitely beautiful, gentle, kind, a good listener, curious, brilliant, nonjudgmental, accepting, strong, powerful. Sam is riding the crest of a wave.

Katie: Read the first part of that again.

Gail: Sam is gone, dead.

Katie: Is that true? "Sam is dead"—can you absolutely know that that's true?

Gail: No.

Katie: Show me death. Get a microscope and show me. Put the cells of a dead body under the lens, and show me what death is. Is it anything more than a concept? Where does Sam live? Here [touching her head and heart]. You wake up and think of him; that's where Sam lives. You lie down at night; there he is in your mind. And every night, when you go to sleep, if you're not dreaming, that's death. When there's no story, there's no life. You open your eyes in the morning, and the "I" begins. Life begins. The Sam story begins. Did you miss him before the story began? Nothing lives but a story, and when we meet these stories with understanding, we *really* begin to live, without the suffering. So, how do you react when you think that thought?

Gail: I feel dead inside. I feel terrible.

Katie: Can you see a reason to drop the story "Sam's dead"? And I'm not asking you to drop your story, this idea that you hold so dear. We love our old-time religion, even though it doesn't work. We devote ourselves to it day in and day out, in every culture of the world.

Gail: Yes.

Katie: Inquiry doesn't have a motive. It doesn't teach a philosophy. It's just investigation. So, who would you be without the story "Sam's dead"? Even though he's mentally living with you all the time.

Gail: He's probably here more now, right now, than he was when he was in his body.

Katie: So who would you be without the story?

Gail: I'd appreciate the fertilizer. And I'd love being where I am, rather than living in the past.

Katie: So turn it around.

Gail: I'm gone, *I'm* dead, when I go into my story about Sam dying.

Katie: Yes.

Gail: I really see that now. Are we done?

Katie: Yes, sweetheart. And we always begin now.

Terrorism in New York City

After the events of September 11, 2001, the media and our political leaders said that America had begun a war against terrorism and that everything had changed. When people came to do The Work with me, I found that nothing had changed. People like Emily were frightening themselves with their uninvestigated thoughts, and after they found the terrorist inside them, they could return to their families, to their normal lives, in peace.

A teacher of fear can't bring peace on earth. We have been trying to do it that way for thousands of years. The person who turns inner violence around, the person who finds peace inside and lives it, is the one who teaches what true peace is. We are waiting for just one teacher. You're the one.

———

Emily: Ever since the terrorist attack on the World Trade Center last Tuesday, I've been terrified that I'll be killed in the subway or in my office building, right near Grand Central and the Waldorf. I keep thinking how scarred my sons would be if they lost me. They're only one and four years old.

Katie: Yes, sweetheart. So, "Terrorists could attack you in the subway."

Emily: Uh-huh.

Katie: Can you absolutely know that that's true?

Emily: That it's possible, or that it will happen?

Katie: That it will happen.

Emily: I can't know that it will happen, but I do know that it's possible.

Katie: And how do you react when you think that thought?

Emily: I feel terrified. I already feel sad about my loss, for myself, my husband, and my kids.

Katie: And how do you treat people on the subway when you think that thought?

Emily: I feel shut down, very shut down.

Katie: How do you treat yourself when you think that thought and you're on the subway?

Emily: Well, I try to repress the thought, and I focus a lot on reading and doing what I'm doing. I'm tight.

Katie: And where does your mind travel when you're tight and you think that thought as you're reading on the subway?

Emily: I just keep picturing my children's faces.

Katie: So you're in your children's business. You're reading a book on the subway full of people, and in your mind you're seeing the faces of your children with you dead.

Emily: Yes.

Katie: Does this thought bring stress or peace into your life?

Emily: Definitely stress.

Katie: Who would you be on the subway without that thought? Who would you be if you were incapable of thinking the thought "A terrorist could kill me on the subway"?

Emily: If I couldn't think the thought . . . you mean if my mind wouldn't do it? [Pause] Well, I would be like I was last Monday, before the attack happened.

Katie: So you'd be a little more comfortable on the subway than you are.

Emily: Much more comfortable. I grew up on the subways. I'm actually quite comfortable on the subway without that thought.

Katie: "A terrorist can kill me on the subway"—how would you turn that around?

Emily: I can kill myself on the subway?

Katie: Yes. The killing is going on in your mind. The only terrorist on the subway in that moment is you terrifying yourself with your thoughts. What else did you write?

Emily: I am furious at my family—my husband, my parents, all of us live here in New York City—for not helping me make a contingency plan in case the terrorism here gets worse, finding a place where we can all meet outside the city, getting our passports updated, some money out of the bank. I'm furious at them for being so passive, for making me feel crazy for trying to make a plan.

Katie: So, "I am furious at my family"—let's just turn that one around. "I'm furious . . ."

Emily: I'm furious at myself for not helping me make a contingency plan?

Katie: Can you see that? Quit being so passive. Get a contingency plan, not just for you and your children and husband, for your whole family in New York. Get a plan for everyone.

Emily: I am trying, but they're making me feel like I'm nuts for doing that. I'm angry about that.

Katie: Well, apparently they don't need a plan. And they don't want a plan. You're the one who needs a contingency plan, so make a contingency plan for the evacuation of New York.

Emily [laughing]: That sounds so funny.

Katie: I know. I find that so often self-realization leaves us only with laughter.

Emily: But I'm still angry that they made me feel like a nut.

Katie: Can you find it, that part of you that is a nut?

Emily: Well, I did do the same thing with Y2K, so I guess they've been through this with me before. I *am* a bit on the paranoid side.

Katie: So they're right, according to their world. They have a point. You could work on your contingency plan in peace, not expecting them to want to go.

Emily: I'll make my kids go.

Katie: Because they're small, and you can put them both under your arms and run for it. Buckle them in the car and just drive.

Emily: I think I'd better learn how to drive. I don't have a driver's license.

Katie [laughing]: You're angry at your family because they don't have a contingency plan, and you don't have a driver's license?

Emily [laughing]: Now that is ridiculous. I can see that. I'm judging them, and I can't even drive if I need to. How could I not have seen this?

Katie: Now, let's say you have the license, and the tunnels and bridges are all closed. You need to get another plan. You need to get five more jobs so you can buy a private helicopter.

Emily [laughing]: Okay, okay.

Katie: But they wouldn't let those fly either.

Emily: No. Definitely not.

Katie: So there you are. Maybe that's why your family doesn't bother with a contingency plan. They notice that the tunnels were shut down; planes weren't allowed in the air last week; there was no way out. Maybe they understand that. Maybe you're the last to know.

Emily: That really could be.

Katie: So it just leaves us to find peace from where we are. To make a contingency plan work, from what I've seen of reality, you need to be psychic, so you can know ahead of time when to evacuate and where to go that would be safe.

Emily: Part of me thinks I should get out now. But then of course the problem is where is safe? Talk about needing to be psychic . . .

Katie: So you need to work on your psychic abilities. And from what I've seen, psychics don't win the lottery.

Emily: That's true.

Katie: So, "You need a contingency plan"—is that true? Can you absolutely know that that's true?

Emily: I guess I can't know that that's true any more. It's kind of a relief.

Katie: Oh, honey, just feel it. Maybe that's what your family knows.

Emily: I think I'm not such a good planner after all. There is no plan to have.

Katie: Of course not. You can't outsmart reality. Where you are right now might be the safest place in the world. We just don't know.

Emily: I honestly never thought of that.

Katie: So who would you be without the thought "I need a contingency plan"?

Emily: Less anxious, less on alert, lighter. [Pause] But also more upset. [Crying] Sad. Very, very sad. All those people died. My city changed. There's nothing I can do.

Katie: Okay, so that's the reality of it. There's nothing you can do. That's humility. For me, that's a sweet thing.

Emily: I'm just so used to being proactive, to making things happen, at least for the people close to me, to protecting them.

Katie: And feeling in control. It works for a while. But then reality catches up with us. But if we take all that amazing ability, that proactiveness, and mix it with humility, then that's really something. Then we can be clear and helpful. "I need a contingency plan"—turn it around.

Emily: I don't need a contingency plan.

Katie: Feel it. Can you see how that could be just as true? How it could be even truer?

Emily: Could be. I can see that it could be truer.

Katie: Oh, sweetheart. Me, too. That's why I'm always so comfortable where I am. When you run in fear, it's square into the wall. Then you look back at where you were, and you see that it was much safer. And without a contingency plan, when something happens, it just comes to you what to do. You can find everything you need to know right where you are. And in reality, you already live that. When you need a pen, you reach over and you take it. If there's not a pen there, you go get one. And that's what it's like in an emergency. Without fear, what to do is just as clear as reaching and picking up a pen. But fear isn't so efficient. Fear is blind and deaf. Let's hear what else you've written.

Emily: Okay. *I think the terrorists are so ignorant in their hatred and their need to feel powerful. They are so desperate to hurt us. They'd do anything . . . why not poison or car bombs? They're evil, ignorant, and yes, they're successful and powerful. They can destroy this country. They're like locusts, everywhere, hiding, waiting to hurt us, disrupt us, kill us.*

Katie: So, "These terrorists are evil."

Emily: Yes.

Katie: Can you absolutely know that that's true?

Emily: I think I can know that they are ignorant. They're ignorant about the effects of violence on us.

Katie: Can you absolutely know that that's true? That they're ignorant about that? This is a good one, sweetheart. Can you know that they're ignorant about pain and death and suffering?

Emily: No. They're not ignorant about that, because they've probably experienced it. I can't know that that's true, but I think they probably have. And that's what they're reacting to. But they're still ignorant about the fact that violence never works.

Katie: Or they're not ignorant. They believe a thought that's the opposite of yours: that violence works. That's what they think the whole world has taught them. They are in the grip of that thought.

Emily: But it doesn't work, really. To hurt another person, you either have to be ignorant, confused, or a psychopath.

Katie: You could be right, and a lot of people would agree with you, but what we're looking at here is not the right or wrong of it. So let's go back to what you read and turn it around.

Emily: I think the terrorists are so ignorant in their hatred and their need to feel powerful.

Katie: Turn it around.

Emily: I am so ignorant in my hatred and my need to feel powerful. That's true. I needed my contingency plan to make me feel powerful.

Katie: Yes, and how does it feel to hate?

Emily: Well, it does empower me for the moment. I mean, it makes me feel less helpless.

Katie: And then what happens when you hate?

Emily: I'm stuck. I can't get past it, and it's consuming.

Katie: And you have to find a way of defending that position. You have to prove that you're right about your hatred. That it's valid and worthwhile. And how does it feel to live that way? How do you react when you think the thought that they're evil and ignorant?

Emily: In the context of what we're saying, it feels pretty false, actually. I'm not sure that I even feel that way anymore.

Katie: But from their position, their hatred is absolutely valid. They're willing to die for it. It's a matter of right. That's what they believe. They're crashing their lives into buildings.

Emily: Yes.

Katie: Their hatred is no obstacle to them. That's what it's like when we're attached to a concept. And that concept is "You are evil, and I'll die to take you out." It's for the good of the world.

Emily: I can see that.

Katie: So continue with the turnaround.

Emily: I am evil in my ignorance . . .

Katie: . . . of where these people are coming from. They know the suffering it's going to bring to their families when they kill themselves intentionally.

Emily: Okay.

Katie: They're not ignorant on one level, and on another level of course they are, because their thoughts just leave more suffering. So continue to turn around what you wrote after the evil and their ignorance.

Emily: They're evil, ignorant, and yes, they're successful and powerful.

Katie: And I . . .

Emily: I am evil, ignorant, successful, and powerful?

Katie: Yes. In all your righteousness.

Emily: Oh, okay. My contingency plan is right, and other people just don't get it.

Katie: So let's continue. "They're like locusts"—turn it around.

Emily: I am like locusts, everywhere, hiding, waiting to hurt me, disrupt me, kill me?

Katie: Yes.

Emily: My thoughts are like locusts.

Katie: Exactly. Your uninvestigated thoughts.

Emily: Right.

Katie: I don't see any terrorists in this moment except the one you live with: yourself.

Emily: Yes. I see that.

Katie: I live in peace, and that's what everyone deserves. We all deserve to end our own terrorism.

Emily: I can understand the arrogance of doing what I've been doing.

Katie: That's where I see the possibility of change. Otherwise, we're like ancient, primitive beings—all willing to die for a cause.

Emily: How are we all willing to die for a cause?

Katie: Well, sweetheart, if someone comes after your children . . . Just watch it.

Emily: Okay. Yes.

Katie: I mean, you're even angry with your parents because they won't get a contingency plan. And feel what it feels like to go to war against your own family.

Emily: Yes.

Katie: What's the matter with them? You would grab them, with them screaming, "I just want to be left alone." You grab them and haul them out

—to where? For all you know, you move them to the very community that gets hit.

Emily: That's true. That's arrogant, too. Crazy even.

Katie: What else did you write?

Emily: I don't ever want to see an ash-covered person again as I did that day walking home. I don't ever want to see another face mask or a look of shock... Part of the problem is that the media kept showing images of the towers falling over and over again. It felt like it was happening for a whole week.

Katie: "Part of the problem was that the media kept showing it over and over"—turn it around.

Emily: I kept showing it over and over.

Katie: Yes. "I want the media to stop"—turn it around.

Emily: I want me to stop.

Katie: So work on you. Your mind is the media.

Emily: I'm not sure how.

Katie: You could begin by putting those images in your mind up against inquiry. Because in reality, there's no one in front of you covered with ash right now. It's not happening here, except in your mind. [Long pause] Okay. Let's go back and take a look. Describe the ash-covered person in your mind. Describe the one who has the most charge for you. The person you actually saw.

Emily: Well, the one who has the most charge for me was the man who walked by my office building when I was sitting outside waiting for my husband a couple of hours after the World Trade Center towers fell. I work in midtown, so the guy had walked more than sixty blocks. We saw a lot of other ash-covered people when we walked home, but this guy was dressed in an expensive, well-fitted business suit, carrying his briefcase, and he was wearing one of those breath masks that you see on television. And he was absolutely gray—his entire head, his suit, his shoes, his briefcase were covered in ash. The ash was untouched. He was like a zombie, just walking, not looking around. He must have been in shock. He had obviously walked all the way from what was the World Trade Center.

Everything was sunny, and everything here in midtown seemed normal, and then this ghost walked by. That hit me harder than any other image that day. It hit me hard. I thought, "Now it's entering my world. It's here."

Katie: Good, sweetheart. Now I want to look at it with you. "He was like a zombie"—is that true?

Emily: He certainly looked like it.

Katie: Of course he did: Look who's telling the story. The man had his briefcase with him. He thought to take it. Maybe he was simply walking home. There were no subways running. Maybe he wanted to get to his family to let them know he was all right.

Emily: Yes.

Katie: He was being perfectly intelligent. He had on a breath mask. You didn't.

Emily: Hmm.

Katie: So, for all you know, he was doing better than you were.

Emily [after a pause]: That could be. I was nowhere near the disaster, sitting there feeling incredibly stressed-out and afraid.

Katie: "The man was like a zombie"—how do you react when you think that thought?

Emily: I feel horror, as if the world were ending.

Katie: And who would you be, watching that man, without the thought "He is like a zombie"?

Emily: I'd just think, "There's a man covered in ash. I hope he's close to home."

Katie: A really *smart* man. Not a zombie. He got out of the building and even remembered his briefcase. What to do came to him in an instant. I don't think he had a contingency plan: "If the plane hits and if I get out, I think I'll pick up my briefcase as a contingency plan and walk home."

Emily: He had walked sixty blocks or whatever it was. I guess he was an instant symbol in my mind of what had happened.

Katie: Yes, but he could just as easily be a reminder of how efficient you can be when some disaster happens. He had his briefcase. He'd made it for sixty blocks. But how were you doing when you saw him?

Emily: I actually felt like I was going into shock.

Katie: Yes. He was doing fine. You were like a zombie, and you projected it onto him. If you needed someone in a pinch, and you saw yourself standing there and him standing there, who would you go to for help?

Emily [laughing]: I'd go to him. Amazing. But I'd definitely go to him.

Katie: Okay, sweetheart. So, gently, let's turn it around. "I'm willing ..."

Emily: I'm willing to see another ash-covered person.

Katie: Yes, even if only in your mind—because you haven't seen anyone since then walking around like that, except inside you. So reality and the story never match; reality's always kinder. And it's going to be fun to watch how this plays out in your life, especially with your children. They'll learn from you that they don't have to be on guard and have a plan; they'll learn that they'll always know what to do. They'll see that where they are is okay and anywhere they're going is fine. And without the fearful story "I need a contingency plan," various good moves might come to you: a place to meet up with your husband in case the phones don't work. Learning to drive might be useful as your kids get past the toddler stage, keeping a few maps and some other things handy in the car. Who knows what a calm mind will come up with?

Emily: Thank you, Katie. I see that.

Katie: Oh, honey, you're welcome. I love how you don't settle for anything but the pure truth of it.

You move totally away

from reality

when you believe that there is

a legitimate reason

to suffer.

13.

Questions and Answers

When people ask me questions, I answer them as clearly as I can. I'm glad when they tell me that these answers are helpful, but I know that the truly helpful answers are the ones they find by themselves.

Q: I feel overwhelmed by the number of judgments I have. How could I ever possibly have time to investigate all my beliefs?
A: Don't undo all of them. Just undo the belief that's causing you stress now. There is never more than one. Undo that one.

If you really want to know the truth, there is no idea that can't be met with understanding. We're either attaching to our concepts or investigating them. How do I know which one to work with? Here it comes now.

One of the things that I understood about the thoughts appearing inside me was that I was someone to be trusted with them. I was the vessel that they could appear in and finally be met with unconditional love. The same thoughts also came to me through my children, when they were free to tell me how they felt. They came through every other form of communication. They couldn't come fast enough for me, because I knew what to do with them. From my children's mouths or from my mind, I put them on paper, and I inquired. I treated them as what they were: visiting friends, neighbors I had misunderstood, who were kind enough to knock on my door again. Everyone is welcome here.

Judge your neighbor, write it down, ask four questions, and turn it around—just one at a time.

Q: Does freedom always come right after you do The Work?

A: It does in its own way, but you may not recognize it. And you may not necessarily notice a change on the particular issue you've written about. For example, you may have written out a Worksheet on your mother, and the next day you find that your obnoxious neighbor—the one who's been driving you crazy for years—no longer annoys you, that your irritation with her has completely disappeared. Or a week later, you notice that for the first time in your life, you love to cook. It doesn't always happen in one session. I have a friend who did The Work on being jealous of her husband because their little boy preferred him to her. She felt a small release after doing The Work. But the next morning, while she was in the shower, she felt everything give way and began to sob, and afterward all the pain around the situation was gone.

Q: What does it mean if I keep needing to do The Work on the same thing over and over again?

A: It doesn't matter how often you need to do it. You're either attaching to the nightmare or investigating its validity: no other choice. The issue may come back a dozen times, a hundred times. It's always a wonderful opportunity to see what attachments are left and how much deeper you can go.

Q: I've done The Work many times on the same judgment, and I don't think it's working.

A: "You've done The Work many times"—is that true? Could it be that if the answer you think you're looking for doesn't appear, you simply block anything else? Are you frightened of the answer that might be underneath what you think you know? Is it possible that there's another answer within you that could be as true or truer?

When you ask "Is it true?" for example, you may not really want to know. It could be that you'd rather stay with your statement than dive into the unknown. Blocking means rushing the process and answering with your conscious mind before the gentler polarity of mind (I call it "the heart") can answer. If you prefer to stay with what you think you know, the question is blocked and can't have its life inside you.

Notice if you move into the next story before letting yourself fully experience the answer and the feelings that come with it. It can be helpful to catch thoughts that begin with "Well, yes, and . . ." or "Well, yes, but . . ." Thoughts like this indicate that you're shifting away from inquiry. Do you really want to know the truth?

Are you inquiring with a motive? Are you asking the questions to assure yourself that the answer you already have is valid, even though it's painful? Do you want to be right, or to prove something, more than you want the truth? It's the truth that set me free—for richer, for poorer, in sickness and in health. Acceptance, peace, letting go, and less attachment to a world of suffering are all *effects* of doing The Work. They're not goals. Do The Work for the love of freedom, for the love of truth. If you're inquiring with other motives, such as healing the body or solving a problem, your answers may be arising from old motives that never worked, and you'll miss the wonder and grace of inquiry.

Are you doing the turnaround too quickly? If you really want to know the truth, wait for the new answers to surface. Give yourself enough time to let the turnarounds find you and time to experience their effects. If you choose, make a written list of all the ways that the turnaround applies to you. The turnaround is the grounding, the reentry into life, as the truth points you to who you are without your story. It's all done for you.

Are you letting the realizations you experience through inquiry live in you? Live the turnarounds, report your part to others (so that you can hear it again), and make amends, for the sake of your own freedom. This will certainly speed up the process and bring freedom into existence as your own life, now.

Finally, can you really know that inquiry is not working? When the thing you were afraid of happens and you wonder why there is little or no panic, stress, fear, or suffering—that's when you know it's working

Q: *When I'm doing The Work myself, and I sense that I'm blocking inquiry, what can I do?*

A: Continue, if you're up for it. I know that if even one small honest answer or turnaround is allowed to surface from inside you, you will enter a world that you don't even know exists. But if your intention is to be right, rather than to know the truth, why bother continuing? Just realize that the story you're sticking to is more valuable to you now than your freedom, and that that's okay. Come back to inquiry later. You may not be suffering enough, or you may not really care, even though you think you do. Be gentle with yourself. Life will bring you everything you need.

Q: What if my suffering is too intense? Should I still do The Work?
A: Suffering is caused by attachment to a deeply embedded belief. It's a state of blind attachment to something that you think is true. In this state, it's very difficult to do The Work for the love of truth, because you're invested in your story. Your story is your identity, and you'd do almost anything to prove that it's true. If you're hurting, put your proof on paper and investigate that proof. I refer to The Work as checkmate. Inquiry into self is the only thing that has the power to penetrate such ancient concepts.

Even physical pain isn't real; it's the story of a past, always leaving, never arriving. But people don't know that. My grandson Racey fell down once when he was three years old. He scraped his knee, and there was some blood, and he began to cry. And as he looked up at me, I said, "Sweetheart, are you remembering when you fell down and hurt yourself?" And immediately, the crying stopped. That was it. He must have realized, for a moment, that pain is always in the past. The moment of pain is always gone. It's a remembering of what we think is true, and it projects what no longer exists. (I'm not saying that your pain isn't real for you. I know pain, and it hurts! That's why The Work is about the end of suffering.)

If a car runs over your leg and you're lying in the street with story after story running through your mind, chances are that if you're new to The Work, you're not going to think, "'I'm in pain'—is it true? Can I absolutely know that it's true?" You're going to scream, "Get the morphine!" Then, later, when you're in a comfort zone, you can sit down with a pen and paper and do The Work. Give yourself the physical medicine and then the other kind of medicine. Eventually, you can lose your other leg, and you won't see a problem. If you think there's a problem, your Work isn't done.

Q: There are thoughts that I feel I shouldn't think—nasty, perverted, and even violent thoughts. Can The Work help me to not think them?
A: How do you react when you believe that you shouldn't think certain thoughts, and you do? Ashamed? Depressed? Now turn it around—you *should* think them! Doesn't that feel a bit lighter, a bit more honest? Mind wants its freedom, not a straitjacket. When the thoughts come, they aren't

meeting an enemy who is opposing them, like a child who comes to her father, hoping that he'll listen, and instead the father screams at her, "Don't say that! Don't do that! You're wrong, you're bad!" and punishes her when she approaches. What kind of father is that? This is the internal violence that keeps you from understanding.

I can't meet you as an enemy and not feel separate, from you and from myself. So how could I meet a thought within me as an enemy and not feel separate? When I learned to meet my thinking as a friend, I noticed that I could meet every human as a friend. What could you say that hasn't already appeared within me as a thought? The end of the war with myself and my thinking is the end of the war with you. It's so simple.

Q: Is inquiry a process of thinking? If it isn't thinking, what is it?
A: Inquiry appears to be a process of thinking, but actually it's a way to *undo* thinking. Thoughts lose their power over us when we realize that we aren't doing the thinking anyway. Thoughts simply appear in the mind. What if there is no thinker? Are you breathing yourself, too?

The mind can only find its true nature by thinking. What else is there? How else is it going to find itself? It has to leave clues for itself, and it comes to realize that it has dropped its own breadcrumbs. It has come out of itself, but it hasn't realized that yet. Inquiry is the breadcrumbs that allow it to return to itself. The everything returns to the everything. The nothing returns to the nothing.

Q: It seems that when I really go inside, my answer to "Can I absolutely know that it's true?" is always "No." Is there anything we can know for certain?
A: No. Experience is just perception. It's ever-changing. Even "now" is the story of a past. By the time we think it or tell it, it's already gone.

From the moment we attach to a thought, it becomes our religion, and we keep attempting to prove that it's valid. The harder we try to prove what we can't know is true, the more we experience depression and disappointment.

In question 1, the lie can be seen and admitted. When we ask "Is it true?" we often come to find out—as we investigate the statements on our Worksheet, sentence by sentence—that none of what we have written is true. That is meeting each thought with understanding. We innocently believed our own thinking. We didn't have a way to understand that it wasn't true.

When you ask yourself question 1, your mind begins to open. Even to consider that a thought may not be true will let a little light into your mind. If you answer, "Yes, it's true," then you may want to ask yourself question 2, "Can you absolutely know that it's true?" Some people get very agitated, even angry, when they say, "No, I can't absolutely know that!" And then I might ask them to be gentle with themselves and just experience that understanding for a moment. If they sit with their answer, then it does become gentle, and it opens to infinite possibilities, to freedom. It's like stepping out of a narrow, smoky room into open space.

Q: *How can I do The Work if no one around me is doing it? Won't they see me as detached and uncaring? How will my family be able to adjust to my new way of thinking?*

A: No one around me was doing The Work when I began; I did it alone. And yes, your family could see you as detached and uncaring. As you come to see what isn't true for you, and as you experience question 3 ("How do I react, what do I say and do, when I believe that thought?"), there is such a shift inside you that you may lose the most essential agreements with your family. "Charlie should brush his teeth"—is it true? No, not until he does: You have ten years of proof that he hasn't been brushing his teeth regularly. How do you react? For ten years, you've gotten angry, you've threatened him, you've given him "the look," you've gotten frustrated, you've laid guilt on him. Now the whole family is telling Charlie to brush his teeth (just as you've taught them to do through your example), and you're no longer participating. You're betraying the family religion. When they look to you for consent, you can't give it. So now they may begin to shame you for not shaming him, just the way you taught them to do. Your family is an echo of your own past beliefs.

If your truth now is kind, it will run deep and fast within the family and will replace betrayal with a better way. As you continue to find your own way in inquiry, sooner or later your family will come to see as you yourself do. There's no other choice. Your family is a projected image of your thinking. It's your story; nothing else is possible. Until you love your family without conditions, even as they shame Charlie, self-love is not a possibility, and therefore your Work is not done.

Your family will see you as they see you and will leave you to work on them all. How do you see *yourself*? That's the important question. How do you see *them*? If I think that they need The Work, then *I* need The Work. Peace doesn't require two people; it requires only one. It has to be you. The problem begins and ends there.

If you want to alienate your friends and family, go around saying, "Is it true?" or "Turn it around" if they're not asking you for help. You may need to do that for a while, in order to hear it for yourself. It's uncomfortable to believe that you know more than your friends and to represent yourself as their teacher. Their irritation will lead you deeper into inquiry or deeper into your suffering.

Q: What do you mean by "Don't be spiritual—be honest instead."
A: What I mean is that it's very painful to pretend yourself beyond your own evolution, to live a lie, any lie. When you act like a teacher, it's usually because you're afraid to be the student. I don't pretend to be fearless. I either am or I'm not. It's no secret to me.

Q: How can I learn to forgive someone who hurt me very badly?
A: Judge your enemy, write it down, ask four questions, turn it around. See for yourself that forgiveness means discovering that what you thought happened didn't. Until you can see that there is nothing to forgive, you haven't really forgiven. No one has ever hurt anyone. No one has ever done anything terrible. There's nothing terrible except your uninvestigated thoughts about what happened. So whenever you suffer, inquire, look at the thoughts you're thinking, and set yourself free. Be a child. Start from the mind that knows nothing. Take your ignorance all the way to freedom.

Q: You've said, "When you're perfectly clear, what is is what you want." Suppose I save all month to go to a good restaurant so I can eat grilled lemon sole. The waiter brings me braised ox tongue. What is is not what I want. Am I confused? What does it mean to argue with reality?
A: Yes, you're very confused. If you were clear, what you'd want is braised ox tongue, because that's what the waiter brought. It doesn't mean that you have to eat it. How do you react when you think that he shouldn't have brought you braised ox tongue? Until you project that you have to eat it, or that you don't have enough time to reorder, or that you have to pay for what you didn't order, or that there has been any kind of injustice,

there's no problem. But when you believe that he shouldn't have brought it, you might become angry at him or feel some form of stress. Who would you be without your story as you face the waiter? Who would you be without the thought that there's not enough time or that the waiter made a mistake? You might be a person loving the moment, loving the apparent mistake. You might even be calm enough to repeat your original order with clarity and amusement. You might say, "I appreciate you, and what I ordered was grilled lemon sole. My time is limited, and if you can't serve me the grilled lemon sole and have me out of here by eight, I'll need to go elsewhere. I prefer to stay here. What do you suggest?"

Arguing with reality means arguing with the story of a past. It's already over, and no thinking in the world can change it. The waiter has already brought you the braised ox tongue; it's sitting in front of you on a plate. If you think that it shouldn't be there, you're confused, because there it is. The point is, how can you be most effective in this moment, given that what is is? Accepting reality doesn't mean that you're going to be passive. Why would you be passive when you can be clear and have a wonderful, sane life? You don't have to eat the braised ox tongue; you don't have to keep from clearly reminding the waiter that you ordered grilled lemon sole. Accepting reality means, in fact, that you can act in the kindest, most appropriate, and most effective way.

Q: What do you mean by "There are no physical problems—only mental ones"? What if I lose my right arm and I'm right-handed? Isn't that a huge problem?
A: How do I know I don't need two arms? I have only one. There's no mistake in the universe. To think in any other way is fearful and hopeless. The story "I need two arms" is where the suffering begins, because it argues with reality. Without the story, I have everything I need. I'm complete with no right arm. My handwriting may be shaky at first, but it's perfect just the way it is. It will do the job in the way I need to do it, not in the way I thought I needed to do it. Obviously, there needs to be a teacher in this world of how to be happy with one arm and shaky handwriting. Until I'm willing to lose my left arm, too, my Work's not done.

Q: How can I learn to love myself?
A: "You're supposed to love yourself"—is that true? How do you treat

yourself when you believe the thought that you're supposed to love yourself, and you don't? Can you see a reason to drop the story? And I'm not asking you to drop your sacred concept. Who would you be without the story "You're supposed to love yourself"? And "You're supposed to love others"? Just another toy—another toy of torture. What's the direct opposite? "You're *not* supposed to love others." Doesn't that feel a little more natural? You're not supposed to love others yet—not until you do. These sacred concepts, these spiritual ideas, always turn into dogma.

Q: What do you mean when you say that you are my projection?
A: The world is your perception of it. Inside and outside always match—they are reflections of each other. The world is the mirror image of your mind. If you experience chaos and confusion inside, your external world has to reflect that. You have to see what you believe, because you are the confused thinker looking out and seeing yourself. You are the interpreter of everything, and if you're chaotic, what you hear and see has to be chaos. Even if Jesus, even if the Buddha, were standing in front of you, you would hear confused words, because confusion would be the listener. You would only hear what you thought he was saying, and you'd start arguing with him the first time your story was threatened.

As for my being your projection, how else could I be here? It's not as though I had a choice. I am the story of who you think I am, not who I really am. You see me as old, young, beautiful, ugly, honest, deceitful, caring, uncaring. I am, for you, your uninvestigated story, your own myth.

I understand that who you think I am is true for you. I was innocent and gullible also, but only for forty-three years, until the moment when I woke up to the way things really are. "It's a tree. It's a table. It's a chair." Is it true? Have you stopped to ask yourself? Did you ever become still and listen as *you* asked *you?* Who told you it was a tree? Who was the original authority? How did they know? My entire life, my entire identity, had been built on the trust and uninquiring innocence of a child. Are you this kind of child? Through this Work, your toys and fairy tales are laid aside as you begin to read the book of true knowledge, the book of yourself.

People tell me, "But Katie, your happiness is all a projection," and I say, "Yes, and isn't it beautiful? I love living this happy dream. I'm having a wonderful time!" If you lived in heaven, would you want it to end? It doesn't end. It can't. That is what's true for me, until it's not. If it should change, I always have inquiry. I answer the questions, the truth is realized within me, and the doing meets the undone, the something meets the nothing. In the balance of the two halves, I am free.

Q: You say that The Work will leave me without stress, without problems. But isn't that irresponsible? Suppose my three-year-old child is starving. Won't I see her from a position of no stress and think, "Well, that's reality," and just let her starve?

A: Oh, my! Sweetheart, love is kind; it doesn't stand still and do nothing when it sees its own need. Do you really think that violent thoughts, such as the ones that come with problems, are necessary to feed a child? If your three-year-old is starving, feed her, for your sake! How would it feel to provide for a starving child without stress or worry? Wouldn't you be clearer about how and where to find the food that is available, and wouldn't you feel elation and gratitude for it? Well, that's how I live my life. I don't need stress to do what I know to do; that's not efficient, the way peace and sanity are. Love is action, and in my experience, reality is always kind.

Q: How can you say that reality is good? What about war, rape, poverty, violence, and child abuse? Are you condoning them?

A: How could I condone them? I simply notice that if I believe they shouldn't exist, I suffer. They exist until they don't. Can I just end the war in me? Can I stop raping myself and others with abusive thinking? If not, I'm continuing in myself the very thing that I want to end in you. Sanity doesn't suffer, ever. Can you eliminate war everywhere on earth? Through inquiry, you can begin to eliminate it for one human being: you. This is the beginning of the end of war in the world. If life upsets you, good! Judge the war makers on paper, inquire, and turn it around. Do you really want to know the truth? All suffering begins and ends with you.

Q: Always accepting reality sounds like never wanting anything. Isn't it more interesting to want things?

A: My experience is that I do want something all the time. It's not only interesting, it's ecstatic! What I want is what is. What I want is what I already have.

When I want what I have, thought and action aren't separate; they move as one, without conflict. If you find anything lacking, ever, write down your thought and inquire. I find that life never falls short and doesn't require a future. Everything I need is always supplied, and I don't have to do anything for it.

What do I want specifically? I want to answer your question, because that's what's happening right now. I respond to you, because that's what love does. It's an effect of the original cause: you. I love this life. Why would I want something more or less than what I have, even if it's painful? What would I do with it that could be better than what I'm doing right now? What I see, where I am, what I smell and taste and feel—it's all so fine. If you loved your life, would you want to change it? There is nothing more exciting than loving what is.

Q: You sometimes say, "God is everything, God is good." Isn't that just one more belief?

A: *God,* as I use that word, is another name for what is. I always know God's intention: It's exactly what is in every moment. I don't have to question it anymore. I'm no longer meddling in God's business. It's simple. And from that basis, it's clear that everything is perfect. The last truth—I call it the last judgment—is "God is everything, God is good." People who really understand this don't need inquiry. Ultimately, of course, even this isn't true. But if it works for you, I say keep it and have a wonderful life.

All so-called truths eventually fall away. Every truth is a distortion of what is. If we investigate, we lose even the last truth. And that state, beyond all truths, is true intimacy. That is God-realization. And welcome to the reentry. It's always a beginning.

Q: If nothing is true, then why bother? Why go to the dentist, why treat myself for illness? I'm quite confused. Can you clarify this?

A: I go to the dentist because I like to chew. I prefer it when my teeth don't fall out. Silly me! If you're confused, inquire and find what's true for you.

Q: How can I live in the Now?

A: You do. You just haven't noticed.

Only in this moment are we in reality. You and everyone can learn to live in the moment, as the moment, to love whatever is in front of you, to love it as you. If you keep doing The Work, you will see more and more clearly what you are without a future or a past. The miracle of love comes to you in the presence of the uninterpreted moment. If you are mentally somewhere else, you miss real life.

But even the Now is a concept. Even as the thought completes itself, it's gone, with no proof that it ever existed, other than as a concept that would lead you to believe it existed, and now that one is gone too. Reality is always the story of a past. Before you can grasp it, it's gone. Each of us already has the peaceful mind that we seek.

Q: I find it very hard to tell the truth, since the truth is so changeable. How can I be consistent in telling the truth?

A: Human experience is constantly changing, though the place of integrity never moves. I say, let's begin from where we are. Can we just tell the truth as it appears now, without comparing it to what was true a moment ago? Ask me again later, and I may have a different truthful answer. "Katie, are you thirsty?" No. "Katie, are you thirsty?" Yes. I always tell what my truth is right now. Yes, no, yes, yes, no. That's the truth.

My cousin once called me at two in the morning, very depressed, and said that he was holding a loaded pistol to his head and that the hammer was cocked. He said that if I didn't give him one good reason why he should stay alive, he would blow his head off. I waited for a long time. I really wanted to give him a reason, and no good reason came to me. I waited and waited, with him on the other end of the phone line. Finally, I told him that I couldn't find one. And he burst into tears. This evidently was the truth he needed. He said it was the first time in his life that he had ever heard integrity and that was what he was looking for. If I had concocted some reason, because I believed that he shouldn't kill himself, I would have given him less than the only thing I really have to give, which is my truth in the moment.

I have noticed that people who do The Work for a while get really clear about the truth as they see it. It becomes easy to stand in it and easy to be flexible and change their minds. Being honest in the moment becomes a very comfortable thing.

Do you know anyone who hasn't changed his mind? This door was a tree, then it will be firewood for someone, then it will return to air and earth. We're all like that, constantly changing. It's simply honest to report that you've changed your mind when you have. When you're afraid of what people will think if you speak honestly—that's where you become confused. "You changed your mind?" Yes. "Is there something the matter with you?" Yes, I changed my mind.

Q: Is it true that I can't hurt another person?

A: It's not possible for me to hurt another person. (Please don't try to believe this. It's not true for you until you realize it for yourself.) The only person I can hurt is myself. If you ask me point-blank for the truth, then I'm going to tell you what I see. I want to give you everything that you ask for. The way you receive my answer is the way you hurt yourself with it or help yourself with it. I'm just giving you what I've got.

But if I think that saying something to you would cause you to hurt your own feelings, I don't say it (unless you tell me that you really want to know). If I think I'm unkind to you, I'm not comfortable within myself. I cause my own suffering, and I stop for my own sake. I take care of myself, and in that you, too, are taken care of. My kindness ultimately has nothing to do with you. We're all responsible for our own peace. I could say the most loving words, and you might take offense. I understand that. What I realize is that the story you tell yourself about what I say is the only way you can hurt yourself. You're suffering, because you didn't ask four questions and turn it around.

Q: So many people, so many souls, are becoming enlightened now. There seems to be a universal collective hunger for this, a common awakening, as if there is only one organism, one being, waking up. Is this your experience, too?

A: I don't know anything about that. All I know is that if it hurts, investigate. Enlightenment is just a spiritual concept, just one more thing to seek in a future that never comes. Even the highest truth is just one more concept. For me, the experience is everything, and that's what inquiry reveals. Everything painful is undone—now, now, now. If you think you're enlightened, you'll love having your car towed away. That's it! How do you react when your child is sick? How do you react when your husband or wife wants a divorce? I don't know about people collectively waking up. Are you suffering, now? That's my interest.

People talk about self-realization, and this is it! Can you just breathe in and out happily? Who cares about enlightenment when you're happy right now? Just enlighten yourself to this moment. Can you just do that?

And then, eventually, it all collapses. The mind merges with the heart and comes to see that it's not separate. It finds a home, and it rests in itself, as itself. Until the story is met with understanding, there is no peace.

Q: *I've heard that people who are free don't have any preferences, since they see everything as perfect. Do you have preferences?*

A: Do I have preferences? I am a lover of what is, and that's what I always have. "It" has its own preferences: the sun in the morning and the moon at night. And it appears that I always have a preference for the thing happening now. I prefer the sun in the morning, and I prefer the moon at night. And I prefer to be with the person in front of me now. As soon as someone starts asking questions, I'm there. He is my preference, and there's no one else. Then when I'm talking to another person, she's the one, and there's no one else. I discover my preferences by noticing what it is that I'm doing. Whatever I'm doing: That's my preference. How do I know? I'm doing it! Do I prefer vanilla over chocolate? I do, until I don't. I'll let you know as we place our order at Ben and Jerry's.

Q: *Do all beliefs need to be undone?*

A: Investigate all the beliefs that cause you suffering. Wake yourself up from your nightmares, and the sweet dreams will take care of themselves. If your internal world is free and wonderful, why would you want to change it? If the dream is a happy one, who would want to wake up? And if your dreams aren't happy, welcome to The Work.

There is only

one problem, ever:

your uninvestigated story

in the moment.

14.

The Work in Your Life

I have often heard beginners ask what would happen if they did The Work on a regular basis. There is often the fear—as we've seen in some of these dialogues—that without a story, they wouldn't be motivated to act and wouldn't know what to do. The experience of those who do The Work— parents, artists, workers in schools and offices, in government, prisons, and hospitals—is that the opposite is true. Inquiry naturally gives rise to action that is clear, kind, and fearless.

When you begin to meet your thinking with understanding, your body follows. It begins to move by itself, so you don't have to do anything. The Work is about noticing our thoughts, not changing them. When you work with the thinking, the doing naturally follows.

If you sit in a chair and have a great insight, is that the end of it? I don't think so. Doing The Work is only half the process; the other half happens when the insights come to life. Until they live as action, they're not fully yours.

The Work will show you where you've got your happiness backward. When you think that people should be kind to you, the reverse is true: You should be kind to them and to yourself. Your judgments about others become *your* prescription for how to live. When you turn them around, you see what will bring you happiness.

The advice you've been giving your family and friends turns out to be advice for you to live, not us. You become the wise teacher as you become a student of yourself. It stops mattering if anyone else hears you, because *you're* listening. You are the wisdom you offer us, breathing and walking and effortlessly moving on, as you make your business deal, buy your groceries, or do the dishes.

Self-realization is the sweetest thing. It shows us how we are fully responsible for ourselves, and that is where we find our freedom. Rather than being other-realized, you can be self-realized. Instead of looking to us for your fulfillment, you can find it in yourself.

We don't know how to change; we don't know how to forgive or how to be honest. We're waiting for an example. You're the one. You are your only hope, because we're not changing until you do. Our job is to keep coming at you, as hard as we can, with everything that angers, upsets, or repulses you, until you understand. We love you that much, whether we're aware of it or not. This whole world is about you. Theories have no value. Pain is not a teacher until you investigate and realize its cause.

So, to put The Work into action, begin with the voice inside you that's telling us what to do. Realize that it's telling *you* what to do. When it says, "He should pick up the socks," listen to the turnaround "I should pick up the socks," and just do it. Stay in the flow that's effortless and unending. Pick them up until you love it, because it's your truth. And know that the only important house to clean is your mind.

Not to pick up the socks can be deadly. It's how you stay in the war zone. What a bonus: You were waiting for everyone else to do it, and there you were, right under your own nose.

There is no peace in the world until you find peace within yourself in this moment. Live these turnarounds, if you want to be free. That's what Jesus did, what the Buddha did. That's what all the famous great ones did, and all the unknown great ones who are just living it in their homes and communities, happily and in peace.

At some point, you may want to go to the deepest pain inside you and clear it up. Do The Work until you see your part in it. And then go to the people you've judged and apologize; tell them what you've seen about yourself and how you're working on it now. It's all up to you. Speaking these truths is what sets you free.

So I invite you to look at the nightmares that you've suffered through and survived, and to see that freedom really is possible in your everyday life. Your story is the only thing that's painful, and life has to mirror back to you what you believe is true. There's no exception to that.

You may be afraid to go deeper into The Work because you think that it's going to cost you something valuable. My experience is the opposite: Without a story, life only gets richer. Those who stay in The Work for a while discover that inquiry is not serious and that investigating a painful thought just turns it into laughter.

I love that I'm free to walk in the world without fear, sadness, or anger, ready to meet anything or anyone, in any place, at any time, with arms and heart wide open. Life will show me what I haven't undone yet. I look forward to it, and I look forward to seeing you walk with me.

Just keep coming home

to yourself.

You are the one

you've been waiting for.

Appendix:
Self-Facilitation

The following are examples of self-facilitated Work written by people who were upset by their thoughts about a friend or a lover. They illustrate the depth inquiry can go to when you take the time to write your answers thoroughly and honestly.

My Boyfriend's Handicap or Mine?

The Written Statement: *I'm saddened and angry because Allen can't walk and we can't do normal "couple" things together.*

Is it true? Yes.

What's the reality? The reality is that Allen is in a wheelchair and he can't walk.

Rewritten Statement (arrived at with the prompt "What would I have if Allen could walk?"): My life would be better if Allen could walk.

Can I really know that that's true? No. I can't know it at all.

How do I react when I believe the thought that my life would be better if Allen could walk? I feel like a martyr. I feel sorry for myself. I feel envious of other couples. I feel cheated and panicky. I feel like a part of my life is never lived out—especially sexually. I long for things that are difficult or impossible for us to do, like travel to nonhandicap places. I worry needlessly and endlessly that somehow I'm making a mistake loving this man as I do. I doubt God, even though Allen is the man he puts in front of me over and over again to love.

What does it feel like to believe the thought? Crazy, alone, a freak, constant addictive thinking that constipates me. My chest physically hurts so much that it feels like someone is standing on it. I get mad. We stand out. We're queer and abnormal—never the ideal.

How do I treat Allen when I think that my life would be better if he could walk? I'm cold and distant. I'm uncomfortable. I hold back loving thoughts, things that I really want to share with him. I don't make love to him. I expect him to do all the work sexually. I act like I know more than he does about how to take care of himself.

How do I treat myself? I think I'm crazy, that there's something wrong with me because I love a man in a wheelchair. The worst thing I do is I don't let myself love him fully. I tell myself I'm codependent. I get so distracted that I drink. I read too much, or I don't read at all. I try to work some angle with another man, usually in my head and sometimes with a real man. I tear myself up with dual thinking: "Is it right? Isn't it right?" I can't sleep. I act like it doesn't really bother me to my family and friends, and I get defensive and hard. I won't let myself think about all the wonderful things we have together. I look for theories to prove I'm right— astrology, double-Capricorn stuff, metaphysical bullshit. I feel ashamed of myself for not following my heart. I won't go with him to New Mexico, because of my brilliant career, my fabulous house, and my cats.

Can I see a reason to drop the thought that my life would be better if Allen could walk? Yes. All of the above reactions.

Can I find one stress-free reason to keep the thought? Not one.

Who would I be without the thought that my life would be better if Allen could walk? A woman in love with a man named Allen.

Rewritten Statement Turned Around: My life would not be better if Allen could walk. That feels just as true.

Original Statement Turned Around: I am saddened and angry because I can't walk. Yes. Sometimes I stop myself from going places, and then I blame Allen. I get angry thinking that I can't get up and walk where I want to. We *can* do normal "couple" things together. True. What Allen and I do is normal for us. So I stop us from enjoying our normal "couple" things by comparing us to other couples and thinking that their normal should be our normal.

Janine Shouldn't Lie to Me

The Written Statement: *I don't like Janine because she lies to me.*

Is it true? Yes.

What is my proof that this is true? She told me that the class would be limited to thirty people. There were fifty-five people. She told me that she would send me tapes by the end of the week. She sent them a month later. She told me that she felt sure she could arrange an earlier ride to the airport. When the time came, she said that there was no ride available for me.

Does any of this proof really prove that she lies to me? Yes.

Can I absolutely know that it's true that Janine lies to me? Yes.

How do I react when I believe the thought that Janine lies to me? I feel out of control and helpless. I can't believe anything she says. I feel frustrated. I get very uptight whenever I am with her or even thinking about her. I am always thinking of how I would do her job better than she does.

Rewritten Statement (arrived at with the prompt "What's the 'should'? "): People shouldn't lie.

Is it true? No—they do!

How do I treat Janine when I believe the story that people shouldn't lie, and she does? I see her as phony, unreliable, incompetent, and uncaring. I treat her with mistrust and coldness. I see everything about her—words, gestures, actions—as lies. I am short with her. I don't like her, and I want her to feel my dislike and disapproval.

How does that feel? It feels out of control. I don't like myself. I feel guilty and wrong.

Who would I be (in the presence of Janine) without the story that people shouldn't lie? I would see Janine as doing her best and actually doing very well, considering the huge amount of information she is handling for so many people. I would be more caring and helpful to Janine. I might take the time to chat with her and get to know her. When I close my eyes and see her without that story, I really like her and want to be her friend.

Rewritten Statement Turned Around: People should lie. Yes, they should, because they do.

Original Statement Turned Around: I don't like myself because I lie to Janine. That's true. I told her that I couldn't get a later flight. That airline was sold out, but I didn't try the waiting list or another airline. The truth is that I lied. I wanted to take an earlier flight. I don't like Janine because I lie to myself (about Janine). Yes, that's truer. I tell myself a lot of lies about Janine when I draw conclusions about everything she says and does. It's not Janine that I don't like—it's the stories, the lies that I tell myself about her that I don't like. I do like Janine because she doesn't lie to me. That's true also. I really don't believe she has ever intentionally told me anything that was not true. She is passing along information she's been given, and she can't know if it will change or not. And I really do like her.

I am the cause

of my own suffering

—but only all of it.

Contact Information

To find out more about The Work of Byron Katie, contact:

The Work of Byron Katie Foundation
P.O. Box 667
Manhattan Beach, CA 90267
Phone: 310.760.9000
Fax: 310.760.9008
www.thework.org
E-mail: info@thework.org

The Work of Byron Katie Foundation, Europe
P.O. Box 1276
1400 BG Bussum
The Netherlands
Phone: +31.35.694.7290
Fax: +31.35.694.7230
E-mail: euro@thework.org

The Work of Byron Katie Foundation offers events throughout the world. The Foundation also provides educational materials free to all who request them. The Work of Byron Katie Foundation, a 501(c) (3) not-for-profit organization, is supported by donations and gratefully accepts your tax-deductible gift.

For information about The School for The Work with Byron Katie, visit www.thework.org or e-mail theschool@thework.org.

For audio- and videotapes, visit www.thework.org or contact:
> Audio Literature
> 1.800.383.0174

Look for the audio version of this book in your local bookstore.

If, as you read the dialogues in this book, you have realizations that seem remarkable, please e-mail them to realizations@thework.org. You are invited to deposit them in this e-mail bank to help us track the power of inquiry. Include your statements or stories, the questions you used, what you realized, and, in cases where you specifically acted on your turnarounds, please describe those, too.

Notes to the Introduction

P. ix, *The more clearly you understand yourself and your emotions, the more you become a lover of what is:* The Ethics, Book 5, Proposition 15. A more literal translation: "He who clearly and distinctly understands himself and his emotions loves God, and does so the more, the more he understands himself and his emotions." Spinoza's term *God*—he often says "God-or-nature"—actually means "ultimate reality" or simply "what is."

P. x, *"we are disturbed not by what happens to us, but by our thoughts about what happens":* Epictetus, *Encheiridion*, V. Two other relevant statements: "Nothing external can disturb us. We suffer only when we want things to be different from what they are." (*Encheiridion*, V) "No one has the power to hurt you. It is only your own thinking about someone's actions that can hurt you." (*Encheiridion*, XX)

P. xi, *To realize your true nature, you must wait for the right moment and the right conditions:* Quoted in a Dharma talk by the great Chinese Zen master Pai-Chang (720–814). See *The Enlightened Mind: An Anthology of Sacred Prose*, ed. Stephen Mitchell (HarperCollins, 1991), p. 55. I have been unable to identify the sutra.

P. xiii, *admission is always free:* All one-day events sponsored by The Work of Byron Katie Foundation are offered free of charge. Because of Katie's commitment to share The Work with as many people as possible, she has, several times during the past two years, accepted invitations from groups that do not waive admissions fees. These events are not sponsored by the Foundation.

P. xiii, *Katie often says that the only way to understand The Work is to experience it:* This paragraph was written by my friend and literary agent Michael Katz, who also wrote the section in chapter 10 called "When the Story Is Hard to Find" and edited many passages in this book.

P. xiii, *"Perhaps the most important revelation":* Antonio Damasio, *The Feeling of What Happens: Body and Emotions in the Making of Consciousness* (Harcourt Brace & Company, 1999), p. 187.

P. xiii, *"The left brain weaves its story":* Michael Gazzaniga, *The Mind's Past* (University of California Press, 1998), p. 26.

P. xiv, *Considering that, all hatred driven hence:* From "A Prayer for My Daughter," *The Collected Works of W. B. Yeats, vol. 1, The Poems,* ed. Richard J. Finneran (Scribner, 1997), p. 192. The second line of the stanza reads: "The soul recovers radical innocence."

P. xxiii, *Step aside from all thinking:* From "The Mind of Absolute Trust," *The Enlightened Heart: An Anthology of Sacred Poetry,* ed. Stephen Mitchell (HarperCollins, 1989), p. 27.